"Terrific! You have a gift. I want to meet you."

-Bob Goff, *Love Does* and Restore International

"Donald Miller in a dress!"

-Lynn Vincent,
collaborative author with Todd Burpo *Heaven is for Real*

"On the surface, this is the story of one woman's long and arduous journey through the devastating, mysterious illness and death of her husband -- but in reality, it is so much more than that. It is a gritty account of honor and deep courage alongside great travail; it is a poetic compendium of facing the unknown with dignity and strength; it is a blueprint of what it means to live -- and die -- well; and it is a memoir of profound and abiding faith. Ultimately, *The Truth Swing* is a beautiful and moving opus of uncompromising and undying love."

-Karla Yaconelli,
widow of Mike Yaconelli,
Youth Specialties

After reading an excerpt from *The Truth Swing* in the Westmont College magazine, I asked Francine Phillips if I might quote from her powerful piece during my various speaking engagements. Her story perfectly illustrates the point of my book *Changing Signs of Truth* (IVP 2012), which argues for Christianity based on what Jacques Derrida calls "the Gift" rather than an "economy of exchange." Francine's profound insight and beautiful prose brought me to tears.

-Crystal Downing, Ph.D.,
Distinguished Professor of English and Film Studies at Messiah College (PA)
and author of *Salvation from Cinema* (Routledge 2015) and
the award-winning *Writing Performances:
The Stages of Dorothy L. Sayers* (Palgrave Macmillan 2004).

"Your story kind of blew me away. I lost my wife of 20 years to a heart attack in 2003. I know the truth that God loves us and will care for us from my experience. I have shared that in ministry as a Director of Visitation and Senior Adult ministries, but your journey has taken you way beyond where I have been and challenges me to learn more."

-Phil Wegener,
Sudden Valley,
Washington

"The Truth often takes a long, long time to discover. What we once thought or assumed to be true we learn, over time and with experience, was either false or just an illusion. With one exception – the Truth about how I am incredibly cherished and adored and valued and loved by God. In the end, that is all I really *need* to know."

-Gail Sheffield Way,
former student,
Westmont College

"Wonderful writing. I'm sorry to read about your husband's death, but thought the theological depth of your writing amazing and made me proud that we studied theology together."

-Scott Grandi,
former student,
Denver Theological Seminary;
Missionary in Taiwan

"Today, Uncle Mike became alive again. I heard his voice, his laugh and his stories, felt his resilience and passion. I cried my way through large portions of the reading, especially in his journal entries, seeing how he clung to God, even though all this 'was happening to him."

-Katheryn de Arakal,
graduate student,
Azusa Pacific University

"Just read your articulate and moving book. Thank you for sharing your innermost thoughts. What a refreshing perspective on John 3:16. We share some similar feelings and reading your work, it felt like you reached into the deepest part of me and wrote down just what you saw and heard. I will be keeping this in a special place always to reread when those moments come, linger and as a reminder. It will give deeper and continued honesty in those mornings together with Him.

P.S. What a heavenly party we will have one day."

-Linda Veninga,
entered heaven December, 2014,
Elk Grove, California

The
Truth Swing

It's Not What They Taught
Me in Sunday School

Francine Phillips

WESTBOW
PRESS®
A DIVISION OF THOMAS NELSON
& ZONDERVAN

WestBow Press books may be ordered through booksellers or by contacting:

WestBow Press
A Division of Thomas Nelson & Zondervan
1663 Liberty Drive
Bloomington, IN 47403
www.westbowpress.com
1 (866) 928-1240

ISBN: 978-1-5127-3352-5 (sc)
ISBN: 978-1-5127-3353-2 (hc)
ISBN: 978-1-5127-3351-8 (e)

Library of Congress Control Number: 2016903433

Print information available on the last page.

WestBow Press rev. date: 09/28/2016

Additional books by Francine Phillips

Conscience of the Community – Rev. George
Walker Smith with Francine Phillips

Leading at a Higher Level – Larry Stirling with Francine Phillips

Fight City Hall and Win – Roger Hedgecock with Francine Phillips

America's Finest City: If We Say It Enough We'll Believe
It – Roger Hedgecock and Francine Phillips

Blog: Writing to Get Through
Francinephillips.com

Contact Francine Phillips at write.now@cox.net

ACKNOWLEDGEMENTS

M Y HUSBAND DIED FIVE years ago. I finished the first draft of this book within nine months with the help of my band of writers, Lynn Vincent, Suzy Haines, Anita Palmer, Beth McNellen and various others who joined and left our group. They had convinced me to make a U-turn and return to writing non-fiction. To write what I know. Thank you for getting me started on the writing.

What I knew was a devastating and painful experience. There was no gloss on the process, no miraculous healing, no reward for faithfulness, and no punishment for being a sinner. There was just loss on all sides. I depended, first and foremost, on Sandy Gold who was my rock and my shield. When I said, "It could be worse," she was the one who said, "But the things it could be worse than keep getting more terrible." On Beth and Scott McNellen, who were my mirrors and my comic relief. On Carol Sonstein, my wise and practical friend who dragged me to holocaust films that provided visual images of horror and taught me that suffering can be redemptive. She also insisted that finding an East Coast-trained physician was paramount; Tibetan even better. She goaded me and continues to encourage me to take better care of myself.

Thanks to the men who met and prayed with Mike weekly – among them Mike Atkinson, Noel Becchetti, John Cumbey, Andy Fredrickson, Doug Johnston and for Craig Knudsen's pastoral care. Thanks to the women in GriefShare who let me be open about my despair and for my new friends at Journey Community Church who stood beside me – April King, Tommie Potter, Gail Nelson Bones, Susan Fuller and many more. And my *Write Your Journey* students who listened and applauded when I read each chapter then responded with gripping and poetic stories of their own lives.

I got encouragement as I tried to finish the book. First from Kathleen Kerr who, even though not my editor, stayed engaged and believed in the writing. Westmont College published excerpts in its magazine and the responses I received kept me writing. The San Diego Christian Writer's Guild awarded me Best Unpublished Manuscript recognition – an encouragement but also somewhat of a dubious honor that spurred me on to publication. Renee Fisher helped me see the value in self-publishing and, finally, God bless the amazing Bob Goff who read it and said, "You have a gift."

Thanks to my brilliant, creative and fun family. Even those who reject prayer, I'm sure, sent up prayers through the years of illness and the years afterward. To Anna Canrinus, who lost her dad at age 10 to illness and, finally, to death at age 17 -- you are brave and beautiful. I hope that someday you will rediscover your faith in God. I hope you all do. In the end, there's nothing else.

Praise you, Father, for your great and enduring love.

Francine Phillips, February 2016

God So Loved Me

*For God So Loved the World that He Gave His Only
Begotten Son, that whosoever believeth in Him should
not perish, but have everlasting life.* John 3:16.

JOHN 3:16. JUST READING the reference brings to mind a chorus of small children memorizing it in a sing-song tone, stumbling over the "whosoever" while the teacher waves her hand like a music conductor and mouths "that means you!" And the room is getting hot and stuffy and my dotted Swiss dress is starting to scratch the back of my knees and one of the boys is always too loud on the word "Begotten" and what does a six year-old know about perishing anyway. Life is already everlasting to a six-year-old in Sunday school. Especially everlasting in a dotted Swiss, too-tight dress.

So somehow, the impact of the scripture's amazing truth gets lost. Somehow we don't get the picture that God loves the world and if we simply believe we become eternally alive.

Usually the idea is more like, God so loved a few who were holy, as he did in the time of Noah. Or God so loved those who were predestined to be part of the Kingdom of God, a chosen remnant, as he did the nation of Israel. Or God loved the good little boys and girls and gave them toys at Christmas. Or God loved the ones who will sacrifice their lives on some kind of cross the way Jesus did. Or God loved those who were attractive, well-dressed with styled hair. Or God loved those who would speak in tongues and be filled with the Holy Spirit. Or God loved those who acted cool and were able to play rock music for his glory and reject other rock music. Or God loved those who loved him back.

That's not the message here. God loves THE WORLD—with its brokenness, sin, murder, deceit, foolishness, power plays, gossip, plastic surgery, gang initiations, the war in Vietnam, ethnic cleansing in Bosnia, the Peace Corps, the Marines torturing naked Iraqis, the Syrian refugees, the lawyers, the Walmart employees and the teenaged shoplifters.

The love comes first, regardless of our response. God loves you. God loves me.

CHAPTER I

The "I Want" Prayer

For God So Loved the World that He Gave His Only
Begotten Son, that whosoever believeth in Him should
not perish, but have everlasting life. John 3:16.

BECAUSE GOD SO LOVED me, Mike sailed into my life.

I was coming up to forty, a single mom for nearly eight years. My marriage to my seminary boyfriend had broken and died mostly because, like many Christian virgins at twenty-five years of age, the only thing I had been taught about being a wife came from Proverbs 31. Neither of us had read chapters 1-30, which explains the importance of wisdom. I was blessed with two incredible children, Molly and Jesse, who had to compete for my attention after a demanding day on the job. My father died and left me a little money, so we moved to a wonderful property with woods, a pool, and a pond. I had a lot—great kids, an interesting job, a cool home, and incredible women friends. I held writers' salons, parties, painting gatherings, readings; and I planted a garden.

But I wanted a man.

Sleeping alone is one of the most painful parts of being a single woman. Just the act of turning down the covers, getting in alone, and turning out the light by yourself is something that those who aren't alone don't understand as the loneliest moment of the day. Whether you take a good book to bed with you, a little sip of Scotch, or a bowl of Rocky Road

1

ice cream, nothing is like sharing the warmth of the bed with a man. It just isn't.

So I prayed for a husband. I told myself I needed a "helpmate," which is Christian code for sex partner, even though you try to convince yourself that it's really someone to cut wood for the fireplace, fix the car, help wash dishes, and sit in the driver's seat. Bottom line, I wanted a man. And I wanted God to bring me one.

Not that I had been alone that much. In fact, I had just been through a final break-up with my artist boyfriend after four off-and-on years of whisking the kids away for their dad's weekend and scurrying downtown to his loft to hang out with the sounds of shouting on the sidewalk, sirens in the night, Van Morrison soulfully providing back-up vocals. A million miles from cold, stuck Cheerios, homework papers, lunch boxes, and alarm clocks. That getaway to another world was fun while it lasted.

Now I wanted a man in my world.

It's a mistake that many divorced women make who have financial security and a certain professional identity. Most are looking for a guy to come into the world they have made for themselves and simply help.

My girlfriends and I were like that. We were the *'80s Ladies* that gritty K.T. Oslin sang about. We were women who owned our homes and had obtained success, recognition, and job satisfaction. We got together for poetry readings, gala events, lots of glasses of wine on the patio, and laughter over our worst dates ever.

Over the years we had refined our criteria for a mate. I shared our findings, once, with a male friend.

"We have narrowed it down to two requirements," I said. "Solvent and capable of love. Is that too much to ask?"

He thought for a moment. "Actually, it could be."

We didn't want to particularly change our worlds—just have help with the ones we had created. Husbands to explain things to the pool man, accompany us to the plays that we like, give us a kiss on New Year's Eve, hold us at the end of the day. We thought marriage was 50/50 and we could probably talk the right guy out of wanting his 50 percent because we were smart, successful, and brought home the bacon.

God so loved me.

CHAPTER 2

Cheering the Pain

THE SUN WAS OVERHEAD bathing San Diego with warmth while a light breeze kept the August heat under control. On the playing field, young boys with shoulder pads, thigh pads, cleats, and helmets with face bars blocking their vision half the time scurried through practice drills. On the perimeter, cheerleaders bounced, kicked their legs high into the air, shook pom-poms over their heads, and shouted with abandon.

My back hurts...
My skirt's too tight...
My hips shake...
From left to right...
Warriors don't take no jive...
Warriors, hey! we are alive!

I loved that cheer. When the girls would practice it I could not stay seated. One of the other moms, an office worker at the local cable company, was my co-conspirator. We would jump to our feet, shout the words, bump rumps, and laugh our heads off, to the everlasting humiliation of our daughters. Life was exceptionally wonderful at that moment.

Because the reality was, my back *did* hurt. My skirt *was* too tight. Life was hard. What those little girls, with their beautiful kicks and perfect cartwheels, didn't see was that their cheer was my psalm, my *yea-though-I-walk-through-the-valley-of-death, I-will-fear-no-evil-for-thou-art-with-me* psalm — with a triumphant amen: We are alive!

That August, four times a week, we repeated that psalm again and again, entering the hilarity of it and disregarding what others might think seeing a tall, mousy white woman and a short, obese black woman shouting, swaying, clapping, and collapsing on each other in a gale of giggles to beat away the pain.

By the time the Pop Warner season began and settled into three practices a week and games every Saturday, our days had become rhythmic. Make sure uniforms are washed, socks found, shoes spotless, and snacks in the cupboard by Friday night. Pile in the car, who needs a ride, where did I put those directions to…what field? Where is Jesse's game? When is Molly cheering? Get in the car! GET IN THE CAR!

I was alive. So much so that when I saw the six-foot-four-inch blond guy who was polite, laughed loud and hard, showed open affection to his son, and helped out in the snack bar, my sad, broken, artist-loft-missing heart lifted its head, wiped away a few tears, and noticed.

I wasn't the only one.

A Pop Warner football field, as it turns out, is Mecca for single women with sons. Mike was a magnet for every cute cheerleader-turned-grown-woman but-still-wearing-low-cut-tank-tops in the stands. Me? I was the local newspaper editor with large red glasses, a waist that was fast crossing the "no belts" line, and permanent bags under my eyes. But I could tell he was watching me.

I kept my distance. During one game, I was standing at the chain link fence watching the field. He came down and stood about four feet away. My chest tightened and I held my breath. I kept my eyes fixed on the Mighty Mites ramming into each other like bumper cars. Mike looked straight ahead.

After a few more tension-filled moments, I simply walked away. I breathed out with a whoosh that set me coughing. Tears came to my eyes, then rolled in streaks down each cheek. I was terrified.

So afraid, in fact, that for weeks into the season I knew his name but never spoke it. He knew my name but never spoke it. We would say hello at games, or I would sit near his circle of parents, but we had never actually been introduced. It was a little ridiculous by October, as the season was winding down, that we both talked to everybody else and not each other. I watched the cute moms flirt with him. He watched me.

My mother drove to San Diego from Los Angeles one day and we went to practice so she could see the kids for a while, then took off to have a soda on the patio of a nearby restaurant.

"Hey, Mom," I said, driving my car into the parking lot. "Did you see that tall, blond guy?"

"No, I'm not sure I did," she said.

"Well, I think I'm going to start dating him."

There, I said it out loud. The words were out there and the fear that had been stifling my heart for months was spoken. Pulling into a space, I immediately plowed into the car next to me, setting alarms screaming in every direction.

God so loved me.

CHAPTER 3

Shameless Flirting

I HAVE NO IDEA HOW big God is. The expanse of the universe is beyond me. Big Bang. Separating sky and sea, earth rising up, the sun setting with a gorgeous streak of orange melting into purple. Stars in an Arizona sky. The bumper sticker scolding me that My God Isn't Big Enough. How do they know?

Some people are into the Big God thing – look at the soaring cathedrals with hushed interiors, or giant churches with giant parking lots. Twenty-thousand Koreans bowing in prayer at the same time.

And I've met some who think that God is infinitely small – a divine spark and nothing more. An unexplained frame on the video of their very important lives that mysteriously shows up and is gone in a blink; only discernible in the replay. As if God is somehow lucky to have them around to see the glimpses and those glimpses somehow make them God, too.

Please.

When Mike came into my life, my expectations of God were about the same as my expectations of men. *Lord, keep me solvent and capable of…well, some kind of connection.* After a failed marriage, a failed church experience, a failed ministry, and a failure to read, pray, meditate, or listen to him — and despite hearing in Sunday school examples of how God cares about us and responds — I had a hard time grasping that he felt about me the same way he felt about Sarah, Leah, and Martha in the scriptures or even Grandma and the woman at church who sings.

So when I saw Mike and saw what was coming, I was terrified. I mean, I know I had asked God for a guy. I just didn't think that when I had asked God for a man, he would bring me a *man*. Wow! Mike was a gift wrapped in a deep, deep voice and a big smile. Inside was a sense of humor, intelligence, a love of books, plays and art, kindness to kids, the ability to listen and a drive to work hard.

God so loved me.

I decided to solve the introduction issue by having a pool party at our house for the team. Not only that, I was going to flirt with him. Yes I was. I could be just as flirty as those sexy, cheery moms.

On a hot, Saturday, hands sticky with melting red vines, in dirty white shorts, a Hawaiian shirt with a blue visor shading my eyes, I walked right up to Mike.

"Are you coming to the pool party?" I asked.

Mike looked down at me and smiled. He laughed and the sound was a deep bubbling brook, calm but alive with motion, washing over me like baptism.

"Yes, we'll be there," he said.

And here's where I pulled out all the stops with the flirt. I took a deep breath and I looked him straight in the eye for the first time in three months.

"Good."

Wow. Hold me back. Call me Jezebel.

CHAPTER 4

Hello, My Name is...

THIRTY-TWO SCREAMING NINE YEAR-OLDS did cannonballs off the slick flagstone deck. Parents mingled with each other and downed beers on the patio, their backs to the mayhem.

Mike and I were the only ones watching the pool. He never took his eyes of the boys while I repeated the, "Don't run!" mantra every few seconds like clockwork. Finally I noticed he took his eyes off the boys to watch me a few times. And to watch me watching him. I needed help.

Finally, I took a push broom, walked over to Mike and said, "Would you mind sweeping up some of the puddles on the stone? Somebody is going to get hurt."

Three months of cringing shyness disappeared like vapor.

"Sure," he said and stood up. He took the broom and then extended his hand to me, and said, "By the way, my name is Mike."

Looking up into his kind face, I swallowed hard and said, "I'm Francine," and shook his warm, huge hand.

It turned out Mike was a yacht guy. He owned his own business, Yacht Outfitting, fixing high-end sailing and cruising yachts. He looked like he had created a pretty cool life for himself, wearing shorts and Hawaiian shirts every day, comfortable around both multimillionaire owners and humble immigrant laborers.

Mike had traveled hundreds of miles across the seas -- cautious, confident. At the helm. He was comfortable being at the helm and loved the sparkling expanse of San Diego Bay and the heaving challenges of the Pacific Ocean. He admired the people who devote themselves to battling the elements for fun, more willing to spend their vacations afloat in cramped quarters and uncertain conditions than in luxury hotels or golf resorts. Mike served his clients with confidence and they loved that he could fix things, while they could merely buy them.

A couple of weeks after the pool party, I called my friend Ginger, who lived on a yacht. San Diego is a small town disguised as a city and the yacht community is a close neighborhood.

"Do you know Mike Canrinus? He owns Yacht Outfitting down on Harbor Drive," I asked.

"I think I've met him," she answered tentatively.

"Well, can you ask around about him? I don't want to go out with an ax murderer or anything."

It didn't take long for Ginger to call back.

"He's well thought-of and most people call him a real family man. He loves his family."

No! No! Make it go away! God, please, make it all go away! I'm afraid. I can't go down this road again! A way of escape! You promise a way of escape!

Next I talked to my friend Carol.

"What does he drive?" she asked.

"I don't know, some kind of white truck, I think."

"You mean you haven't looked in his car? You have to look inside his car."

The football practice was nearly over. Any minute hot, thirsty, tired boys would be scanning the stands for their parents. I slipped out of the bleachers and walked up to the parking lot above the field. There it was. White truck. I strolled past and glanced in. Clean, not messy. Sunglasses, a clipboard, tool box mounted in the back. No axes. No ax murderer.

No obvious way of escape!

As I turned around, Mike was right there. Did he see me look inside his truck? I went bright red, mumbled something about not remembering where I parked. As I stumbled back down the rise I could hear Jesse hollering, "Mom!"

I can't do this! Blushing? Looking in cars? What is this, junior high? No. I am not doing this. I'm a serious woman with an important career. I'm editor of the newspaper, for heaven's sake. I am NOT doing this.

God so loved me.

CHAPTER 5

Christmas Miracle

Christmas Day.
Away in a manger
No crib for a bed,
The little Lord Jesus
Lay down his sweet head.
The stars in the sky
Look down where he lay;
The little Lord Jesus
Asleep on the hay.

I T'S THAT SIMPLE.
   Knowing who God is, who Jesus is, who you are and how it all fits together takes the rest of your life. And let me give you a hint. He's not asleep on the hay.

It was a gorgeous day – warm with a little crisp breeze. The eucalyptus tree by the back door towered above the yard, while the Fuertes avocado leaves rustled on the branches and underfoot. The sky was wide and blue. A couple of tomatoes and a cauliflower were left in the garden. I plucked them up and smelled my hands, soaking in the fragrance of the tomato stalks and peace on rich, fertile earth.

Mike was coming over. He had called first.

"Hi, this is Mike."

"Hey, Hi… How's it going? Merry Christmas."

"Oh, thanks, everything is good."

"Good."

"So, uh, what are you doing today?"

"Oh, not much. We opened presents last night. The kids are at their dad's."

"My kids are at their mom's."

"Oh."

"Yeah, I don't have anything planned."

"Oh."

Silence.

"Would you like to come over?" I asked.

."Sure," Mike said. "I would like that."

"O.K., why don't you come over at about 10:30 and we can have brunch and sit on the patio. I have some peaches canned from this summer and they would be great over pancakes. Then we can sit on the porch or play a game or something, or maybe we can take a walk. I love taking walks in this neighborhood, everything is so beautiful. I take a walk every morning. Or maybe we can play a game or do a puzzle or something. Do you like books? I was thinking about reading on the porch in the sun. Do you like to read?

Silence. Deep laugh.

"I love to read. I'll see you at about 10:30."

"Okay."

"Oh, can I bring my dog?"

I hate dogs. What would a giant man have, a retriever, Jack Russell?

"Well, of course you can."

"Great. Higgins and I will see you later."

Higgins?

"O.K… Bye."

"Bye."

I called Carol immediately, wished her a Merry Christmas and she said something about Hanukkah in return. Then I told her Mike was coming over for the day. We discussed the various implications of this and she told me to just stay calm.

"Oh, and he's bringing his dog."

"His what?"

"His dog."

"Well," said Carol, "you must really like this guy because you hate dogs."

I did like him a lot. We had been on one date since the pool party -- a double date with his daughter and son-in-law. We sat in the back seat like a couple of kids and went to dinner on the bay, then window-shopped in La Jolla. Mike held my hand crossing the street. I loved a man holding my hand to cross the street.

But being alone together? All day? I started shaking and tears came to my eyes. I sat in my living room, stared at the walnut tree out the window, then bowed my head.

Lord, thank you for coming to earth. Thank you for the angels and the wise men and the shepherds and the star. I don't feel you anymore and churches make me crazy and I don't like being a Christian anymore, but I know that you are here. You've listened to me forever. Thank you for Mike coming over. Please, please, please don't let me like him unless you want this for me. If this isn't going to work out, please, please have him walk away. Because I can't. I can't walk away from this guy. He's too handsome, too kind, too funny and he likes me. Help me, O God. Amen.

I had no business praying, of course. I hadn't set foot in a church for almost ten years, and I'd pretty much decided that God discarded me over the divorce anyway and I had no right to talk to him.

Following the divorce, my ex-husband had married a woman from our Bible study. It didn't seem right for our two children to have to yo-yo back and forth from different churches every weekend. They needed to be in one church, with one fellowship of people who knew them and would know them until they were out of high school. It was the least I could do for them. So every Sunday I drove Molly and Jesse to church, dropped them off, and watched as they went inside. Through tears I waited as they ran inside to little circles of friends, then I put my car in reverse and kept my head down near the blue steering wheel until I had made a right turn onto the road.

A white truck pulled into my driveway. Mike was wearing jeans, a plaid flannel shirt, and a big smile. His green eyes squinted in the sunlight and his blond hair shimmered. Mike held a bouquet of flowers in his hand. When I opened the door, he wrapped me in a warm hug.

"Merry Christmas, Francine. I'm so glad to be here."

A tiny white, yappy poodle scampered through the house like a cyclone. I similarly ran around nervous, chattering away, trying not to get close, trying to get close. We ate a perfect brunch on the patio. From the table we plucked plums and ate them off the tree. We played cards. Told each other our stories. He listened. I laughed.

As the afternoon started to fade and streaks of pink and red surrounded the clouds, we went over to the swing bench I had put up overlooking the lower half of the yard. We sat side by side and I wasn't shaking anymore. Our legs dangled and we rocked it back and forth.

"This, Mike, is a special swing."

"It is?"

"That's right. It's a Truth Swing. Whenever we sit here, we have to tell the truth, no matter what."

"Ahh, I like that idea."

He looked me in the eye, then put his strong arm around my shoulders and leaned back. I curled into him.

He let out a long sigh and said, "I think we'll be sitting here a lot."

That was pretty much all it took. Even though we shook hands when he left, Mike later told me that all he could think that about were my lips and how soft they would be and he couldn't believe that we spent the whole day together without one kiss, let alone lying naked under the Christmas tree.

God so loved me.

CHAPTER 6

Surprise

B Y THE TIME THE next Christmas season came twinkling around, Mike and I were a "couple." The six amazing kids — his four (Vanessa, Melissa, Teresa, Nick) and my two (Molly and Jesse) —- had gotten used to us starting to make "family" decisions. We had pool parties at my house some weekends and sat around the outdoor fire ring telling stories. At his house we watched television, created gourmet dinners (Mike as chef), and sat at the dinner table hearing teenaged boyfriend drama and dispensing love and advice. After dark he sometimes crept up to my patio outside my bedroom and knocked quietly on the door. I always let him in.

At the beginning of December, Mike suggested that we drive up to the Bay Area to meet his family – his sister Kate and her family, and his mom, Dorothy. On the way, we spent a night in Santa Cruz, a favorite town for both of us, at the charming Babbling Brook Bed and Breakfast Inn.

I giggled as we walked into the room. It was like stepping into a bouquet of flowers, with fussy wallpaper, lace curtains, antiques and delicate paintings. This was a real switch for Mike, who loved the simplicity and streamlined surface of yachts. He was a good sport as we set our suitcases in the mirrored armoire, then flopped onto the high bed. He giggled too.

I got up and opened the French doors leading out to a winding brick path and lush garden.

"Come on," I said, "let's see where this goes.

"O.K.," Mike let out a groan and he got to his feet and followed me out the door.

Holding hands, we walked the pathway as I pointed out flowers.

"Look at those impatiens, they are gorgeous! Oh, the agapanthuses look great against that bougainvillea! And the begonias, they're huge!"

It was, in fact, a cavalcade of color on each side, then we turned a corner and there was a sparkling white gazebo. I felt like a princess finding a treasure in the deep wood.

"Come here," Mike said, drawing me into the center of the gazebo. He put his arms around me and held me a long, long time. I heard his heart beating and felt his warm breath in my hair. Then he looked down and leaned in to give me a soft, long, tender kiss.

"I love you."

It was my fairy tale moment. Forty-one years old and I felt 18. A lovely, handsome, tall, blond sweetheart loved me. And for the first time since we met, I actually believed it.

"I love you too, Mikey."

Then I said, "Let's take a picture!"

So I spent the next five minutes fussing with the time delay photo feature set on a rock wall about five feet away. We gave it several tries, running into place, kissing under the gazebo and holding it until we heard the click. Mike played around with backbend kisses, and other silly poses and that night, in the darkness of that frilly room, Mike said it over and over again.

"I love you."

The next day we headed over the hill to Palo Alto to meet Kate, her husband, Don, and their girls at their beautiful, light-filled home. I liked her immediately and listened to them reminisce about cousins and uncles and their dad.

Across the street, Mike's mom, Dorothy, had an assisted living apartment in a nice complex. We said goodbye to Kate and went to meet her. As we walked over, Mike explained that he also had a second family he wanted me to meet, the Earleys. Betty, Charley, and their five daughters essentially adopted Mike throughout his high school years.

"I went to dinner with them one night and never left," explained Mike. "They simply took me in. Betty gave me ice cream privileges and Charley finally had someone to tinker under the hood of a car with. The girls treated me like a brother. All I had to do in return was take their dateless friends to their proms. It was ideal."

For Mike, it was a lifeline. When he was a twelve, he had pretended to be sick one day and stayed home from school. Not wanting to leave him alone for long, his mother had hurried through her errands in her VW bug. She was hit head-on by a truck. She was in a coma for months. Mike's dad shouldered her care and recovery while maintaining his position as football coach and high school principal. Mike just stayed out of the way.

"I was embarrassed by her in my teens," Mike told me. "She was in a wheelchair; her clothes didn't fit right and she smelled funny. Mom could only repeat a few words, and squawked like a broken bird. She drooled and had to be fed. I didn't want to be anywhere near her."

We walked across the street to Dorothy's apartment, where she had lived since shortly after Mike's dad died. She was feisty, had been in that wheelchair for forty years, still played bridge every week, and attended the board meetings of her facility. As we sat with her outside, I was very moved as Mike touched her raw, cracked hands tenderly. He spoke to her about things of the past —family jokes and legends. She nodded her head and repeated one of her few words with a smile, "Mike, Mike, Mike..."

Suddenly an ambulance with siren blaring raced up the street and Dorothy stiffened. She tried to turn her wheelchair away and started screaming, "Help, help, help!" Her sobs and fear took us all to that instant of impact — that moment when a brilliant, educated teacher, who knew John Steinbeck and carried her intellectual sophistication with grace, became a brain-injured paraplegic unable to express nuanced thoughts or feelings.

Mike held her in a tight hug, "It's okay, Mom. Everything is okay."

After Dorothy calmed down we lingered as long as we could before walking back to our car.

Behind the wheel, Mike fought back tears. I rubbed his arm and his shoulders, and kissed his neck, As he drove away. I whispered, "It's not your fault, it's not your fault."

"I wasn't really sick," he said, letting the tears fall. "I wasn't sick..."

By the time we got to Charlie and Betty Earley's house, the mood had brightened. I'd caught on to the fact that this was the family meeting that was going to be a tougher test.

"Hi, this is Francine," Mike said, putting his hand on my back and drawing me into that circle of warmth. Betty hovered around, gave him a hug and me a smile.

"Want some ice cream?"

After eating a bowl of vanilla, I walked around their garden of well-tended grass, fruit trees, and roses. We sat in the den as they showed pictures of Mike as a teen. He really was as tall and skinny as he had claimed. Mike went off somewhere with Betty while I listened to Charley tell story after story of the shenanigans the kids would pull, and the trouble they would be in with the priests at their school.

I couldn't help feeling that I was undergoing some kind of initiation. Charley smoked cigar after cigar and sipped scotch in his chair next to me until the smoke and the tenseness of the day became overwhelming. My head ached and I started to feel sick to my stomach.

"I've really enjoyed meeting all of you," I finally said and stood up. "But I'm afraid I'm going to have to say goodnight. I'm exhausted."

I crawled into the twin in a bedroom still decorated with the girls' high school mementos. Later, when Mike came quietly into the dark, he leaned over me and kissed my cheek before he settled into the other twin.

"They love you," he said.

"Well, they're great," I answered, "and they certainly love you."

Just then I felt a lurch deep in my stomach.

"I don't feel so well."

I got up and made a dive for the bathroom, kneeling before the turquoise toilet and barely opening the lid before I spewed out cigar smoke and ice cream and dinner and Dorothy screaming and being polite and feeling scrutinized. Afterward, I rinsed my mouth. I tiptoed back into the dark room.

"I think it was just the cigars," I whispered and nestled against a pillow.

Mike was already asleep.

God so loved me.

CHAPTER 2

All is Calm, All is Bright

Silent night
Holy night.
All is calm,
All is bright
…Sleep in heavenly peace.
Sleep in heavenly peace.

CHRISTMAS DAY. AGAIN.

The white plastic wand slipped out of my hand and skidded across the bathroom floor. I held my breath and held back tears. Then I bent over, picked it up, and turned it right side up. A pink stripe. An unmistakable pink stripe.

It had been twelve years since a similar white plastic wand had heralded change. Those days it was exciting to find a romantic way to tell my husband, to surprise my parents, to be pregnant at the same time as my sisters. I leaned over Mike's toilet and threw up again – heave after heave after heave. When I sat back on the edge of the tub, my mouth felt like both poison and sandpaper, taste buds recoiling from the bile that fought its way up to my throat one last time as I flung to my knees and released it into the porcelain.

ame time the white wand slipped off the sink and rattled on the ... I found myself on my knees, head bowed, hands above my head ...ing the toilet tank and staring at the pink stripe while I gasped for air.

Ahhh...the position of the contrite heart. Here I am, Lord, exactly where you want me, right? You want me on my knees one way or another. Well you've got me there. What now?

God so loved me.

I got to my feet, brushed my teeth, pulled up my jeans and took the pink-striped wand with me out the door, where Mike was waiting.

Then I burst into tears.

Mike took me in his arms and rocked me while I let the sobs come. Then he pulled me back, dried my cheeks with his huge hands and said solemnly, "I thought we decided not to give each other anything for Christmas."

Smiling up at him through my red, puffy eyes, I couldn't help but laugh.

"Can we take another test? I just don't believe it."

"Believe it."

"I can't believe it. I'm forty-one. I can't be pregnant."

"I know. I'm forty-five," he said. "I've been trying to tell my girls how to avoid this for the last ten years."

We got dressed to go to my family's big Christmas gathering. We decided that we would not tell anyone about the results and just keep it to ourselves. Just as we were going out the door, I said, "Mike, maybe we should take the test one more time."

"You're pregnant."

I got in the car and realized I was still holding the wand. I shoved it into the glove box and put on my seatbelt. A few miles into the trip, I opened the glove box and looked over at Mike.

"We don't need another test, sweetheart. You're pregnant."

"I don't believe it."

God so loved me.

The rest of the day was like one of those dreams where you feel like you are outside of yourself. It was the first time that Mike had met my whole extended family and he charmed them all, laughing it up with the other husbands and helping clean up the dishes; listening intently to my mother's stories and helping Aunt Betty to her chair. He played games with the cousins and made sure I was comfortable, whirling around the family like a busy elf, leaving admiration and good will in his wake. We sang our traditional, "Twelve Days of Christmas" with each small group acting out a day and ending in hilarity. Five golden rings. Four calling birds, three French hens, two turtle doves and (big finish) a part-ridge-in-a-pearrrrrr-tree!

This man – this kind, handsome man – loves me. I'm carrying his child, my family loves him. He's a good man. Wow.

At the end of Christmas Day, Mike and I bustled into the car with presents for my kids in the trunk, goodbyes and well wishes sincerely rendered. As we started down the road we were silent, taking in all in. I was trying to think of something loving and romantic to say when Mike spoke up, eyes straight ahead.

"We found out who killed Fat Ray." He said it with kind of a question mark, like I would somehow know how to respond.

"What?"

"We found out who killed Fat Ray. I got a call from my friend who's a Hell's Angel and they got the story."

I took a moment. Suddenly I was light years away from a silent, holy night.

Whose life am I in? I can't believe that I sitting in a car with someone who can say that sentence – We found out who killed Fat Ray – who can form those words into a meaningful sentence. What am I doing next to this man? Who is he? This is not my life. I am the good girl. I don't get pregnant until I am married. I don't know people called Fat Ray, especially a dead man named Fat Ray and especially a murdered dead man named Fat Ray whose murder was solved by Hell's Angels.

Sleep in heavenly peace, Fat Ray. I'm pregnant.

"Uh, so Mike, who *did* kill Fat Ray?"

CHAPTER 8

A Penny's Worth of Faith

Before I met Mike, my sister once said to me, "You need to marry a man with five children who wants a wife to stay home. Or an accountant."

Well, real life isn't that simple. A family with lots of kids can't afford for the wife to stay home, and, besides, I loved my career as a writer. And Mike was no accountant. If Mike and I were going to make a home and family, it was going to have to include buying a new home, moving, juggling two businesses, six kids, a dog, two cats, and, as it turned out, a new baby.

Piece of cake.

Not that I didn't have my doubts. The closer Mike and I got to a real commitment, the more I tried to seek God — way after the fact, of course. Should I marry this scary big guy? I prayed for some direction even though some would say God wouldn't give me direction unless I repented, broke up, stopped having sex, and dipped myself in the pool seven times.

God so loved me.

If you are familiar with the story of Gideon, the very reluctant prophet called by God to boldly denounce the sins of wayward Judah, then you know the slick method he used to "know God's will." He asked for a sign.

Knowing God's will is big with many believers, even to the point where they discuss his "perfect" will and his "provisional will." I've never really gotten into the difference. All I knew was that I was in need of reassurance, big time. Should I marry Mike?

Then a miracle happened.

Okay, a little one. A tiny, even silly, one.

I used to think that miracles happened to those of great, profound faith. Careful reading of the dealings of God and people, however, demonstrates that miracles happen when our faith is incredibly weak. Think of a faithless Abraham, a retreating Moses, Elizabeth, barren and doubting. If anything, miracles are a last option for those who need the most propping up, overcome with fear and disbelief.

And, by the way, miracles don't necessarily dispel disbelief. You figure that out when you confront the "free will" argument against belief in God. You know, people who say, "Well, why doesn't God just do something big and awesome enough so that *everyone* will have to believe in him?"

Besides the fact that God did lots of big and awesome things, the truth is, there is nothing that can make anyone believe if they don't want to believe. Not even miracles. It didn't happen with Christ standing there in front of everybody raising the dead and it sure can't happen today. It's up to us to take the leap.

So, to bolster my once-strong and still-flickering faith that God would show me his will, I asked for a sign.

I got one.

I found a penny.

The day after I prayed for a sign, I walked from my front door to the car and there, on the driver's side of the cracked driveway, I spotted a penny.

Then came the miracle part. I heard a voice, loud and clear, saying, "This is my gift to you. Mike is my gift to you. Marry him."

Not exactly a burning bush. But then it got weird, as many spiritual things do when they intersect with reality. The next day, I found another penny.

"This is my gift to you. Mike is my gift to you. Marry him," I heard.

The next day, I found another penny. And the next and the next and the next and the next and the next and the next. It was my secret, between me and the God of the entire universe who loved me. Every day.

Same promise. Another penny. I started to believe that God was paying attention.

Mike and I were sitting on the Truth Swing. The day was crisp and the slope toward the pool was covered with crackling avocado leaves. The branches of the plum tree were bare and black. Overhead the tops of the pines swayed. I shivered and moved closer to Mike – his long legs reached the ground to swing us and his arm draped over my shoulders. He wasn't smiling.

"What are you thinking about?"

He turned his head and looked toward the back fence.

"I've been thinking that maybe having this baby will be too much. We already have six kids between us and it's going to be such a hard thing to pull everyone together as it is. I love you and I want to marry you and build a life together and I want to make it as solid as possible."

He turned and looked me in the eyes.

"I don't think that a baby is going to help us do that."

I looked into his eyes, his face, so kind and sincere. And, of course he was right. A baby at our age would make everything infinitely more complicated.

I held Mike's face in my hands and looked up at him.

"I don't have a problem with making this choice," I finally said. "I absolutely believe that women have to make responsible choices about pregnancy. But I don't take it lightly and I need to think about it."

"What should we tell the kids?"

"I want it to be a teaching moment for them, whatever happens. Let's get them together and let them know that we are considering all the options."

"That sounds right to me," said Mike.

That night we gathered everyone together at Mike's, had a fun dinner and then sat everyone down – four girls and two boys, ranging from ages twenty to twelve.

"We want you to know that we are trying to work through the decision to have the baby or not," Mike said. "We'd appreciate it if you'd give us some time to think everything through and decide what's right for the family."

You could hear a pin drop. The girls looked at each other; the two twelve-year-old boys looked down.

I finally spoke out.

"I love you all and I'm really looking forward to the time when we can all create a home together," I said. "This is something that Mike and I have to both want if it's going to be a strong foundation for the family. So we want you to know that over the next few weeks we will be thinking and talking about what to do."

There was silence again. One of the girls suddenly stood up and clapped her hands once. "OK, then, let us know what you decide."

The kids scrambled away from the living room and, after doing the dishes, Molly and Jesse and I drove home in silence.

Once they were tucked in, I walked outside the back door and sat on the stone wall. The sky was filled with stars and a cold wind swept through the bare branches overhead. I leaned forward, closed my eyes and listened.

When I opened my eyes, there, next to my hand, was a penny. I stared at it a long time, then picked it up. "This is my…"

Before I could hear for the umpteenth time that Mike was a gift to me, I stood up, and threw the penny as far as I could and watched as it became lost in a pile of dead leaves and decaying pinecones.

CHAPTER 9

Choice

THE BEDROOM WAS DARK. Outside crickets kept a rhythmic chant. Beyond the bedroom door was a private brick patio with a high wooden fence. Stepping stones wound a path down to the hot tub. Another unmarked path of sorts had been worked through the trees and bushes beyond the wood fence to a dirt driveway crowned with arches of tree branches.

A driveway where a truck could hide from the road, from the windows of the kids' bedrooms upstairs, or from the driveway. Even a white truck.

I was awake at the first sound and the crickets became silent. Tires on the dirt and rock ground to a halt. Headlights went dark.

The knock at night.

I opened the door and was swept up into an embrace that took my breath away.

"What are you doing?" I whispered.

"I miss you."

His kiss was homey and comfortable. This was neither a fairy tale nor romance novel. This was a real man, a good man, coming to see me. Missing me. Wanting me. The knock in the night worked its magic. We snuggled close and soon our snores became a soft counterpoint to the renewed cricket staccato.

What are you doing? The voice rang through my head and my eyes opened wide. I sat up like a shot. It was God asking the real question, but not giving the answers.

What was *I doing? Who was this person? Who was I? Forty-one years-old with a thickening waist, skin tight around a womb that held growing tissue and blood. Cells splitting and doubling every day. A baby! I have a fulltime career, a man who loves me and four almost-stepchildren that I'm trying to get to trust me, plus my own two getting to that eye-rolling stage.*

But I do want a baby. I don't feel finished. I feel like there will always be a "his" and "mine" without the "ours." I can do this. I can do a baby. I've done it for years alone. If I have to be alone again, I'll do it. Lord, help me figure this out.

Morning brought the elephant in the living room into sharp focus. Mike brought me coffee, toast, and an omelet on a tray. I sat up and fluffed the pink pillowcases. He went to pick a rose from outside but as he was coming through the doorway, I threw off the covers and made a beeline for the toilet…head first. Mike was patient while I brushed my teeth and tongue and wiped my mouth with a towel, then sat on the edge of the bed.

"We have to talk," I said. A relationship-killer if I ever heard one. I wasn't even embarrassed by the cliché.

He stared at me, didn't flinch, didn't whine, didn't look away.

"It's not so much about the baby," I started to explain. "I'm pretty old to be wanting a baby. The thought of picking up a diaper bag and carrying it around until I'm forty-two is not a happy thought. But it's about the family."

I shifted on the bed. " Here's what I don't get. How can we say we want to try to blend a family and be a new family and not have the one thing that can really make us one, our baby together? It just doesn't make sense to me."

Mike listened, thought a moment, then framed a response carefully. His deep, soothing voice finally spoke.

"There is also the potential that every one of the other kids may feel instantly left out," Mike said. "We don't want everyone else to feel abandoned or not a part of a family and that only the baby matters to us. Where will that leave us?"

It was a good point. His kids' mother had moved to another state. My two were reaching that age when they disconnect anyway and don't feel that they matter to anyone, let alone a career-mom with a hot husband, three step-daughters who were all homecoming queens and a son who is a confident athlete.

I looked up into Mike's calm face.

"My gynecologist is a friend. I'll call her about my decision."

"Don't you mean *our* decision?" Mike's voice was tight, no longer a melodious lullaby.

I looked him in the eye.

"It's my body. It's happening to me. I will be the one throwing up every morning, sticking to healthy eating, not drinking wine, assuming the responsibility.

"You will get to choose whether or not to be responsible to raise this child," I continued. "Engaging with family will always be a choice for men. They get to choose every day for the rest of their lives!"

I took a breath and swallowed. Mike was looking down.

"My choice is right now."

"And you're going to make it alone? Without me?

"Me and God. We are going to make this choice."

Scripture tells us that words are as powerful as a sword and it's so true. I could see the cuts in Mike's hurt eyes.

"My choice is now," I repeated to Mike.

God so loved me.

CHAPTER 10

Little Star

"HELLO, DOCTOR'S OFFICE."

"Hi, this is Francine Phillips. Can I have an appointment, please? Is there any way that you can fit me in today?

"What is your name?"

"Francine Phillips"

"Can you hold please?"

The phone switched to "hold" status and at first there was silence. I was just thinking "thank goodness there isn't music" when there was a loud drumbeat and Whitney Houston's voice hit the key change.

…And I — I…will always love you.

You.

I will always love…

The voice abruptly broke into the line.

"Dr. Jean-Murat can see you at 1:30 p.m. today.

"Okay, great! I'll be there. Thanks."

I heard a dial tone, but in my mind I was hearing Whitney go higher and higher and higher with "You…..ou….ou…ou…ou!"

Which "You" was I singing to? Was my commitment to Mike or to the baby?

I had no idea.

The office looked like any other. Green. Comfortable chairs. On one wall was a photo collage of babies and moms and thank you notes. Among them was Dr. Carrolle's soft black face lost in a huge white smile, her eyes twinkling.

Carrolle was one of my successful-single-women cohorts. A native of Haiti, she was the granddaughter of a voodoo practitioner but she embraced Western medicine, practiced as a gynecologist and obstetrician, taught belly dancing, and opened a school for girls in Haiti. I had written about her in *San Diego Women* magazine and immediately signed up as her patient.

Carrolle's practice redefined gyno for me. Having a girlfriend at the other end of that metal thing made it so much more endurable. She talked rapidly in her lilting Haitian voice, pulling syllables at random, musically, punctuated with laughter like a bell choir playing Christmas carols.

"So, you are pregnant. How do you feel? What is your man like? Is he a good man?"

"Mike is a really good man," I answered first. "I feel okay, actually, except for throwing up every morning. It was that way with my other kids, too. I threw up on the day they were born."

"So, you did not plan for this to happen, is that right? How old are you?

"Forty-one."

"Not so old. I can take good care of you."

I paused and looked at her joyful face. I wondered what she would say about my next sentence.

"That may not be necessary. I'm thinking of terminating the pregnancy."

Carrolle looked directly at me.

"You don't want a baby with this man?"

It was the perfect question. *The* question. I sidestepped it as well as I could.

"Oh, it's not the man, it's a lot of things. We already have six kids between us. We're older – I'm seeing light at the end of the tunnel when it comes to parenting. We're not sure that a baby is the best choice."

She was still looking right at me.

"I'm…I'm not sure that he wants a baby with me."

My voice caught and I hung my head.

Carrolle let out a deep sigh, then gave me a hug.

"I can still take care of you. But you have to make this decision soon." She locked her eyes into mine. "I will give you until Monday, Francine. For you, I will do this on Monday. After that, I cannot."

I nodded. "I'll know by Monday."

She walked out the door and I dressed quickly. Monday. The photo collage of the happy baby mamas was a blur on my way out the door.

It was Friday. Tonight I had a book signing. I hurried home to get ready. I fed the kids, ran out the door, and flew down the freeway. My co-author and I were sitting on metal chairs for two hours smiling and signing our names to a popular book about San Diego politics. Finally there was a lull. I looked over at him and then looked away.

"Uh, there's something I need to tell you…"

"You're pregnant," he said instantly. I think it was meant to be a joke because it was such a cliché, something from a soap opera. I wasn't quite sure how to answer, but decided to go for it.

"Yes, I am, actually."

He didn't pause for even a split second.

"Wow! That's great!" He was genuinely enthusiastic. "Mike's a really great guy. You're a good couple. This is great!"

"Really?" I put my hand on his arm. "I'm not so sure. I'm thinking of ending the pregnancy."

He spoke with command, as he always did. He lifted his chin and looked down at me. "Francine, have this baby. Marry Mike. You need to do this, and you'll be fine. This is great!"

We started packing up books and he took the boxes from me. "No, no, no. Let me do that. You go on home. You go marry Mike and have that baby."

I left quickly. That was a surprise. I had told two people outside the family about the pregnancy and the world hadn't collapsed on top of me.

The next day was cool and bright and the kids and I headed into the yard. After an hour of raking leaves, we scooped everything into trash bags and cooled off in the swimming pool. The little belly that I carried around in my after-forty body still showed in my black one-piece suit with one small difference. It was hard, not flabby. I floated on my back while

Molly and Jesse did cannonballs off the diving rock. Floating. That's what babies feel. Just floating.

Later that afternoon as I walked around in a wet bathing suit, flip-flops and a beach towel cleaning bathrooms, the phone rang. I perched myself on a patio chair and answered.

"Hello?"

"Hello, darlin'; this is Hap. How are you doin'?"

Hap. Hap was Mike's ex-mother-in-law. She was a matriarch of her family and was wise and loving. She adored Mike and when he separated from her daughter, he moved in with Hap.

"I needed to create a family center, and it needed to be near Hap. Near Grandma," Mike had explained. "The girls didn't feel like they could go home with the boyfriend there, so we created a space where they were welcome and relaxed."

Mike smiled his big smile, "It was fun. I got to stay in the room with the cowboy bedspreads and the bucking bronco lamp."

So Hap ended up being a big part of our lives. She was my champion from the beginning, was part of all of our celebrations, and became surrogate grandma to my two kids.

This all flashed through my mind as I pictured her kind face.

"Hi Hap. Is everything O.K.?"

"Oh, sure. I called to make sure that everything was O.K. with you."

I nestled closer into the patio chair cushions and sighed.

"Well, we're trying to decide about this pregnancy."

The breeze stirred up through the plum tree and I could see the Truth Swing swaying, as if the Holy Ghost was rocking and listening in.

"You know, Francine," said Hap. "Men are all alike. They just don't understand about a baby. They don't seem to think it's real until they hold it in their hands."

"Oh, I think Mike knows it's real."

"He has no idea. If there is one thing I know about Mike it's that he loves kids. Trust me, Francine. You go ahead with this pregnancy. Mike will come around. As soon as he sees his baby, he'll melt like butter."

"Do you really think so?"

"I know so."

Tears started to well up into my eyes. Hap was a religious mixture of Catholicism, mysticism, psychic phenomenon, and Southern hospitality. She was an unlikely prophet, but I wondered if God was speaking from her lips straight into my heart. I looked around for a penny, but there was none in sight. I felt so alone.

"Well, thanks Hap. I really appreciate the call."

"Trust me, darlin'. He'll come around."

"We'll see…"

Why didn't Mike call? He knew I had been to the doctor.

I tucked Molly and Jesse into their beds that night, smelling their skin and trying to remember them as wiggly infants.

It was not hard to recall Molly's liquid sparkling eyes, rosy cheeks, and curly long hair. "Are you holding a doll or is that a baby?" strangers used to ask. Now she was a teenager, awkwardly tall but still beautiful enough to take your breath away.

Jesse was nearly twelve and his bunk bed was covered with toys and dirty, crumbled balls of T-shirts and socks. He had been a bundle of energy as a toddler – on the go at all times. He was late to start talking but once he started he never stopped.

"It's not so much the questions that are annoying," my friend Carol had said. "It's the pitch! The tone! If he could just learn to lower his voice."

Mom! Mom! Mom! Mom! Mom! I remembered distinctly his staccato squeak that was finally starting to tone down. Jesse had been tough duty. Could I do that again? A decade older?

I called my sister.

"So, Joleen. You had a baby in your forties. If you had to do it over again, would you do it?"

I was surprised by the long pause.

"Well, it seems like we just dragged her around with us going to the boys' games and practices. I feel like she didn't really get the magical childhood. It's just hard to do the same things – make a teepee or get out crayons – when you are an older mother. All the other mothers are cute and young and full of energy while you're teaching a teenager to drive. You're getting into shouting matches until midnight instead of reading nursery rhymes at eight o'clock with a music box playing *Twinkle, Twinkle Little*

Star in the background. It's not the same. There's no *Twinkle, Twinkle Little Star.*"

"Hmmm. Well, that's something to think about."

She changed her tone. "Oh, Fran, just go ahead! Why not? Isn't it kind of late to stop it at this point? It'll be fun."

"It's not too late," I said shortly, annoyed. "I have two more days to decide."

"Oh." Joleen said. "I hope you can figure it out.

"Louis," she hollered to her husband, "She has two days to decide…"

"Stop it!" I said sharply. "Don't have side conversations while I'm talking to you! You always do that!"

"What? Oh. Sorry. But Louis —"

"Listen, I've got to go," I said. "Thanks for your opinion."

"— Louis says have the baby."

"I've got to go."

I hung up. My head started hurting at the back and the pain was coming around to the sides. Tears welled up and overflowed and my nose started to run. I grabbed the Kleenex box and took out five or six tissues and sat on my bed, blowing, wiping, blowing more.

Still crying, I got into a roomy night gown and crawled under the covers. Why was I crying? Why didn't Mike call?

I woke up. The room was not completely dark. It felt like about 2 a.m. I had left the blinds open and the streetlight filtered through the trees, leaving soft, gently-moving shadows on the leafy wallpaper until I felt like I was in a forest. Crickets scratched their lyrics to one another against their legs outside the window. Everything else was hushed. I arranged the pillows and sat up in bed.

Suddenly, to my right, a tiny light glowed among the stars outside. I stared in amazement as it fell from the sky. The light suspended for a moment outside the window glass, then floated into the room. The light was a warm, white ball, reminding me of Tinkerbell, but different. Softer.

The pinpoint of light drifted playfully around the room, dancing its way near my face. I was transfixed. My skin was cold and I held my breath. Then I heard a quiet voice. The voice of a little girl.

It's all right, Mommy, the voice said sweetly. *I don't have to be born. I'm perfectly fine. I'll be fine. You don't have to have me.*

I stared. The light flickered and grew brighter. It circled in front of my head, then swirled and swooped its way to the window. The next second it was through the window and soaring high, high up into the dark sky. I watched until it disappeared.

I wasn't sure I could move. For a long time I stared out the window, tears streaming down my face.

Twinkle, twinkle little star
How I wonder what you are!
Up above the world so high.
Like a diamond in the sky.
Twinkle, twinkle little star,
How I wonder what you are!

CHAPTER 11

The Consequences

For a long time I sat up and stared out the window.

What just happened? Was that my baby girl?

The double-hung wood and glass window embedded in the thick plaster walls of my bedroom looked out over a hand-built brick patio. It was tucked behind an old wooden fence and hidden by a tall canopy of pines. Beyond, the winding two-lane road was silent.

Beyond the treetops, the black sky, thick with stars, seemed like a different universe, very far away. I searched for a special star, one that might be brighter or closer or winking at me. But they were just hanging there as a reminder that the sky holds so much more than we know. So much more.

What just happened?

I closed my eyes and gulped, my throat suddenly dry, my arms and legs tingling.

Uh... God, is that you?

The question echoed in my head. The silence of the room was broken by crickets and the rustling of some animal in the brush near the fence. A motorcycle in the distance grinded its way toward the neighborhood and changed gears near my driveway, then sped away.

Everything was back to normal.

Everything had changed.

I had just been given a pass to keep my life manageable, under control, planned and on an even keel. I could stay in my comfort zone. Chaotic, yes, but chaos of my own making. No baby, just happily ever after with a kind, funny, gorgeous man. A man who held my hand.

"It's O.K., Mommy."

Suddenly nausea washed through me. I pushed aside the covers and ran to the bathroom. I fell to my knees as I lifted the toilet cover and felt my insides roiling in waves. I blindly grabbed a wash cloth and wiped the bitter bile from my lips. Carefully, I got up and started to brush my teeth, hoping not to trigger a gag reflex. I pulled on my old terrycloth robe and dragged myself upstairs to the kitchen.

Without thinking I put the coffeemaker away under the counter and set the kettle on the stove. Putting a teabag in my favorite mug, I grabbed the water at the first shriek of the whistle, poured it into my cup and leaned over the fragrant steam. Glancing over at the empty spot where the coffeemaker used to sit and then down at my tea, I realized what I had done.

I'm going to have a baby.

The sun started to streak through the trees when I was still trying to think through the implications of this decision. If I was going to have this baby, then I had to face the likelihood that I would have to raise her by myself. The wisdom and calm that I had come to depend on in Mike would be missing from my life. No doubt I would be afraid, as always.

God would be there, but that doesn't really cut it at the 2 a.m. feeding when my nipples feel like they are being torn from my breasts or when I jam my finger trying to strap the car seat while the other two children are fighting over getting to sit in front or in back. When the crying won't stop no matter how much you are rocking and you forgot your slippers and your feet are freezing. When you run out of formula and there's no one to go to the store.

Once, in a poem, I called it "parenting without a net."

God so loved me.

Because I thought I had learned that whatever God was, God was *not* a safety net. That was for sure. And what was all that stuff about the penny and Mike being a gift? Choosing the baby meant losing Mike.

"It's O.K., Mommy."

My little girl had come to me and told me that she didn't need to be born. She came from the sky, in twinkling starlight, and spoke to me in her tiny voice. Remembering that moment kind of trumped everything about Mike — the deep voice, the warm hugs, the soft kisses; the man who wanted to hear my voice the last thing at night, and his amazing children whom I loved, his yappy poodle, and most certainly the penny.

Of course you need to be born, little star.

I'm going to have a baby.

CHAPTER 12

Follow Me or Die

THE NEXT MORNING I threw up.

Get used to it.

Later I picked up the phone.

"Dr. Jean-Murat's office."

"Hello, this is Francine Phillips. I'd like to make an appointment."

"What is your name, please?"

"Francine Phillips."

"And what is the nature of the appointment?"

"I'm pregnant. She knows."

"And what is the purpose of your visit?"

I'm going to have a baby. I'm going to give up the beautiful man I LOVE for a tiny lump of flesh no bigger than my finger. The man who loves me, who is kind and sweet and funny and extremely handsome because of a baby voice in a speck of light. I'm letting him go because I want God back and I thought he was telling me one thing and now I think He's telling me something else and I'm completely confused about that part, but I know that I'm going to have this baby. Is that a good enough answer for you!

"I'm not terminating the pregnancy. Be sure to let her know that, O.K.?"

Pause.

"I can have her see you at 2 p.m. tomorrow."

"Perfect, thank you."

I breathed deeply. *That went well.*

The next part not so much.

I looked out the window at the oaks, bare and vulnerable against the blue skies. Protective leaves had long ago fallen and lay in mounds, dry and withering. I glanced at the pool and instantly flashed back in time. Imaginary boys were jumping and splashing and running alongside the water, and there was Mike extending his huge hand. His smile, the Truth Swing, his warmth surrounding me and the feel of his flannel shirt when I buried my head into his chest. The knock in the night.

God so loved me.

I got up and poured more hot water into my teacup and put both hands around it as I sat down again, thinking about Mike and letting it sink in what was probably going to happen. He was going to walk away, I just knew it. I was so afraid.

Once, a few years earlier, I had been part of a day-long seminar that included a team-building exercise in which each group was assigned a disaster scenario. My team's challenge was a plane crash in Alaska. We had to learn to listen and evaluate ideas, show leadership, practice persuasion, and decide upon a course of action with many alternatives leading to possible death. There were elaborate maps showing obstacles, or settlements, that could be helpful or could be blind alleys. It took hours to complete the exercise and we knew each other's strengths and weaknesses at the end of that time.

Recently I had explained the whole thing to Mike and suggested that maybe we try something like that to get to know each other better.

Mike looked amused, and patted my hand. His eyes twinkled and he answered me in his deep voice.

"Follow me or die."

"What?"

"It's simple. It would not take three hours. Follow me or die."

"That's it?"

Mike leaned into me.

"I spend many weeks every year on a little floating piece of wood and canvas in the middle of the ocean. I check everything three times. I know the risks for miles around. I weigh all the options before the first sail goes up. I've been very good at what I do and at staying alive, sweetie. Follow me or die."

I was about to call Follow Me or Die.

The phone rang twice.

"This is Mike!"

"Hey Mikey, how are you?"

"Fran! I'm great! What's up?"

The normalcy of his voice was like a punch in the stomach. We hadn't spoken in days.

I'm okay. Except for the throwing up."

Silence.

"I've decided to go ahead with the pregnancy. This amazing thing happened that I'd like to tell you about. Any chance you can come over tonight?"

My voice kind of caught in my throat and I realized that I was hoping against hope. After all, basically I was telling him that I was choosing the baby. I would rather have the baby without him than him without the baby.

And we both knew it.

"I'm kind of slammed tonight. Sorry."

"I have a doctor's appointment at 2 p.m. tomorrow. Would you like to come with me?"

"No, Francine. No, I don't think I would like that."

I could hear the hurt in his voice and imagined his green eyes small and sore.

Please. Please, please, please! I know we can do this. I know that it will be hard but we can make a family. We can make everyone feel included and loved and special. Because these kids are special, every one of them. They are God's gift to us. You are God's gift to me. He tells me every day.

I tried to sound very calm and unemotional, just as if I was describing the normal course of events. Not like a raving, pregnant nut.

"Well, Mikey, I'd like very much to see you, if you could make some time. Our baby appeared to me last night in a twinkle of light. It's a girl. I'd like to tell you about it."

Pause.

"We'll see. Uh, I've gotta' go."

"Well, bye, then. Mikey, I love you."

"I've gotta' go."

Click. Follow-Me-or-Die hung up. I felt empty.

I got up and poured more hot water into my tea cup, and again put both hands around the cup until the warmth radiated up my arms and into my heart. Mike was not going to be able to do this. He was not a man of faith and would never understand how to take the leap that this would require. Not a leaper, Mike. A planner, yes. With contingencies for his contingencies. But this was a wild jump to a place where he would have to completely trust me, not his plans, not his judgment. Me. Based on a penny and a twinkle. No way.

I understood, I really did. But I was already across the chasm reaching back to him and that went against everything about him.

Finishing my tea again, warm and teary, I straightened my back and felt some resolve. I could do this alone. I could watch him walk away from me. Tears welled up and my arms were suddenly cold again.

I didn't follow and I wasn't going to die.

Anyway, isn't that Jesus' line?

Follow me?

CHAPTER 13

In Sickness and In Health

When you walk through a storm
Keep your head up high
And don't be afraid of the dark
At the end of a storm is a golden sky
And the sweet silver song of a lark
You'll Never Walk Alone

This song, *You'll Never Walk Alone*, composed by Richard Rodgers and Oscar Hammerstein for the musical, *Carousel,* has been an anthem for singers and an inspiration for listeners. I first heard it in my mother's rich alto as part of the Mothers' Singers – a choir put together by the Dahlia Heights Elementary School PTA. She loved singing it. She wasn't the only one.

Here are the artists who have recorded *You'll Never Walk Alone:*

The American Tenors
Ed Ames
Gene Ammons
Angelis
Louis Armstrong
John Arpin
Chet Atkins
Joe Augustine

The Bachelors
Michael Ball
Shirley Bassey
Laurie Beecham
The Blind Boys Of
Alabama
Blue Haze
Pat Boone

Brooklyn All-Stars
C W S Glasgow Band
Glen Campbell
José Carreras
Johnny Cash
Eddie Chamblee
Ray Charles
Enrique Chia
Kelly Clarkson
Richard Clayderman
Jan Clayton
Perry Como
Ray Conniff
Barbara Cook
Michael Crawford
Czech Symphony Orch.
Doris Day
Muriel Dickinson
Plácido Domingo
The Drury Land
Theatre Orch.
Jimmy Durante
Billy Eckstine
Simon Estes
Eileen Farrell
Ferrante & Teicher
The Five Blind Boys Of
Alabama
The Flamingos
Renee Fleming
Myron Floren
Florida Boys
Nettie Fowler
Sergio Franchi
Aretha Franklin
Paul Freeman
Jane Froman
Bill & Gloria Gaither

Judy Garland
Lesley Garrett
John Gary
Gay Men's Chorus
of L.A.
Gerry & The
Pacemakers
Wayne Gratz
Byrdie Green
Lee Greenwood
Guy & Ralna
Roy Hamilton
Sam Harris
Linda Hibberd
Katherine Hilgenberg
Burt Holiday
Jason Howard
Engelbert Humperdinck
Ferlin Husky
Imaginations
The Imperials
Mahalia Jackson
Vern Jackson
Joni James
Jon Jang
Papa Bue's Viking
Jazzband
Christine Johnson
Meg Johnson
Shirley Jones
Tom Jones Michael
Junior
Kamahl
Fiona Kimm
The Knickerbockers
Patti LaBelle
Mario Lanza
The Lennon Sisters

The Lettermen
Liverpool FC
London Theatre Orch.
John MacNally
Johnny Maestro
Bill Medley
Melodie
The Mighty Clouds
Of Joy
Brett Mitchell
Mormon Tabernacle
Choir
Jim Nabors
Tom Netherton
Olivia Newton-John
Martin Nievera
The Oak Ridge Boys
Daniel O'Donnell
101 Strings Orch.
The O'Neal Twins
Frank Patterson
Mike Pender
Peter Pan Kids
Bernadette Peters
Elvis Presley
Billy Preston
Johnny Preston
Colin Pryce-Jones
John Raitt
Boots Randolph
Eric Reed
Jerry Reed
Joanna Riding
The Righteous Brothers
Rev. Cleophus Robinson
Robson & Jerome
Rodgers &
Hammerstein

Richard Rodgers
Daniel Rodriguez
Kevin Rowland
Robin S.
Tony Sandler
The Sentimental Strings
Nina Simone
Frank Sinatra
Johnny "Hammond"
Smith
Kate Smith
Keely Smith
Smoking Popes
Dorothy Squires
Jo Stafford
The Starlite Orchestra
Starsound Orchestra
Barbra Streisand
Enzo Stuarti
J.D. Sumner
Grady Tate
Dame Kiri Te Kanawa
Bryn Terfel
Claramae Turner
Gordon Turner
Conway Twitty
Ronan Tynan
Malcolm Vaughan
Regine Velasquez
Gene Vincent
Fred Waring & His
Pennsylvanians
Dottie West
Andy Williams
James Williams
Kevin Williams
Roger Williams
Jackie Wilson

Women's Chorus Of Dallas
Finbar Wright
Tammy Wynette
Glenn Yarborough
Norma Zimmer
Nonoy Zuniga

In my book, any song that can attract singers like Mahalia Jackson, Perry Como, Gerry & The Pacemakers, Placido Domingo, the Peter Pan Kids, Patti LaBelle, and the Smoking Popes has a certain breadth of appeal.

It's the theme song for the doctrine of God Helps Those Who Help Themselves. And, even better, it avoids mentioning God altogether. What could be more perfect for early twentieth century America, where we also had to pack up our troubles in our old kit bag and smile, smile, smile?

As if we are in control.

Because the truth of the matter is, holding your head up high is exactly the wrong thing to do in a storm.

In the Bible, the Book of Matthew, Chapter 8, tells about Jesus and his posse of followers crossing the Sea of Galilee. The disciples had seen healings and miracles but they didn't really understand what was going on. They couldn't see that God was present among them in Jesus. Hadn't figured out that they themselves might need saving at some point.

So Matthew writes that a storm came up and started whipping their little fishing boat around until waves were crashing over their heads. Jesus was asleep. But once that boat started taking on water, they ran over to wake him up.

"Lord, save us!" they cried. "We're drowning!"

Some of us kind of like our God to be asleep. Just off in the distance; there but not there. Certainly not interfering. But when the storm comes, some people have the sense to cower and beg and not wander around thinking that hope in their hearts is going to somehow end in the sweet silver song of a lark.

The people doing that *do* walk alone. Really alone. And the sky where they are walking to is pitch black and ends in a chasm of misery.

"Lord, save us!"

Jesus woke up and did just that.

* * *

"Lord, save me!"

The day was overcast and a chill set in within those thick plaster walls. I put on a coat and some thick boots and tromped around the property picking up small branches and placing them in a faded shawl to bring back to the house. Once inside, I wadded up sheets of old *Daily Californian* newspapers, where I had been the editor, and jammed them together over the grate. Then I crisscrossed the branches over them in just the right amount to mix air and fuel. With the snap of a match, it all went up in flames.

I pulled the rocking chair right up next to the hearth and wrapped myself in an afghan my mother had made and started to rock. My mother. Hmm. This would be a tough one. She really liked Mike. Well, who didn't?

I didn't know how Molly and Jesse would react. After over a year of having Mike in their lives, loving them, losing him would be hard. Probably they would blame me, but I think they might love the baby.

Mike's kids. I would miss their laughter and frivolity – it was so infectious and new to me, the stuffy, serious writer.

Well, at least I wouldn't have to get caught up in the dating thing again. That was it for me. Over. Pregnant, 41, two pre-teens and a broken heart. Stick that on a dating profile.

O.K. Lord, looks like it's going to be just you and me.

Finally, I went to pick up Molly and Jesse from their schools. We got through homework and I made the chicken cacciatore that I had made for Mike on that first Christmas dinner, just so I could savor the onions and garlic and wine taste and remember wanting to know the taste of his kiss.

I resolved that I would not linger on this breakup. I was not going to take refuge in being a victim. I was a woman; this was the life I was making for myself. No regrets whatsoever. After I tucked the kids in bed, I again stoked the fire and made a cup of tea. There was a penny on the kitchen counter. I picked it up and rubbed it between my fingers, then let it slip into my pocket.

When the room was finally starting to get warm I heard rustling outside. The driveway gate was being opened and it scraped the asphalt and pushed aside cracking leaves. Then I heard tires outside the window. My heart started beating faster but I stayed in my rocker, hoping against hope.

Could that be Mike? Was he going to say that he loved me or that he never wanted to see me again? My hands started trembling.

Through the lace curtains I could see a white truck rumble onto the driveway.

My heart beat faster.

Footsteps on the walkway.

Faster still.

A knock.

Stepping towards the door, the wood floor creaked as I made my way across the room. My head was down. By now everything was trembling.

Opening the door slightly, Mike pushed it wide and gathered me in his arms. He pulled me tight against him and just held me, swaying and whispering.

"I'm sorry, I'm sorry."

"I know. It's okay."

Tears were in his eyes.

"I'm so sorry."

"I love you, Mikey."

"I love you, Frannie. So much. So much."

We held hands and moved to the couch. After a moment he asked the question I had been dreading.

"Would you really rather have the baby without me than me without the baby?"

I felt sheepish, but lifted my head and looked at him.

"I guess…yes, that seemed like what I had to do. I love you so much. There is just no way I could *not* have your child."

"Even if it meant losing me?"

"Even if it meant that, but I hoped that you would still love me. And that you would love her."

Mike looked at me and sighed. His face looked worn and I knew this was hard for him.

"Well, I would rather have you with the baby than not have you at all. You are the world to me and if that's what you need, that's what we'll do."

My head hung down for a moment. When I lifted it up, I got to taste that kiss one more time and we spent a long time holding each other, watching the fire, and then holding each other more. He was tall and warm and soft and strong and I fit just right into his arms.

Mike was back. He still loved me. We were going to be a family.

Thank you Jesus!

You can go back to sleep now.

God so loved me.

* * *

We put a down payment on a house and decided that it was time to elope. We ran away to Las Vegas like two wayward teenagers. I refused to embarrass my mother by having a wedding that involved guests from the Baptist church celebrating her divorced, pregnant 41-year-old daughter. Better to just get this done.

Fortunately, my cousin, Paul, was the pastor of the cathedral-like First Presbyterian Church of Las Vegas, where we would be married. Still, the queue at City Hall to get the marriage license was as colorful as any Vegas chorus line – young servicemen and their younger girlfriends, old men and gaudily-dressed hookers. The block was surrounded by chapels of every sort, limousines pulled up to the loading curb as part of numerous wedding packages offered by garish billboards. Mike and I giggled. The wedding was the next afternoon.

We stayed at a simple hotel off the strip Paul knew about and I took a nap while Mike went to get a haircut. Inside the room was a huge basket of flowers, fruit, and chocolate sent by my two sisters in support of our "secret" wedding.

Mike came back smiling.

"The barber was a cool guy. He retired here a few years ago."

Mike made a friend wherever he went.

"I almost invited him to the wedding."

That made me laugh, so typical of Mike and a huge part of why I loved him. As it turned out, just the two of us stepped into the hushed chapel of the huge church under the spectacular stained glass window. My cousin stood at the front with Mike, both of them grinning. Paul's wife, Joan, played the organ and I waddled down the aisle. Their daughter was the sole guest. She took pictures.

Our vows were as fervent as any bride and groom.

> *To have and to hold,*
> *From this day forward,*
> *For better, for worse,*
> *For richer, for poorer,*
> *In sickness and in health,*
> *To love and to cherish,*
> *Until death do us part.*

We had a beautiful dinner holding hands and sharing dreams at the top of Caesar's Palace. Back in our room, I crawled under the covers. Mike looked a little nervous.

"Uh, I'm going to go down to the casino. I'll be right back."

It felt like a slap.

"You're leaving me alone on our wedding night?"

"I'll be right back."

After the door shut, I went to the basket and got out a handful of chocolates, carefully pulling back the foil and letting them slowly melt in my mouth. Silent tears fell down my cheeks until sleep overcame me.

The next morning we returned to the church, this time taking a seat near the back with hundreds of congregants. Paul entered with dark flowing robes and climbed up to the pulpit. It was Easter Sunday and I was determined to begin our marriage in the presence of God.

Sometime around the fourth hymn, Mike leaned over and whispered, "This is great! Now I can never forget our anniversary. It's the day before Easter."

I looked at him to see if he was kidding. He wasn't.

"Hate to break it to you, Mike. But Easter comes on a different Sunday every year. Our anniversary is April 10."

After the long drive home, Mike dropped me off. The house we bought was still in escrow, so for the next six weeks I lived at my house with my kids and he lived at his house with his kids. Every night we called each other.

"Good night, wife."

Good night, husband."

After a week or two, Mike joked, "You, know, this isn't all that bad. Maybe we should keep it like this."

I rubbed my aching back and pulled up the socks I wore to keep my feet from freezing.

"I don't *think* so."

I still found a penny every day and heard God speak, *Mike is my gift to you.* I was grateful to have a husband who was a wonderful father and loving man who was respected by everyone in the community.

I wonder what it will be like to live together?

CHAPTER 14

Knocking on Heaven's Door

MOLLY WAS IN HIGH school when I began to miss God more and more. There was a hole in my heart. I couldn't admit that it was the gaping "God-shaped hole" that Blaise Pascal insisted we all have inside that only God can fill. Just little things that did not jibe with the way I was raised and the way I had once conducted my life that caused a little discomfort. Something didn't fit.

I wanted to pray and, for the first time in a long time, I felt that God was listening for my voice.

The baby, Anna, was about four years old now, and every once in a while I would look at her and remember teaching Sunday school to Molly at that age. A bright little face being reassured that God was with her every minute of the day and loved her. Teaching her that God was reliable and there, particular important to Molly when her daddy was not. Where was that Sunday school teacher? Where was that reliable God?

Now there was a new daddy in the home, plus brothers, sisters, cats, a dog, and a baby. In a big house at the top of the hill with a view of the sky as wide as the world. I saw God in that sky every morning in the whitest clouds and every night in the fiery sunset. Wasn't that enough?

One Sunday Molly said, "Mom, would you come to church with me? Dad doesn't go anymore since he and Lynn broke up."

I was surprised but I had kind of seen it coming. It didn't take much hesitation to jump in.

"Sure."

It had been ten years.

God so loved me.

Going back to my old church felt odd and uncomfortable. I held my breath and walked down the stairs to the small, basement sanctuary. Same music, same families, same dedicated band of believers trying to do church in some sort of righteous way, to raise kids to know and love God.

I joked with the pastor about a 10-year statute of limitations on staying away from your ex-husband's church after a divorce. He looked worried. For the most part, the more I came, the more I felt, "What is SHE doing here," just under the surface.

One Sunday, I couldn't hold in my tears.

"Are you okay?"

Mandy Stone, a talented artist with an "unchurchy" wisdom, sat down next to me. I heaved an uneven sigh.

"Mandy, there's just no place for me here. I don't fit anywhere. There's no room."

I bowed my face in my hands and my shoulders shook.

Mandy's soft eyes connected with mine. "I'm so glad you are here. I don't fit in either, and I've been coming forever." She swallowed as I looked surprised. "And you know what? Jim hasn't been sure of his faith for years."

"What! He plays the piano for the church! He knows all of the hymns by heart! He closes his eyes as we worship."

"Yeah, I know. That's his only way of connecting with what's going on at church. He really doesn't know what he believes about God anymore."

Then Mandy couldn't help a little grin. "Some people would be shocked and horrified if they knew."

Well, that worked. If Jim Stone could sit and play so expressively and beautifully during worship with cold darts of doubt in his heart, maybe I could keep sitting in the pews alone and wonder what I was doing there.

Because the truth of the matter was, I had grown up giving service to the church and didn't really feel comfortable just sitting there taking it all in. It wasn't church unless I was serving — giving my five loaves and two fishes, or was it two loaves and five fish? Either way, the belief had been drilled into me that if you give everything you have to the service of the church, God will multiply it and it will become a miracle. Give and it will be given to you, full measure, pressed down, shaken together and running over. In other words, God isn't trying to cheat you. But I no longer knew what I had to give.

The book of Hosea in the Old Testament serves to demonstrate the lengths God will go to woo us back into his loving arms. Hosea was a prophet, one of the few men and women God chose to make real-life, real-time revelations to the greater community. Hosea had the unlucky calling to marry a prostitute and love her. She mocked him, left him, and slept with other men publicly, scorning his manhood and probably making more money than he did. We only read about it now, but in the days of Hosea, it was out there for everyone in the community to see and gossip about.

Hosea begged her to come back. He loved her all the more, shouting that he would meet her on her own terms and seduce her back. His love was bigger than all the humiliation she made him suffer, and he forgave it all, no matter what. To the everyday person down the street watching this drama, it was pretty embarrassing that Hosea had no conditions, no punishments. Where was his pride?

Today's church is often pretty much the same way. Too many churchgoers are waiting for sinners to earn approval before they offer them love. They hold back and reserve judgment, forgetting that God warned his followers not to judge at all, ever. Not even for the sake of having pride.

Especially *not* for the sake of having a little pride.

So I kept going, flapping around like a dying fish on the dock with no place to serve, no sense of belonging. Not understanding that God loved me desperately, without pride. It never occurred to me that it was okay for me to simply receive. I had not been taught to receive.

Mike tolerated my absence on Sunday morning, usually by going down to the yacht club and checking his boats. He would come back smelling of sea and sunshine and diesel. But sometimes he came with me to the little basement church service. He listened intently, keeping a firmly closed mind about their take on spiritual truth.

Maybe it was the fact that spiritual truth was clothed in shorts and Hawaiian shirts that made it unrecognizable to him. The church was anything but traditional. Banjos, guitars, clapping, square dancing, skits, games, camp, potlucks and church-at-the-beach. Mike was raised in the

Catholic tradition that required dressing up, wearing veils and robes, and creating a Sunday persona opposite the reality of Monday through Saturday. It required compartmentalization, which Mike loved.

In fact, Mike was a master at compartmentalization. We had eight different bank accounts, just so that everything could be separated into Household, Yacht Outfitting, Write Now (my writing business), and Rental — each with checking and savings. In addition, we had four Charles Schwab accounts. Each month was a paperwork tsunami.

I put everything on the computer and tried to diligently keep up. This was not my strong suit. Mike would smile, wave it off, and then we would have massive end-of-the-year data entry marathons. Not pretty. I tried to explain that we could have just a few accounts and do all the separations through computer categories, but it was no-go. Eventually I gave up trying to computerize our accounts at all. Our finances became a source of pain that we stuffed down below the crises of everyday life. I was a writer, he was a yacht guy; nobody had married an accountant.

But slowly, to my surprise, God was given a compartment in Mike's life. Not in the wheel house, but somewhere aft. As Mike began to attend church more regularly, he enjoyed talking about things of the universe; God's existence; right and wrong; Jesus' divinity. At times I would ask him to pray with me as we lay in the dark. I would hold his huge hand, rest my head on his shoulder and close my eyes, feeling like I was in the safest place in the world. I would pour out my heart to God and Mike would join me in an "Amen," then give me a hot kiss. Prayer as aphrodisiac.

Other times Mike and I would engage in the argument about God in the ten seconds we had at night after the kids were asleep and we were still awake. Finally, after listening to Mike's same series of doubts about God for the umpteenth time, I asked him.

"How long have you had these doubts, Mike?"

"Since I was about eighteen," he said.

"Well, you're fifty. Are you planning to resolve this or just die wondering?"

The church bought an old property, gutted most of it and remodeled and landscaped it into an attractive, welcoming place. There were suddenly more people, an exploding and lively youth group, an expanded music ministry, church skits and dramas and a strong Sunday school for Anna.

Mike was impressed that everyone had pitched in to build the church, including our Jesse, who spent the summer being a "go-fer." Pastor Craig painted every wall. This was something real. Wood and concrete. Commitment.

Mike changed from being a doubter to becoming a seeker.

About this time Craig was holding an annual seeker's class — a discussion place for those wanting to explore what following Jesus was all about. Mike attended, made friends with everyone, of course, and began to come with me to church more often. He started to sing some of the songs. He started talking to some of the other men.

The Apostle Paul, in his advice-giving letters from prison to the churches he had started across the Middle East and Northern Africa, reminds the new Christians to "forsake not the fellowship of others." He doesn't say, forsake not the sermon, forsake not the women's tea, forsake not the Christmas Eve service. It's the community that makes all the difference in the life of the Christian. People are going to lead you to God. And not the ones you might expect.

Bruce and Lurene Stevenson were an older couple with a life-long faith. Bruce was tall like Mike, and loved the ocean. Before retiring to San Diego, Bruce had been a high school principal near Los Gatos and knew Mike's father, Fred, who had been the principal at Los Gatos High School. Bruce had owned a sailboat and had spent years enjoying San Francisco Bay and the sea. Here was a soul mate for a man in search of his soul. Every Sunday Bruce would seek out Mike to greet him and chat.

Mike really enjoyed Bruce and Lurene, so we made plans to take them sailing one Sunday after church. It was a glorious, sunny, brisk afternoon. We got on board our shared yacht, *Insurgent*, and took off out of San Diego bay toward the Pacific Ocean, sunlight skittering off the rippling water. Lurene and I were fine at first, both bundled in jackets and watching these two men navigate the sailboat, turning, filling the sails, skimming across the water and having the time of their lives. Lurene and I were turning green, but Bruce was ecstatic.

"You have made my *year*!" Bruce shouted as we headed back. "This has been fantastic."

I was impressed with Mike's kindness to share sailing with someone who could no longer manage to sail on his own.

Mandy and Jim Stone became another touchstone for us. Jim was not only gifted in music, he was also gifted in math and science and had a wicked sense of humor – devastatingly sarcastic with a gentlemanly touch. Mike really liked him.

Mandy started a visual arts team to help her with church décor and visual worship and there I finally found my niche of service — a place to fit in and express my own take on God through evocative worship. I started to feel like a part of the church – a part of the body of Christ. Like the wayward wife of Hosea, I was lured and wooed back to Christ.

Jim and Mandy hosted a monthly dinner for about eight couples and Mike and I became regulars at their beautiful home surrounded by trees, natural stone and filled with art, music and a sense of welcome that was unsurpassed. Over the years, other groups had tried studying the Bible or using set curriculum. Those groups drifted apart. Ours had dinner once a month for years and years where we experienced unconditional acceptance and love, told stories and shared our struggles. Out of all that time, I remember only one night that we actually talked about God. Yet we all knew that somehow he was there among us.

During this time, Mike became more intrigued by this church thing. Unbeknownst to me, he called Jim one day and asked him to lunch. They met down at a restaurant near the Yacht Outfitting office and sat facing the bobbing sailboats and sparkling water. After a few pleasantries, Mike got the heart of the matter.

"Jim," he said, "I've been thinking a lot about Stephen Hawking and the randomness of the universe and the chaos theory of physics. And I was just wondering, how do you rectify all of that science with believing in God? I'm just not sure how to do it. I want to believe, but that is the last thing to get in my way."

So Jim, with his lifetime of church-going, his years of church youth groups and his ability to play by heart every hymn ever written, answered Mike's question with absolute truth.

"I don't," said Jim. "I have no idea if God is real."

CHAPTER 15

Take a Bow

IT WAS AFTER THE annual data-entry marathon that I started to suspect. Over the last few months, Mike had been working harder and longer — staying late at the office, working on the weekends. He was stressed out, snappy, not his usual easy-going self. One night we took up our positions on the love seats that faced each other in the bedroom. The upscale version of the Truth Swing. Talk was in order. I went first.

"Honey, what is going on? Can you tell me? Everything seems to be so hard lately and you are under a lot of pressure. Is something wrong?"

We both were under pressure. My mother had suffered three strokes in three years. Like most parent illnesses, Mom's vulnerability brought out the worst in everyone involved. Although Mike was saintly in listening and sustaining me against constant drama, I was furious in about fifteen directions.

My heart was breaking, watching her inevitably slip away. There were a thousand painful moments.

Alone together one night, resting next to her on her soft bed in her beautiful home, Mom looked at me and whispered, "What happens when we die?"

I grasped her gnarled hand. "Well, most of what I know comes from the Bible and from people who have experienced death and come back. The Bible says we are present with the Lord at once, filled with peace and surrounded by a great light. Some say that loved ones come to meet us and bring us to the presence of God. Jesus is right there with us and we are covered with grace because he experienced life and death as a human so we could be set free from death."

"I believe that," she whispered. "No pain, no more tears."

I was hoping for a break from stress, but days after Mom died, Mike came down with a horrible case of shingles that lasted for weeks. His face was divided exactly in half. One side was yellow and sallow and the other was swollen and red – crusty sores covered him from forehead to chin – in his ears, his eyelids. He was so sick, so helpless. I carefully washed and rinsed his face every few hours, helped him lift a glass of water to his swollen lips, spooned soup into his throat, fluffed pillows and helped him to the bathroom.

He had sustained me for so long that his body finally allowed itself to let down. Finally, after weeks of sleeping, he grew stronger, the inflammation cleared up, and his smile came back.

The inheritance from my mom provided the financial cushion we needed to help the kids through college, put a new roof on the house, and maintain the six aging cars that found a welcome spot on our circular driveway. I was protective of our little nest egg and had a plan that when Anna entered middle school I was going to stop working fulltime and stay home again to write. She was the last of the kids. We knew how important those middle school years would be; it would be my final chance to be there for Anna before she would roll her eyes and push me away.

There was more. Now that my heart had turned toward church, I felt a strong tug to concentrate my attention to writing about faith. I had been successful writing about politics, land use, financial planning and child abuse. Could I be just as successful writing about God? Did he still care? The year to stay at home was becoming more and more important to me. I could pour myself into Anna, craft stories about God and establish my career on a new playing field. It was a great plan. It was my plan. And we were almost there.

Yacht Outfitting was doing well also. Mike had a great crew of employees — "the boys" — who were talented, genius at times, hard-working and fun-loving. It was all coming together for Mike, and the company's reputation was growing.

Starting with helping Hobie Alter build his own custom catamaran, *Katie Sue,* to flying to the Newport, Rhode Island, yacht club to work on a famous yacht, *Victoria,* Yacht Outfitting was on the brink of larger contracts and comfortable success.

Mike decided to add value to his customers by providing a document – an owner's manual – of all systems, history, and trip logs for their boats. He became a distributor for a bow thruster system. The future looked good.

So I really had nothing but a vague suspicion about what was bothering Mike that spring day when the evening sunset cast shadows across the rose garden and we huddled together in our bedroom in front of a fire. I waited for an answer.

Mike nestled his head against a pillow, his long legs draped sideways over the plump cushions of the short loveseat. He didn't look at me. I looked at his skin and it seemed dry. His eyes were red, puffy white bags underneath. He was taking short breaths.

Finally, he sat up and looked me in the eye.

"I need $15,000 dollars."

It was my turn to sit up. I swallowed hard.

"What do you mean?"

My head was going all over the place. I felt that I didn't know this man in front of me.

I waited for an answer.

Mike coughed and spread his hands in front of him.

"I'll be able to pay it back, I have lots of work loading up in the next few months. I need to pay my quarterly taxes and I am just short on cash right now."

Tears sprang to my eyes and my heart sank. This was not the first time our personal finances had bailed out the business. The sun had dropped behind the hills and the room was turning cold. The fire was dying down. I bit my lip.

"Are you sure this is the best thing, Mike? The best thing for the family?"

He stood up. "I don't see any alternative."

"Well, can we at least pray about it?"

Mike looked annoyed. I was just getting started.

"In fact," I said, standing up and setting my jaw. "I think we should pray. Together. Every day."

Mike hung his head.

"On our knees."

"What? On our knees? Why?"

"That is the position of supplication and you and I are going to assume it. Every day. Until Yacht Outfitting is able to put that money back into our account."

Prayer as punishment.

Mike threw his head back and laughed a deep, warm laugh.

"O.K., O.K., we will pray on our knees for Yacht Outfitting. It can't hurt."

"Of course it can't hurt." I turned away and stomped upstairs.

The next morning the alarm came to life at 5:45 a.m. Mike rolled across the bed, climbed over me and slid down to the side on his knees, pulling me and the blankets down beside him. His deep, rich voiced echoed into the pillows.

"Dear Lord."

And that's how it started. Daily prayer, supplication — assume the position. Say the magic words.

In return, God will reward us with more business, greater income, a closer marriage and a happily ever after.

Right?

God so loved me.

CHAPTER 16

Show Me the Money

PRAYER DOES NOT COME easily. It's crowded with pitfalls. Even the Bible has plenty of examples in the Bible of how to do it wrong. There's the old guy in the synagogue in the Book of Luke who loudly prayed to thank God that he was not like "these other sinners," and especially thank God that he was "not born a woman." Not exactly what God has in mind to humbly approach the throne of grace. Then there was the prophet Elijah who prayed for death when his prophecy didn't turn out the way he wanted. Jonah who did the same thing even after he was saved from three days in the belly of the whale. God just laughed at them with compassion.

And even if our prayers aren't wrong, many are simply met with silence — or worse, a big "No." Paul had some kind of creepy infirmity that drove him crazy, so he prayed for relief. Even Jesus asked if he could skip the whole death on the cross agony. Both were turned down. Were they not praying right? If they had said some other words, would that have changed the outcome?

Even the disciples, the twelve followers who were with Jesus day and night and saw him cast out demons and raise the dead, had to be taught a very basic formula for prayer not unlike the way we teach our children to pray "Now I lay me down to sleep," but without the bargaining element.

In fact, the prayer that Jesus taught was devoid of bargaining.

Our Father — the loving kind, not the judging kind — who
lives beyond this world,
Help us to get that you are holy.
We want you, not us, to be in charge on earth,
Just like it is where you live.
Give us today what we need for today
So that we can have hearts of gratitude, not entitlement.
Forgive us for the times we mess up,
Just as we forgive those who mess us up.
Don't let us go thinking that we can do this or that without
consequences;
Deliver us from that kind of evil pride.
Because it's your kingdom,
Your power,
Your glory
And not ours.
Forever.
Amen.
(Matthew 6:9-13, personal interpretation)

If you hear the Lord's Prayer at a wedding or a funeral it may sound different, but that's what it means.

So the prayers of a middle-aged couple from a middle-income neighborhood may seem silly to some. After all, Christians are starving in some areas of the world; murdered in others. Shouldn't they be given first priority? And the sheer volume — so aptly depicted in the movie *Bruce Almighty* when Jim Carey finally hits the "yes to all" button – how does that work? Does God really have time to listen to a reluctant yachtsman forced to his knees by an angry wife?

Or, even more importantly, were we really going to be listening to God?

The summer moved ahead at a crazy pace — kids coming and going, Mike mostly going. He'd gotten involved with a project that he was giving heart and soul to support. A local group called Challenged America was readying a boat for the first-ever disabled crew entry into the Trans-Pacific race to Hawaii. Yacht Outfitting became very involved. Mike personally spent hours during the day and most of every weekend to make the Challenged America yacht seaworthy and accessible for the crew. He got more than $40,000 in donated parts by calling in favors from his vendors. Yacht Outfitting designed a custom seat at the helm to accommodate wheel chairs and many machined, custom parts were installed for navigation, maneuvering sails and operating the galley and the heads.

One night he pulled into our driveway after dark, exhausted. The old door of the truck squeaked and moaned when it opened and his long frame unfolded out of the driver's seat. He'd put in another sixteen-hour day.

"Why are you so committed to this, Mike?" I asked after he came in and sat down at the table while I warmed some food. "Do you think it's because of your mom? Do you think it's your way of giving back to the disabled community because you can't be near her?"

He looked at me for a minute, weighing that possibility in his mind. His tired eyes brightened.

"I think it's just exciting to work on it, to really have something to offer that makes a real difference. We have done some very cool stuff, like hand controls and ways to move around the boat."

He paused, took a few bites and then said, "It just feels like the right thing to do."

I stood and rubbed his shoulders, working out the kinks, then reached my arms around him and hugged him tight.

The summer continued and I spent most mornings in my crowded office, looking out at the giant schefflera tree that hid a deep blue, cloudless sky. I sat at my mother's huge desk that was now mine and opened the computer program that tracked our bank accounts. I found a penny next to the pencil sharpener and opened the middle drawer and brushed it inside, then closed the drawer.

I know, I know. Mike is your gift to me. I get it. It's been ten years.

The task before me was to catch up on our bills, which seemed more of a strain than usual. The expenditures weren't really out of line and the fixed expenses were not out of the ordinary. I switched over to track the deposits.

A book had been finished in May and the last writing payments had been paid to Write Now! On this particular book, I advanced the printing costs and would be taking them out of the sales, so a few thousand dollars more would dribble in. Then I looked at the deposits from Yacht Outfitting. Usually there were three to four thousand dollars a month at the beginning of the year, then income ballooned as summer approached and people got their yachts ready for use.

That's not what the computer showed me today. There had been a large deposit in February. Another in April. And now, with the year half over, the deposits that were usually around $35,000 were now less than $10,000. I stared at the computer and double-checked the figures.

Mike wasn't making any money.

Even worse. Mike wasn't making any money, but he didn't know it.

What's happening to Mike?

CHAPTER 17

What Did You Say?

FOLLOWERS OF GOD HAVE a very odd relationship with money. Yes, that thing that the love of is the root of all evil. First of all, God says that all money belongs to him. We give it back to him in prescribed 10 percent amounts – not because he needs it (it's already his, remember?) but so WE don't cling to every last cent. Churches formed after the resurrection of Christ held things in common. Members sold their goods and gave the proceeds to the church. Church leaders, in turn, took care of the widows, orphans, and the unemployed. Because we are human, power and abuse and favoritism and deceit quickly messed that system up, just like every bureaucracy since.

Jesus asked a guy only identified as the "rich young ruler" to give away his money and follow him. We are told that the man "went away sorrowful." So Jesus makes a throwaway remark to his closest friends that it is easier for a camel to go through the eye of a needle than for a rich person to enter the Kingdom of God. They are stunned. They had just assumed that the rich could have anything they wanted, including the Kingdom. And the rich usually assumed that too.

"Who, then, can be saved?" they asked.

Money meant as much to Mike and me I as the next middle-class family. We had experienced hard times and flush times. Being on our knees before God every morning was something we now practiced regularly, but, to be honest, I thought God would be impressed with us. I thought that bowing on our knees for five minutes was pretty humbling and that surely we would be rewarded for our diligence. Blessings would follow. And I didn't mean a penny a day.

God so loved me.

Summer that year was as beautiful as it gets. The sky from my back porch was bluer than the feathers of the birds that liked to bob and soar from the plum tree on one side of the yard to the peach tree on the other, singing away. More birds than ever, that summer. The nests that were tucked under the porch eaves had emptied by then, scattering young birds throughout the canyon below.

The garden had taken off and I plucked a sprig of leaves from the tomato vine just so I could rub it in my hands, bring it to my face and dive into the fragrance of growth and hope. Black soil, leafy vines, red tomatoes, thick green beans, a few stalks of corn for fun, growing half a foot a day, and celery reaching straight to that sky.

In the late afternoon the cool breeze from the ocean swept through the neighborhood, forcing the hot air higher into the atmosphere and forming a haze that turned the sky pink until the after-dinner sunset deepened the color with streaks of orange, then red, then purple, then night. I stretched across the wide, green hammock with a book and read until my eyes blurred.

Mike was home.

And he looked good. He had a rich summer tan and his blond hair was nearly white from running sea trials of spectacular yachts in the calm San Diego Bay. He'd lost some weight, was fitting into single X instead of double XX shirts, and had a smile on his face. I thought it might be a good time to ask about any deposits that might be headed into the household account.

Before I could bring it up, though, he walked into the living room and turned on the television, sinking into the couch. I followed him into the room, my throat tight.

"I don't feel good," he finally muttered.

"Is there something I can get for you?"

"No, I think I'm going to go see the doctor."

"Can I make an appointment for you?"

Mike craned his neck to look at me.

"That's O.K. Fran. I'll do it."

"Do you want me to come with you?"

"Naw, it's nothing."

"All right, then. Let me know what he says."

Mike unfolded from the couch and stood. He stretched out his long arms and twisted his back to the right and to the left.

"I think I'm going to head on downstairs to bed. I'm beat."

"O.K.," I said, giving him a quick, tight hug. "I'll be down in a bit."

I sat on the couch and stared out the sliding glass doors, open to the porch and the night sky. To anyone else, the evening might have seemed perfectly normal. To me, the whole thing had been baffling. Mike never turned on the television. He never went to the doctor, and he never, ever went to bed before me.

The doctor's appointment took a couple of weeks to be scheduled. They took blood and that took another couple of weeks. More tests. More weeks.

Summer days were ending in shadows earlier and earlier. Anna's cheerleaders, after placing fifth in the nation the year before, had said that this season would be about fun, not competing. The problem was, they kept winning competitions and the season kept going. Mike no longer came to the practices, even though the medical tests showed nothing was wrong with him. The ringing in his ears, tiredness, and slight confusion was getting worse.

"I'm good on paper!" Mike would joke as another test result was announced.

It was a crisp November day when thousands of parents from Southern California, Arizona, Nevada and Hawaii and even more thousands of girls in colorful, swinging skirts, jumbo rollers covered with bright scarves and sparkling pom poms poured into the Sports Arena for the Regionals. They carried makeup bags for cans of hairspray and last-minute lip gloss, and cheered their hearts out filing down the arena steps to their appointed sections. Anna's grin was irrepressible as she locked arms with her squad.

As the routines ticked off one by one, these girls — their last year, their last Regionals — revved up like a jet engine when it was their turn. They took the floor, poised, ready to have fun and work together with flawless precision. The music pounded to life and the routine that we parents had all seen a hundred times was like something new. At the end of three minutes with the final back flips, basket tosses and splits perfectly performed, the smiles were wider than ever. Across the arena, feet pounded and horns pierced the rows of clapping, fist pumping and shouts. The girls were perfect.

I looked down and saw that my phone had lit up. When the pandemonium died down, I covered my ear with the phone and slapped my hand against the other ear. I barely heard Mike's hello.

"Mike, Anna's routine was amazing! I bet anything they will be headed to Nationals. That means we have to raise $2,000 each for 26 girls a month before Christmas to go to Orlando, Florida! It's going to be crazy! Last year all over again!"

"Fran . . ."

"We'll have to make more gift baskets and blankets to sell in the next two weeks . . ."

"Fran . . ."

"What? What is it? Can you speak up a little?"

"Fran. I'm going to ask Molly to take me to the emergency room."

He had my full attention. The screaming thousands around me suddenly sounded far, far away.

"What happened? Are you O.K.?

"I'm O.K. But I had an episode. I don't feel good and I am sick of these weeks going by and being tested one thing at a time. I'm going to that hospital and I'm not coming back until they have done every test that there is — I have to find out what's wrong with me."

The crowd had started to gear up for another performance and I was losing him, but I was able to get one more sentence out to Mike.

"I'll get Anna a ride home and I'll be right there. See you soon."

I handed another parent a $20 bill so Anna could get a snack and a ride home. I fought my way through the crowd to the parking lot and down Interstate 8 toward Longmont Hospital — the community hospital where I had sat with children through bronchitis and broken bones. Finally, I thought, we're going to get to the bottom of what's bothering Mike and fix it.

My cell phone buzzed.

"Hello," I said, feeling tenser every mile toward the hospital.

"Mom! We did it! We're going to Nationals!"

I watched the cars in front of me weave and speed, then slowly blur as my eyes teared up.

"That's great, honey. Good for you. That's great news. I'm so proud of you."

I moved into the fast lane and stomped on the pedal.

What's an "episode?"

CHAPTER 18

The Waiting Room

THE EMERGENCY ROOM WAS populated with huddles of misery — children crying and uncomfortable — seats attached together in long, inflexible rows. Not so easy to comfort anyone over bars of metal in between cold, plastic seats. Who thought this seating would be a good idea in a room full of people in pain?

I went to the window where a woman in scrubs sat at a desk behind thick glass.

"I'm looking for my husband, Michael Canrinus? He was brought here by my daughter a little while ago. I think he's having tests."

"Let me see. What is his name?

"Mike Canrinus."

"Can you spell that?"

"C-a-n-r-i-n-u-s."

The woman did not look at me but clicked the keyboard impatiently. A couple more people got in line behind me.

"He's here, "she said. "He's having tests."

I kept standing there.

"Take a seat."

"Will you call me when I can see him? My name is Francine."

That made her look up to see me face to face, a woman who had presumably lost her mind. She looked back down.

"You can check back with me every few minutes."

The next person in line stepped in front of me as I turned. There was a seat between a woman tending to her father in a wheelchair and a girl screaming into her phone, "I don't know, I don't know!"

I've done my time in ERs. We used to call it "Quality Time" with Nick, Molly, Jesse, or Anna — a guaranteed five-hour window of one-on-one time with a vulnerable child. Time to ask about school or girlfriends or teachers, church or what he or she thinks of sports, music, MTV, the Oscars and *American Idol*. Looking around the room to make up stories about the others waiting and trying to figure out how many will go before it's your turn.

And I'm that woman, of course. That woman who goes up to the window and demands a box of tissues for the convulsing mother across from me surrounded by three little ones crawling all over her, whose nose is a slimy faucet wiped every three seconds by a too-thin arm in a flimsy tee-shirt and no jacket.

The nurses behind the glass give me a cold stare while the intercom phone hung prim and useless.

"Do you have some tissues?" I asked.

There was a pause.

"They're not for me, they're . . ."

"She's a junkie."

"She told me she had irritable bowel syndrome."

"Look, lady . . ."

"She needs a tissue. A box of them."

The nurse handed them over through a small slit at the bottom of the window. I took the tissue box over to the suffering woman and she looked up at me with tearful eyes, yellowed with illness, pupils dilated. Then she doubled over in her seat with fresh tears, fresh slime dripping from her chapped nose. Her children stopped and stared at me to assign blame, then resumed their busy play, oblivious to their broken mommy.

After about an hour and after the sixth turn of going to the window to check if I could be let in, the woman behind the window hit a buzzer and said, "Meet me at the door."

Which door?

I raced to one side of the room where a green door slowly opened. It felt like a contest and if I didn't pick the right door I would be locked out forever. But there she stood with a tiny hot pink sticker that read "Visitor" hanging from her finger. I rushed through the door as it was starting to close, lunged toward her hand and slapped the sticker on my left shoulder.

She turned and started to walk back to her window and before I thought to ask, her head twisted to the side.

"Twelve."

In front of me was a sea of blue-green curtains attached to metal grids with noisy aluminum clips in random states of closure. Number printouts on letter-sized paper were safety-pinned awkwardly to the curtains. Nurses and doctors stood in clumps in the hallway, where some gurneys formed an obstacle course of misery. I passed a frightened child whose parents hovered behind their curtain as if seeking a wall of protection. A blond teenager was vomiting from an overdose as they readied a stomach pump. A young Hispanic male was passed out and drained of color with thick bandages wrapped around each wrist like boxing gloves.

Gingerly passing through the gauntlet, I approached the blue-green curtain-wrapped area with the flimsy number turned sideways. Twelve.

He was asleep. Curled up on his side, face soft with peace. Mike always said that once you've been in the Navy you can fall asleep anywhere, any time, and that was true of him. His closed eyes were still and his handsome face snuggled into his long arm, wrapped around a scrunched up pillow.

"Why do people love to watch me sleep?" Mike once asked me. "They're always taking pictures of me asleep."

"I'm not sure, honey, but it probably has to do with a being a giant of a man who has the ability to look like a sweet little boy that needs protection when his eyes are closed. It's the contradiction that is so beguiling."

Listening to the deep, even breaths interrupted by sharp, startling snores, I backed out of the room and searched for a restroom. The one at the end of the corridor of horror had a sign that said Staff Only. To the left was another double door labeled No Admittance. The only alternative was going back to the ER lobby, where there was no bathroom, then walking outside and around the entire building to the hospital main entrance; then reversing the process, battling the woman behind the glass for entry. By then Mike could have been taken out for another test.

I ducked into the Staff Only bathroom, feeling guilty and rebellious. And afraid. Would they release Mike and not help him if I was caught in the staff bathroom? I got out of there as soon as possible.

Mike was now grinning as wide as the sky, his joy like sunshine. I climbed up next to him and held him tight.

"Sweetheart, how are you feeling? You're freezing."

He turned to his side and put his arm around me.

"Great! We're finally getting somewhere!"

Throwing his head back, he let out a belly laugh. I could picture the sound bounding off the walls with little rays washing over the fevers and the chills throughout the room. His laugh was amazing and powerful and it shook through him so I had to wrap myself more tightly around him. He looked so out of place in the tiny hospital gown, his legs too long for the bed.

I giggled at his joy and was instantly more at ease. We kept laughing and every time we looked at the flimsy blanket and his feet sticking over the end of the gurney and the switches and equipment and the blue-green plastic walls, we'd start up again. Hysterical.

"So what happened?" I finally was able to ask.

"Nothing, really. I get these moments when I feel dizzy and my ears start ringing and I just wanted to find out why. I want to fix it. Once and for all."

"Well, that's what we'll do, then. Once and for all."

Sometime after midnight we were released to wait for the test results at home. We went down the stairs to the coolness of our master suite. Mike stretched out across the width of the California King while I threw a pressed-wood log onto the grate and lit it. By the time we were huddled under the comforter, the fireplace was dancing with flame, beautiful and warm. The freeze from the emergency room was finally thawing, and I entangled my feet with Mike's and rubbed them briskly over his and he rubbed my arms with his huge hands until we collapsed against each other in more giggles. Mike made one last stretch across the bed, then curled into a comfy ball and scrunched his pillow under his head and closed his eyes. I watched the flames flicker and play until sleep covered me like a blanket.

* * *

We'd been waiting about thirty minutes. Mike sat on the examining table while I flipped through magazines on the aqua vinyl chair. Dr. Breslin finally came in and grabbed the rolling stool. He smiled.

"I have good news."

I reached over and took Mike's hand.

"All of your test results are normal," said the doctor, continuing to smile. "Your heart is good, blood pressure is healthy, MRI clear. All of your blood work looked good, so it's very encouraging.

Mike and I looked at each other and he squeezed my hand.

"What about these episodes of dizziness," he asked. "Can you describe them?"

Mike sighed. He'd gone over this at least three times in the ER.

"It starts out with a tightness across my head, then my eyes get sore and the dizziness starts."

The doctor's smile never wavered.

"How long does it last?"

"A few minutes. If I can close my eyes and lean back in my chair for a few minutes, it goes away."

The doctor kept smiling.

"Do you have anything causing you anxiety?"

Mike and I looked at each other. Then I looked down.

"Well, things are not going that well at my business. Times are a little tough for yachts."

Mike looked over at me.

"It's making Fran a little crazy."

"Let's try this," the doctor looked right at Mike. "I want to give you some anti-anxiety medicine to try and then I'm going to get you a referral for some counseling. Maybe this is something that you can work out. You two have a lot going on with all of those kids and maybe just having a place to talk things out can make a big difference."

"O.K., doctor," I finally said. "We'll start after the holidays."

He left the room, still smiling.

It took a minute for Mike and me to even look at each other. We walked to the car in silence.

"Well, that's good news, right?" I looked at Mike, leaning back against the headrest of the passenger seat. I hardly ever asked anymore if he wanted to drive.

"If this is going to make me feel better, I'll try anything," Mike said, eyes closed.

"We didn't ask him about the weight loss."

Mike chuckled. "I think that is part of the good news."

"Oh yeah, good on paper."

"That's me," echoed Mike, not opening his eyes. "Good on paper."

Medical Record (sic)

PATIENT: Canrinus, Michael A.

CHIEF COMPLAINT: Dizzinessx1 month

HISTORY OF PRESENT ILLNESS:

The patient is a 56-year-old gentleman who had had quite an extensive workup it turns out. His chief complaint is a dizziness for one month. He apparently has had an MRI and carotid Dopplers which were negative. The patient reports that his ability to remember things has been deteriorating and he has visual disturbances. He states he is occasionally nauseated and his appetite is poor, but denies any specific symptoms other than that described. He denies any focal weakness. The patient does not know the results of his MRI but states his carotid Doppler scan showed less than 10% disease. He denies polyuria or polydipsia. He denies any focal weakness. Denies chest pain or any shortness of breath.

EMERGENCY DEPARTMENT COURSE:

At this time there are no identifiable abnormalities. I told the patient as well as his wife that we would not likely come up with any answers that might explain his symptoms. The patient is ambulatory without any disturbance in gait. He neurologically is intact at this time. It is very difficult for us to ascertain what his symptoms are due to the non-specificity of findings. Condition is improved. Certainly, should there be any deterioration in clinical condition or worsening symptoms, he should return to the emergency department. His condition is improved.

CHAPTER 19

Best Buy Breakdown

B EFORE WE KNEW IT, the Christmas tree was up, lights hung in swags across the covered porch in back of the house, and I had an idea for the front lawn. Our home was very visible and our family was known by dozens of neighborhood kids and families that spanned almost twenty years of school and sports activities. Easter was a vision of lilies, wreaths and lambs, chicks and bunnies. Halloween was an extravaganza of spiders, black light illuminating ghouls and ghosts and hand-carved pumpkins.

When it came to Christmas my goal was always to make our home welcoming and delightful, but this year I wanted to show a spiritual side to the holiday. Let someone else put up the blow-up plastic reindeer and Santa. My vision was a 10-foot glittering angel — majestic, mystical, and inspiring. I wanted to show everyone the real meaning of Christmas was God entering into our world. The unknown. The unexpected. The glittering archangel – a fabric sculpture –was up and sparkling in floodlights by the end of the weekend.

God so loved me.

Facing a tight budget, Mike and I decided to shop together instead of our usual method of me buying presents all year and hiding them all over the house, then he going out on Christmas Eve and buying more for everyone. With our family, one of the smarter giving strategies was music — it spanned the generations and it didn't have to fit right or be the right color. Mike and I drove down the hill to the local mall where Best Buy stood bright and loud at the end of the parking lot.

"This should be easy. Movies and CDs for the girls, an electronic drum for Jesse, a CD duplicator for Nick, and how 'bout a Karaoke machine for Anna? Isn't that something every ten year-old can use?"

"Wait!" said Mike. "That's what I want you to get me!"

We were laughing when we pulled into the parking space outside the door.

It was a typical San Diego Christmas season — warm, breezy in the evening, beautiful long days that stayed light until after 7 p.m. in backyards that still had coals at the ready next to the barbeque. I had written a Christmas list while lying on the back-porch hammock and was wrapping presents in shorts and sandals.

We jumped out of the car and as the double doors slid open we encountered loud rock music and flashing lights. Christmas on steroids. After only about sixty seconds, Mike turned to me and said, "I've got to get out of here."

"Oh, I know, honey. You should try to shop at Tilly's."

"No, I mean it," he stopped and turned to say. "I have to leave. Now."

I followed him out the door.

What about our joyful bonding time?

The next night was our monthly gathering at Jim and Mandy's house. Their tree was simple and gorgeous. Chunky red and white candles were tastefully arranged around the room with blooming Christmas cactus and poinsettias carefully displayed.

I was whispering with Mandy in the kitchen. ". . .Then he turned to me and said, 'I have to get out of here now.' Something about the lights were bothering him."

"I thought they said it was a stress thing?"

"He couldn't stand the lights."

"Maybe it was the thought of spending the money? Are you sure you agreed on what to buy?"

"It was the lights."

We carried silverware out to the table and stopped talking. Mike and the guys were listening to a story about camping and laughing.

"Mike, you are wasting away!" one of the ladies commented. "How much have you lost now?"

"I think about thirty pounds," he answered, grabbing a handful of candied walnuts.

"More like 50," I interjected. "And he's not even trying. It's completely not fair."

Jim and Mike had their heads together much of the evening. The software company Jim partnered in was stalled. For the first time in his confident career, Jim was concerned about losing his job, and Mike had an inspiration. By the end of the evening, it looked like they had a plan all worked out.

Mike "hired" Jim to do an analysis of Yacht Outfitting. Over the next few months, Jim would assess the strengths and weakness of the company. He would interview the employees, survey clients, and come up with the ideal client demographic that Mike should concentrate on developing. Jim would also look at the financial processes and see if things could be streamlined or handled more efficiently. The plan would allow Jim to be engaged in a project that would help him maintain his management skills and help Mike focus the company to be more productive.

Then they came up with another idea. Mike had just become a regional dealer for a brand of bow thrusters — devices that provided spurts of thrust power that helped navigate boats out of slips or other tight spots. Every February the San Diego Convention Center had a huge boat show and Mike had always taken a day to attend. He'd roam the aisles, connect with owners and vendors and basically talk "yacht" as much as possible. Because Mike made friends wherever he went, he was his best marketing tool. It was decided the next boat show would have a Yacht Outfitting booth. It would have a model of a bow thruster and feature Yacht Outfitting's services. I offered to make a video that could be playing on a laptop to draw customers to the booth. In addition, it would have sign-ups for free diagnostic sea trials, prizes, candy, banners — photos of yachts with testimonials from the owners.

Full of excitement and plans for the future, we looked forward to the end of the current year and had hope for the next. Mike had always kept me at arm's length from the business and I was enthusiastic about having a tiny part in bringing Yacht Outfitting some success. We both trusted

Jim, and secretly I hoped that adding a new plank to the friendship would solidify Mike's connection to the church.

You never know, right? Thank you, God. Thank you! Thank you! Thank you for hearing our prayers.

God so loved me.

CHAPTER 20

New Year's Eve

I<small>T WAS THE LAST</small> day of the year. Finally. After the flurry of Christmas, I looked forward to some alone time with Mike. Having saved some Scharffen Berger chocolate for a special occasion, I got out the blue package and broke it open. Mixing creamy butter and sugar, I poured the melted chocolate into the big glass mixing bowl then poured the blend into a square pan and inserted it into the pre-heated oven. I watched the brownies until they were the perfect balance of chewy and cakey. They cooled on the counter while I got out a fancy tray, a china plate, and two crystal glasses.

With the movie *Chocolat* ready to go in the DVD player and bubbly champagne on ice, it seemed as if we could have a quiet New Year's Eve celebration all to ourselves.

Mike was at the docks. The irony of working on yachts was that holidays were also the days when clients were on the water and discovered all these little fixes that kept Mike in business. His cell phone was constantly ringing as someone drifting across the bay, feet up and sail billowing, would notice that they wanted a new navigation station, or a better sound system, or a second television. None of these conversations could wait until a work day, when they would be long gone from their leisure lives. Mike was on call 24/7.

"My business succeeds because I give them access," Mike would say. "They go with the guy who picks up the phone." He appreciated that same access to the owners as well.

"They can be in the middle of a board meeting and if I say I have to talk about their boat, they'll take the call." It put a sly grin on his face as he said it, knowing that he was at the center of that special magic between man and ocean. Conquering waves, sailing into uncharted waters.

Basically, two kids building a fort. A really expensive, really sophisticated floating fort.

The truck pulled up outside. Mike walked through the door in his shorts and Hawaiian shirt, tan and handsome. But there were puffy bags under his eyes and his large hands rubbed his forehead back and forth.

"I picked up a lot of work for the next couple of weeks."

"That's great," I said as I put my arms around him and we rocked back and forth for a minute. "You must be so tired. Are you hungry?"

"No, I ate something."

"Well, then, let's just take a long shower and get in bed. I have a surprise for you."

His eyes said, *Oh no, what now?* Still, he was willingly led downstairs where candles were lit in the bathroom and fragrance surrounded the bed. I rubbed his back as the hot shower loosened his stiff muscles and we pulled on clean terry robes and stretched out on the freshly washed sheets.

"So," I began, "There is this charming movie called, *Chocolat* that we can watch and I made some brownies with the last of that expensive chocolate that I got in Denver and I bought some champagne. Real champagne. Good champagne. Does that sound fun? Then if we want we can go out on the porch at midnight and listen to the fireworks and holler in the New Year."

Mike smiled. "If I can stay awake that long."

"Well, let's give it a try."

I clicked the remote and the movie started. I brought the tray to bed and poured the champagne.

"Here's to the New Year, Mikey."

"Happy New Year, Frannie."

We fluffed out pillows and settled in to get caught up in the cobblestone streets of Paris, the rich chocolates, the power and prejudice against the unknown, gorgeous Juliette Brioche and rakish Jonny Depp.

After about thirty minutes I asked Mike if he wanted one of those chocolate brownies.

His face was hard.

"I don't like brownies. I hate chocolate."

What?

I swallowed hard. "Okay. Well then, would you like more champagne?"

Mike gritted his teeth. There had only been a couple of times in our marriage that he had raised his voice, but those few times I had seen true rage. He had always retrieved it into control, though. This time he sat up in bed. He took his long arm and swept it across the tray, crashing the crystal glasses to the floor, the champagne bottle flying across the room, slowly emptying onto the carpet while I stiffened in the bed.

"I hate champagne! I hate chocolate, I hate this movie and I hate New Year's Eve!" I had to duck his backswing or he would have caught me in the cheek. I sucked in my breath and felt my heart rise up into a lump in my throat. His eyes were bulging and he looked like his mouth had gone dry.

"Mike!"

"No! Don't say anything! Not a word!"

"But I—"

"I said shut up!

Mike never used that term! What's going on?

I tried again to get up, terrified that I would step on glass. Instead, Mike jumped onto his knees and straddled me, his face red and sweating, his lips snarling.

I bent my arms and tried to put my hands over my face. Quickly, he grabbed a pillow and put it over my nose and mouth, holding it down on either side of my head. My eyes were wide with fear trying to look into his. They were blank with rage.

"Shut up! Shut up! Shut up—" He blurted it out what seemed like a hundred times." He never stopped saying it.

With each repetition he pushed against the edges of the pillow and bounced into the mattress. I managed to push back with my hands enough to get some air but I could tell it was a battle that I would soon lose. Finally the pillow was completely over my face. I screamed his name into the softness hoping that the muffled sound would get through to him.

It worked. Suddenly he rolled over onto his back, sobbing. I ran upstairs. My chest was heaving.

"Lord, help me! Help me! Help me!"

I sank to my knees by the couch and the scream became a whisper. Below I could hear Mike start to breathe more evenly. Slowly I stood and controlled my emotions. After getting the broom and dustpan, I stiffly walked back downstairs to our bedroom, went through the door, and methodically began sweeping the shattered glass until it was in a neat pile that I could brush into the dustpan and deposit into the trash can.

He watched but I could not look at him. I leaned the broom against the wall and pulled a blanket and slippers out of the closet and slowly walked back upstairs, trying to make myself comfortable on the couch. Exhausted and sore, I drifted into a fitful sleep.

The sound of a gunshot woke me with a shock.

What now? My body became stiff and cold.

Then I heard shouts. Noisemakers and another shot. I went out the sliding door and let the ruckus and fireworks from the cul-de-sac below and the bright stars above me bring me back to wakefulness. Happy New Year. Woohoo. Hooray.

I tiptoed down the stairs and peeked into the bedroom.

Mike was asleep, looking like a peaceful child. The demons in his head were quiet. I slipped back upstairs so as not to wake them.

Should auld acquaintance be forgot and never brought to mind?
Should auld acquaintance be forgot in days of auld lang syne?
We'll take a cup of kindness yet,
For auld lang syne.

CHAPTER 21

What Just Happened?

WHEN JESUS WAS ON earth to teach us about God, religion for its own sake was alive and thriving. Centuries earlier, God appeared to Abraham in a burning bush and promised him that he would have more descendants than grains of sand.

Hundreds of years later, when Moses decided to obey God, the Lord rescued the Hebrews from Egyptian slavery, miraculously parting the Red Sea. After that they wandered for forty years in a wilderness that could have been crossed in a couple of weeks if they hadn't been such whiners. God fed them daily manna and quail, provided water from a rock, and then gave them the ten commandments for successful living. Which, in a few more hundred years, mushroomed into a tidy bundle of 600-plus rules, designed to separate the truly righteous from pathetic sinners.

The bad news, however, is that we are all pathetic sinners. No one is more righteous than anyone else. Religion can't help. I'm a pathetic sinner. You're a pathetic sinner. And the good news to the bad news is that once you get it and admit it, there's no more bad news. The bad news is finished. Because God loves sinners.

Mike and I kept our distance from each other the next day. I got up, went to our big, sunny kitchen and made coffee in the same coffee maker, drank from my same favorite mug, waved good-bye to him from the same front door while I turned on the Rose Parade to watch. Kids straggled in at different times from different rooms while I stared at the merriment and listened to the corny chatter of the familiar KTLA team sharing interesting tidbits about high school bands and equestrian units and how many petals it takes to make a woodland scene or rocket ship float down Colorado Boulevard.

Once the first viewing was done and the immediate replay was under way I went down to our bathroom. I left the light off, fumbled for a washcloth and looked into the mirror. Closer. Alongside the New Year's morning bags under my eyes, a long streak of bruise shaded my left cheek. I covered my face with the washcloth and cried. Finally I decided to call Mike.

"Mike. How are things down at the shop?" I tried to keep my voice even. Cordial.

"It's a gorgeous day, the sky is so blue."

"Is it? When do you think you'll be coming home?"

"Uh, I donno. Maybe a couple of hours."

"Can we talk about last night when you get home?"

"What about last night?"

Is he kidding?

"We'll talk about it later. What do you want for dinner?"

"Hey, I got a message that the Wilsons left me a bunch of halibut on their boat that they caught yesterday. Why don't I bring that and we'll put it on the grill."

"I've got some wild rice . . ."

"Perfect. I'll see you in a couple of hours."

"Sounds good. O.K. See you then."

Mike came home big as life, happy and pleased to be bearing several halibut steaks. He quartered them, drizzled them with butter and olive oil and dropped them carefully over hot coals, then added seasoning that made my mouth water. The rice was soft and buttery, the salad was crisp. The fish was light and flaky and meaty at the same time. We stretched out on the patio chairs and watched the night creep across the sky. His smile showed contentment and happiness.

I took away the empty plates and silverware and settled back down at the table with a glass of wine for each of us.

"About last night . . ."

"What about it?" he asked. Then he took my hand. "Look, I know that I get really frustrated about work sometimes. I'll try not to bring it home."

I looked down. "Maybe we'd better give that counselor, Peter, a call and set up an appointment."

"I'm willing to do that," he said.

"I think we have to." I looked into his eyes, while mine started to fill with tears.

"I'll call Peter . . ." he said, his voice trailing as he stood up and went inside.

CHAPTER 22

Two Hundred an Hour

IN THE FOLLOWING WEEKS I threw myself at the task of creating a video for Yacht Outfitting. Mike set up interviews with the employees. I also took footage of the boatyard, the bay, our signs, and Mike himself, explaining the magic of being at sea and the joy of owning a dream. He worked hard on getting ready for the boat show in February and lining up demo equipment for the booth. Days flew by starting new repair jobs, brainstorming with the staff to come up with some creative solutions to problems and always, constantly, answering the phone.

As Jim Stone was diligently doing his review of the company he came up with a demographic for the most desirable client. It needed to be someone who used their yacht often enough to keep it in good condition and someone who wanted to improve it – and the profile boat was at least a hundred footer.

It looked like everything was going in the right direction. Finally I had a finished draft of the video to show Mike. Early the next morning, we sat down at the study dining room table while I flipped open the laptop.

"I think it's whimsical and informative, Mikey. The whole purpose is just to draw people to the booth and give them something to watch while you are talking to someone else."

"Hmmm."

"What?"

"I'm kind of tired-looking," he said, "I don't sound as sharp as I should."

I looked up at him. He rubbed his eyes.

"I think you look approachable and smart. I think people will watch it."

"Okay, load it up."

"I'll get the laptop ready and all you will have to do it push the button. It will be on a loop."

I gave him a quick hug and he started out the door, then called back over his shoulder.

"Oh, I talked to Peter and made an appointment for Tuesday night. Will that work for you?"

"Sure, honey, that sounds good."

Thank you, God. Thank you. Thank you. Thank you. Now we will finally get some help.

The appointment with Peter took place on a breezy evening at a mid-sized office building in Mission Valley – halfway between Mike's office and home. As I pulled up, I saw our green Ford Explorer parked on the shady street. Mike no longer drove the Ford 250 truck; we bought the used Explorer so he could maneuver and park more easily.

Mike was waiting in the outer area, where we sat together flipping through magazines until Peter came out to greet us. Inside the office, Mike leaned back into a recliner. Peter gave us a "homework" assignment to each write down ten things that were causing us the most stress.

Walking out to the cars, the night had turned chilly and Mike put his arm around me.

"This is just a bump in the road, Frannie. Everything is going to be fine."

His voice was deep and soft and being in his arms was reassuring. I almost believed him.

When I got to my car, I opened the door and there, on the threshold was my penny for the day.

Mike is my gift to you, the Lord spoke in my spirit.

I almost believed Him, too.

CHAPTER 23

Breaking Down the Boat Show

THE NEXT FEW WEEKS moved quickly. The date of the boat show had come, sunny and glorious, with shiny yachts filling the convention center and bobbing along the docks. Mike was with his guys from the shop setting up the booth and the demo equipment, and preparing handouts and prizes. The laptop was ready with the three-minute video to wow onlookers so they would want to talk directly to a Yacht Outfitting employee.

As the doors opened, droves of men and a handful of women made their way through the exhibits, jumping on boats, shaking hands with old friends. Mike was completely in his element, his face shining with joy as they discussed navigation systems, bow thrusters, setting up GPS stations and sharing secrets with the best fishing spots between San Diego and the tip of Baja. I left around 11 a.m., happy and hopeful.

At 4 p.m. in the afternoon, I got a call from Dan, the brilliant musician/electrician who helped Mike invent cool solutions to many equipment challenges on our yachts. He was laid back, observant, and had sailed everywhere in the world. On the video we taped him with his bushy, Santa Claus beard, saying, "One thing I've learned is that things that you think are invincible turn out to break down very quickly when you are in the middle of the ocean. I always test everything, test again, and then test again when I install a system. It has to be utterly reliable."

So when I heard Dan's calm voice on the phone, I wasn't expecting what he told me.

"Frannie, you've got to get down here."

"What do you mean? What's wrong?"

"Mike looks terrible."

"Terrible how?"

"He's confused. He can't talk to people. He doesn't understand what is going on around him. He can't find his way around."

What is happening to Mike?

"Is he going to be okay until I get there?"

"We are all keeping an eye on him, but he needs to go home. And we'll take care of tomorrow and the booth breakdown. Just come get him and take him home."

"I'm on my way."

The drive to the convention center was quick and smooth on a weekend but my hands were shaking. I drove in and made my way through the layers of parking and talked my way through security, saying my husband was sick. As I looked past the bright banners and white, gleaming yachts, there was Mike sitting alone at the booth, head down and talking to himself. The laptop was blank. People walked past him, glancing quickly away. His skin was grey and he looked so, so tired.

When I walked up to him, he didn't recognize me. He stood to hand me a brochure so I quickly spoke up.

"Hey, honey! Not feeling so well?"

"Oh, it's you! Hi. No, my eyes hurt and my ears are ringing."

"Well, let's head home. Dan said that he and the guys would finish up the day."

"No, I'm good."

"Come on, Mikey. They said they would get the truck over to the shop. Let's take your soda and find the car. You look thirsty."

Mike looked at his drink as if he didn't know what it was, then grabbed it and took a long gulp. I could see Dan coming over from across the aisle and nodded to him. Taking Mike by the hand, I tried to get him talking and moving.

"I talked to lots of interesting people today, we had some great conversations," he started as I moved him forward.

"Good. You always make friends, Mikey. That's what you do."

"That's what I do," he repeated in a quiet voice.

In the car, I leaned the passenger seat all the way back so he could stretch out as much as possible and put his head back. He closed his eyes and kept them closed all the way home. As we passed through East Village and onto the freeway, zipping through suburban areas to our sprawling home in El Cajon, I couldn't stop thinking of my conversation with Dan.

"How does he look?"

"He looks like death," Dan said evenly.

CHAPTER 24

Forgetful

W E CALLED OUR DOCTOR and they gave us an appointment in two weeks. No big deal, apparently. I guess fifty-six year-old men get confused, turn grey, and forget their wives all the time.

After a couple of days of rest, Mike was eager to get back to work and check his boats and his clients. His color was a little better and he was sharp and aware. There had been more "episodes."

When Mike's birthday came at the end of February, I was at a loss to know how to celebrate. I had bought him several new shirts and pairs of pants in his new size so everything would not hang on him. He loved all of them and picked a new shirt to go to dinner.

We chose a quiet, local Italian restaurant with a great chef and authentic Italian music softly playing. The walls were painted with scenic murals of the ocean and leafy vineyards; I found a parking spot near the entrance and held his hand as we entered.

Settling into a booth Mike asked me to read him the menu and we ordered. Holding hands across the table, I felt awkward. He looked so old. I leaned across the table and kissed his cheek. It was dry and his skin was loose and stretched across his cheekbones. His lips were wrinkled and thin. *Who is this man?*

I asked the waiter to take our picture and we cuddled up in the booth smiling at the lens. There wasn't much conversation and I struggled to think of a way to bring some laughter to the table. It felt uncomfortable and awkward.

Shortly after we got home, Mike went down to bed. I thought I would take a look at the photo from the restaurant and maybe send it in an email to all the kids. Slipping the memory card into the computer, the photo from the restaurant filled the screen.

Mike looked thin and confused and I was uber-smiling with fear and panic reflected in my eyes. Closing the file, I wrote a cheery email, sent it to the kids without the photo, and watched the screen fade to an empty black. Then I dropped to my knees next to the desk.

Oh God, thank you for watching over our family. I know that you love each one and have given me so much with all these amazing kids to be a part of my life.

Please help us find out what is wrong with Mike and make yourself real to him while he can still understand who you are and how much you want to enfold him as your child. I'm so scared that he is losing his mind. I'm so scared of what's coming. I'm so scared.

Father, look upon us with your grace and mercy. Please hold us in your loving arms. Help us to surrender all.

In the name of Jesus,

Amen.

I got up from my knees and went downstairs to bed. Mike was asleep, looking like a vulnerable child.

Please hold us in your loving arms. Amen.

* * *

A couple of days later I was at a church planning meeting for the Easter decorations and ran into our pastor, Craig.

"Craig, do you think Mike is any closer to giving his heart to Christ?"

"Well, Fran, he is enjoying the search, I know."

"How did he do when he took that Seekers class?"

"He asked a lot of good questions. I think he is honestly trying to figure out what he believes. Mike is a very deep thinker and it all has to make sense to him on a cosmic level."

"I know. I think any leap of faith is going to be very hard for him. He's used to being at the helm of his own life. Do you think he should take the class again?"

Craig looked down. Then he looked me in the eye, he spoke with kindness and a touch of amusement.

"Fran, Mike does not need to take the class again. Mike knows exactly what he needs to do about Christ. He just has to make a decision."

I swallowed hard. "Keep praying for him, Okay?"

"Oh, I'm praying," he said. "Lots of us are praying."

Later that evening I got a call at about six o'clock on my cell phone. It was Mike.

"Hi, honey, how are you? Ready to come home?"

"Can you help me with something?" Mike sounded very loud and in command.

"Sure."

"Well, I'm on the corner of Johnson and Main and I can't remember how to get home from here."

I tried to hide the gasp in my breath. The sound of his voice was in such contrast to that sentence that had just come through the phone. He was less than a mile from home and must have gotten off one exit sooner than usual. He had been at the corner of Johnson and Main at least a thousand times in the last ten years.

"Okay. You need to follow Johnson to the east. If you are at the Chevron station, that means take a right. Go through about five blocks until you come to Fletcher Parkway. You'll see the mall on your right and a Burger King on the left and a furniture store on the corner. Turn left at Fletcher Parkway…"

My heart felt like a stone at the bottom of my stomach. I could tell he wasn't tracking with anything I was saying. I was determined to sound normal. Not panicked. I took all of my concentration.

"Why don't I just stay on the phone with you and take it one step at a time?"

"That's probably a good idea. I don't recognize anything."

Why didn't he recognize anything?

"Well. Where are you now?"

"I am at the Chevron station."

"Okay, you'll be home in five minutes."

He let out a huge sigh and I could tell this was reassuring to him.

"Turn right," I said with authority. "The trolley track will be on your left."

"Got it. I turned right."

I swallowed hard.

"Perfect. Now keep going straight. Pass the Home Depot, see it."

"Yeah, I'm passing it."

"Good." I realized I was gripping the phone too hard, trying to picture the streets, the shops, and the lanes he needed to be in on the busy street. In a moment he would need to turn left.

"Now get in the left lane, over by the Burger King. See the next light? Get in the inside turn lane."

"I'm going to turn left?"

"Yes, you want to turn left, but stay in the turn lane on the right."

"What?"

That was so hard to describe. I realized it didn't make sense when I said it out loud, but somehow got him to turn the corner without a mishap. I had to keep going.

"At the top of the hill you'll see Hacienda on the right, just in front of Matt's where we take our cars to get fixed. The sign says La Mesa Auto and Tire."

"Okay, I see that sign. I turn right?"

"Yes, turn right."

"Oh, I know where I am now."

There was a pause and my body was flooded with relief.

Mike spoke with less fear. "Thanks, Fran."

"Sure, honey, no problem. Call me back if you need anything else."

I leaned on the kitchen counter while tears flooded into my eyes. Quickly I splashed cold water onto my face from the kitchen faucet and wiped it with a paper towel. I could hear the truck.

Good, he made the turn into the driveway.

What is happening to Mike?

Tuesday night I drove over to Peter's office for our counseling session. Mike was late, so I took the opportunity to bring up my concerns to Peter. I tried to explain that there was something wrong, but it wasn't really a marriage problem. It sounded lame.

As I was speaking, we both saw Mike through the window as he walked past the office and kept going. A minute later we saw him pass by again going the other way. Mike was lost.

Peter started to say something but I jumped up and opened the door. "Here we are, honey."

Mike came in and sat down, giving Peter a big smile.

He looked at us both and laughed his deep laugh and said, "Let's get started!"

"Let's do," Peter said, relaxing in his chair and we settled into the inner office. "A couple of weeks ago I asked you both to make a list of the ten things that most concerned you in your marriage. Do you have your lists?"

I handed him a piece of paper. My list wasn't not too out of the ordinary – not enough time together, not communicating about money, feeling last in his priorities.

"Mike, do you have your list?"

Mike pulled a yellow work pad out of his backpack and his smile faded only slightly. He looked directly at Peter.

"Well, I thought about it, but I can't write."

"I understand, Mike, that this is hard. But it will really help us find some common ground."

"I know. I know. But I can't write." He looked down at the pad. There were loops and scribbles crossing over all the lines.

"Maybe it's hard to find time, but it's important..."

Before I could stop myself, I grabbed the yellow pad from Mike and waved it in front of Peter's face. My voice got louder with every word.

"He can't write. Did you hear what he said? He can't write. Mike can no longer write. He doesn't have a list because he can't write a list! This has nothing to do with our marriage! Mike can't write!"

By that time I was shouting. Peter's head snapped up, his eyes wide. He looked at Mike.

"I can't write," Mike said sheepishly.

We sat there for a moment, no one speaking. Quietly, Peter finally responded.

"I have a friend who is a neurologist," he said finally. "I think I'll give him a call."

CHAPTER 25

Finding the Right Fix

THERE ARE WRITINGS IN the scripture that tell us Jesus knew about misdiagnosis. There was a blind beggar that he talked to once.

"Who sinned to make this man blind, he or his parents?" asked the religious leaders standing around. Classic misdiagnosis.

"No one sinned," Jesus said. "He was blind so that I could show you all the glory of God."

The man was immediately healed. People marveled.

Or another time, the religious leaders came to beg Jesus to save the life of the sick servant of a Roman commander who was sympathetic to the Jews under Roman rule. Jesus set out to go heal the man but word came that the servant was dead. Then the commander told Jesus that he knew about being a commander and that Jesus just had to say the word and the servant would be healed.

Jesus told the crowd that he had never seen such faith among all of Israel—the nation of people who were supposedly eagerly awaiting the Messiah. But the religious people missed the point. The Messiah wasn't going to restore the political nation. He was, in fact, going to replace it with a spiritual kingdom. The godless Roman soldier believed this, and his servant woke from the dead.

The Bible tells us that the reason that Jesus healed a lot of people when he was on this earth was because he had compassion for them. The blind, lame, lepers, demon-possessed, widows—people desperate for healing because they thought the physical healing was the most important fix. Jesus knew it wasn't what would really change their lives, but he just couldn't help but respond to all the misery. I'm pretty sure that he expects us to feel the same way about the world around us. Respond to the misery, whether there is a spiritual payoff or not.

Time after time after time, we ask Jesus to fix the things that aren't the cause of true brokenness. He'll do it sometimes. Sometimes not. But the true brokenness is what he really wants to fix. And that doesn't always happen by us touching the hem of his garment. Sometimes there is a cross to shoulder and carry up a hill.

Lord, please fix Mike. Please heal whatever is going on in his mind. Help him to turn to you. I know that if he will just surrender his heart to you, everything will be fine. All he has to do is take your hand and everything will be fine.

God so loved me.

CHAPTER 26

He Sees Each Tear that Falls

"I NEED $15,000."

Mike was sitting up in bed. I was leaning against a pile up of pillows, reading. I threw my book down on the bed, breaking the spine.

"What did you say, Mike?"

"I don't think I'm going to be able to make payroll. I've never *not* made payroll." He was sweating. He wouldn't look me in the eye.

Was this some kind of déjà vu nightmare?

"I can't let the boys down. They've been doing brilliant work lately and we are getting streamlined, with Jim's help. I know that there is money out there to collect, but I won't get it in time."

I dragged myself out of bed and put on a heavy robe. I didn't want to be next to him for this conversation. I did not feel safe. I stretched out on the loveseat and faced him.

"No."

"Fran, we have to support the business. What will I do if it goes under? It's all we have."

Didn't he see that the business already was under? The business had not provided any income for almost a year and we were living off my inheritance from my mom and the income from my writing. It was time to talk about it openly.

"Mike, I'm sorry that you are not able to protect the boys. But why are you not willing to protect the family? Giving that money to Yacht

Outfitting is going to put the family at risk. I can't do that. And I can't believe that you would do that, too. Maybe it's time to think about other options for you."

"Saving Yacht Outfitting *is* the best thing for the family! What else is there?"

"But we put in $15,000 last year and you never repaid it to the family. Why should I believe that this is going to be any different?"

"You just have to trust me."

"How am I supposed to do that?"

"Why don't you think I'll succeed?"

"Mike, it's not as if I'm afraid you won't bring in any more money. That's not some scenario that I'm dreaming up. You've already proven to me that you are willing to risk our security for your business. You already did that. I have to look at what is, not what you want to see."

And then there was the unspoken conversation:

> *You don't remember how to get home. You sometimes can't recognize your wife or remember the names of your children. Something is desperately wrong with you and I'm terrified that you are dying. How am I supposed to invest $15,000 in your business?*

Mike flopped back against the pillow and half-spoke and half-whispered. "What am I going to do?"

I was angry. Yacht Outfitting was his idol and I was sick of sacrificing to it.

"You're going to miss payroll. It happens. Sit everyone down and give them the facts. If you really have money coming in, maybe they can help you collect it."

Immediately Mike started shaking and turning from side to side. It was as unexpected and bizarre as if a tsunami had broken through the sliding glass door and filled the room with sickening, destructive forces, wave after wave.

"I forgot to lock a boat."

"What?"

"I made a mistake on a boat. It's going to catch fire. What do I do? What do I do? Call Dan, I'll call Dan. I lost the key. Where is the key? The boat! The boat! It's going to sink!"

Mike's head twisted and turned as the babble poured from him like poison. I drew my legs up on top of the seat and clutched one of the pillows on the seat.

Mike, my kind and smart husband, tossed around the bed, agitated and either re-living or imagining every mistake possible on every yacht he'd stepped foot on over the years. I watched for a half hour, terrified.

It didn't look like the mania was going to subside, so I crawled back to bed next to him. I tried to hold him and sooth him but he was not aware of my presence.

God! Help us! Help us! Where are you?

I started to recite Psalm 23, which I had memorized in fifth grade.

> *The Lord is my shepherd, I shall not want…*
> *He maketh me to lie down in green pastures:*
> *Yea, though I walk through the valley of the shadow of death,*
> *I will fear no evil, for thou art with me…*

As I whispered the prayer, Mike finally began to respond to me. We put our arms around each other and wept together. Finally, I put my arm under his head and soothed his face with my other hand. In a shaking voice, my throat tight and tears in my eyes, I began to sing a worship song that I knew was his favorite,

> *He knows my name;*
> *He knows my every thought;*
> *He sees each tear that falls and hears me when I call.*

Mikey finally hummed along to the tune in his deep, off-key voice and I rested my head on his shoulder; his arm around me. We continued singing the song over and over and over until his breathing was even and heavy, his demons gone, for now.

Over and over. He knows our names. He sees each tear.

Without remembering exactly when, I, too, drifted to sleep.

CHAPTER 27

Harbor Drive

Mike's behavior was fine at times and weirdly strange at others. One of the great traditions that Mike had established with Anna was Saturday at the shop. She would jump in the big truck with her dad and off they went down to the Yacht Outfitting office on Harbor Drive where they would sit on the stairs, watch the bay, and talk about the different boats propped up on pipe "stilts" all over the boatyard.

Anna's "job" was to empty the waste baskets and then file client paperwork in neatly alphabetized folders in the tall, beige file drawers. Sometimes she would run the sweeper over the rugs and dust the desk, careful not to touch any of the piles Mike had constructed across the back. Then he would take out the giant blue Yacht Outfitting check book and write out to *Anna Canrinus* a check for $5.00. She always beamed with pride.

Afterward, the two of them would walk down the block, greet clients and friends, drop by the bank and on the way back, stop for giant burgers and a huge plate of fries at Boll Weevil, a local chain with the best burgers ever.

One day in the fall they walked into the house after a day at the office and Anna run up to me and said, "We saw a bank robber!"

I looked at Mike with wide eyes. "What!?"

Mike was casual about it.

"We were going into the bank when a guy ran out the door and knocked us aside. Turns out he had just robbed the bank. So we gave a description to the police when they came."

"Did you get a look at him?"

Anna answered, "Yes! He had a black sweatshirt and he was about five foot eight with black hair and a mustache."

"Did he get a look at you?"

Anna looked at her dad with a question in her eyes.

"No," said Mike, "He was running away fast. The police caught him a couple of blocks away."

"Wow," I said to Anna. "That must have been an adventure."

"It was!" she said. That was her forensic science phase in life when we all watched *CSI* after dinner together. She thought the whole thing was very cool. Mike was unperturbed.

It was spring. Mike came home from work one night very upset. His eyes had that crazed look that I was seeing more and more often and his head turned from left to right.

"Someone is after me, Fran."

I held my breath. *What now?*

"What do you mean, 'after you'?"

"I keep getting a call from the district attorney's office. I think they are trying to pin something on me."

"Honey, what are you talking about?"

"I just hang up on them."

"You hang up on the district attorney's office?"

"Yeah, they said something about robbing a bank!"

"What!"

"I think they are after me. Maybe it has to do with back taxes. They are out to get me. They are trying to frame me or something."

Mike was pacing, his brow crunched like a frayed rope. I went to the bathroom and plunged a pink washcloth into cold tap water. Then I buried my face in it. This new thing, stepping his toe into the whirling vortex of conspiracy theories, took my breath away. I had to be the calm one. I'm never the calm one. I breathed a quick prayer and then went back into the kitchen.

Lord, help me deal with this. Help Mike to calm down and get rational. Embrace us and watch over us.

I went back to the kitchen. "Mike, can you back up a little? Tell me exactly what happened."

He sat down and I set a tall glass of water in front of him.

"Well, I got a phone call and the woman identified herself as from the DA's office. She asked if this was Michael Canrinus and I said, 'Yes.' Then she said something about me being wanted." Mike looked out the window. "I didn't really understand her, but it was something about the bank."

I sat down next to him and took his hand.

"Honey, do you have her number?"

"No, I hung up."

"Well, maybe I can get it from your phone."

He handed it over and I scrolled down the calls and wrote down several that might be from a downtown office.

"I think I can find out what is going on if I call."

"Don't mention my name or say you know me. Someone is out to get me. They want to say I did something wrong."

I bit my lip. Just then Anna came bounding into the room with smiles. "Hi, Daddy."

"Hey, boo!" He stood up and gave a bear hug, lifting her high off the ground. She sat on his lap at the table.

"Oh yeah, they said something about Anna."

"Who said something about me?" Anna asked brightly.

I intervened. "Dad got a phone call from the district attorney's office. Something about the bank."

Anna got excited. "Oh, was it about the bank robbery?"

Instantly I remembered the incident and the truth started to fall into place.

"Mike, it must have been about the bank robber."

"What bank robber?"

"Dad! We saw that bank robber running out of the bank. Maybe they want us to look at a line-up or testify!" She thought this was awesome.

"I don't remember any bank robber," Mike said. Anna tried to remind him and talked about that day, going step by step while I got out the plates and set the table, but he had zero recollection of any of it.

"I'll call them tomorrow and get to the bottom of it," I said. "Mike, don't worry about it, I don't think anyone thinks that you've done anything wrong."

"Are you sure?"

I held him close and then rubbed his shoulders.

"I'm sure."

We took our time over dinner, listening to Anna ask about boats and hearing the news from the shipyard. It was starting to stay lighter outside, and I suggested that we sit on the patio. Anna hopped into the hammock and rocked while we played a game with her.

"Name twenty-five places that you think you could hide Easter eggs where no one will find them and let's write them down and see if your sisters will figure them out," I suggested.

"My sisters will be here for Easter Sunday?"

"We're having a bridal shower for Teresa the day before. Twenty-two ladies are coming! Then Teresa and Melissa and Molly will be here Sunday for the egg hunt after church. In fact, we better start dying eggs tonight. Want to?"

Mike got up. "I think I have to pass. I'm tired."

"OK, Daddy. We'll make some blue ones with your initials on them," said Anna, "but you have to find them yourself!"

"I always do!"

He always did. Every Easter Mike and Anna enjoyed this ritual of the egg hunt. She would scramble around the rose beds, the bird of paradise, the peach trees, and the ferns, while Mike would lift her up to check out tree branches and secret nooks and crannies in the porch overhang. There was nothing sweeter than watching a six-foot-four bear of a man running around the yard with a little yellow plastic basket and squealing when he found a two-toned, hard-boiled egg which he later slipped into Anna's basket. She never caught on.

I got out a big pot of water and emptied two eighteen-egg cartons into the cold water, thinking about the bridal shower set up, decorating the church for Good Friday *and* for Easter. Should I cook lamb or duckling for Sunday dinner? *And how to explain to the kids that Mike was a little off these days, even though he was good on paper.*

The next day I was able to get hold of the right person at the DA's office. The trial for the bank robber was coming up and she wanted Mike and Anna to testify.

I explained that Mike was having memory loss and didn't recall anything about the incident. Even though I had no medical evidence, she agreed he had acted very strangely on the phone. Still, she wanted Anna to testify.

It caused me to do some soul-searching. It was the first major issue that I had to decide without input from my husband. Did I want my ten-year-old to face down an armed bank robber, so that he would know who had sent him to prison? How long would he be away? What would stop him from seeking revenge? The DA promised that she would only ask Anna to testify if it was absolutely necessary. Later she called to assure me that they would not need Anna to convict the robber.

Thank you, Lord!

The week went like clockwork. The eggs got done, and I took a day off to help set up the stations of the cross in the church — candles and symbols and implements of Christ's last week alive on earth. Did he know, when they were calling him King and the children were laying palm fronds at his feet, that he was going to be dead by the end of the week? Did he know how much it would hurt – that nails would be driven into his hands? Did he know that his mother would watch, weeping, until he took his last breath? Would it help to know or would that be worse?

The coming months were going to be filled with celebrations. Melissa's restaurant was expanding and she had won a blue ribbon for making goat cheese from her neighbor's goat's milk. Jesse was graduating from U.C. Berkeley in May, while Anna was graduating from middle school a few weeks later. Teresa was getting married in June. Nick and Jocelyn were getting married in September, and I was already thinking of a special rehearsal dinner. Rob and Vanessa and the kids were going to move into their new house as soon as it was finished, and Molly was getting her first apartment. Finally, it was my year to host the family at Thanksgiving: usually thirty to forty people. I didn't think that I would be able to fit another thing on the schedule.

God so loved me.

The bridal shower was wonderful — women celebrating Teresa and showering her with gifts was such a joy. I loved filling my home with laughter and excitement, putting beautiful flowers everywhere. Nick and Mike and another friend, Gabriel, sat on the patio for the three hours talking "guy stuff" during the shower. Nick had recently returned from Iraq and I was sure that they had lots to talk about. I made sure they had plenty to eat and drink while we ladies inside filled our dessert plates with cake and peanuts and pastel candies.

When the last gift was open, I went out to check on the boys. Mike had gone downstairs for a nap.

"How was it out here? Were you able to catch up with your dad after being away for so long?" Nick and Mike had always been very close, and I'm sure they had military stories to share in detail.

Nick hesitated and then looked me right in the eye.

"We talked, Frannie, but he didn't track with anything I was saying," Nick said bravely. "He was completely out of it the whole time."

CHAPTER 28

God Loves You and Has a Wonderful Plan...

DAWN WAS MISTY AND quiet as rays of sun pierced the sky and showered light over the lantana bushes with their blossoms bright as ripe oranges. I went upstairs in my robe and made a cup of tea, then went out to the patio to watch the world wake up. Remnants from the bridal shower were scattered in the living room and kitchen. Ribbon, wrapping paper, and a few paper cups and plates that I had missed were tucked under chairs and on counters — hiding like the Easter eggs I would place around the yard after church.

I thought of each child and the difficult work that Mike and I had put in over the years to create a blended family. We wanted to make our home a safe, welcoming place for each of them and yes, there was conflict and there were fights, like every other family. But at the core, I know that this was home to seven amazing kids that God had given to us to love.

And being a family wasn't about how they behaved or followed our "rules" or went to church or didn't have sex or use drugs or if they met our expectations. It was about them being individuals created by a God who loved them. They were gifts to us to also love unconditionally and to learn from and be loved by. We told all but Anna to describe us like this: "We are not your mom and dad, but we are your parents. We love you and this is home."

As pink streaks rose on the horizon, I thought about Mike and tried to figure out what was happening. Was this early Alzheimer's? But it was more than memory loss. Was God forsaking him? Was it demonic, or worse, punishment?

Growing up, I had heard the mantra: "God loves you and has a wonderful plan for your life." It was the lead sentence in an evangelism booklet — a handy pamphlet passed out at campuses and beaches all over Southern California in a campaign to have teenagers pray the "sinner's prayer." The implication was that if you repented and invited Jesus into your heart, life would become wonderful. Your life would follow a plan. No confusion, no worries.

I had always considered it suspect, given realities like the starving Christians in Africa and believers imprisoned in Russia. What was *their* wonderful plan? But there was still this hidden, magical expectation that following God would somehow be rewarded with everything becoming a little easier. God had our backs.

Turns out I had it right. God isn't behind us. He's leading us — we're the ones that take up the cross and follow. And it's hard and painful to carry that cross, even though it results in surrender and surrender results in ultimate joy. Jesus said that the one who loses his life will find it. Not sure I would describe that as a wonderful plan. But somehow, decade after decade, churches hold out this little carrot. Believe and it will go better for you, not just in the next life, but in this one too. Starting now.

* * *

Mike and I stood near the front of the church, Anna between us like an angel in a long pink dress, me in my flowered Easter hat, Mike in his blue pastel silk shirt. Dressed for spiritual success.

Mandy Stone was painting on the platform alongside the pulpit. It was the end of a series where she painted a picture during the sermon that was obscure until the final amen. She was using black ink on a four- by-four-foot hunk of foam core on an easel. I don't remember the sermon or the worship music or the prayers, but at the end of the service we saw a painting of two hands grasping each other; It was Jesus pulling Peter out of the water after Peter's faith failed. When Peter failed to walk on water after taking his eyes off of Jesus. When he jumped out of the boat filled with bravado and halfway to Jesus became a miserable, fearful failure. When Jesus lifted Peter out of his failure and led him to safety.

The painting stood like a huge wayfarer sign as people filed out of the church.

"I need to have that painting," Mike whispered to me. "Go ask Mandy if I can have it."

"Mike, where are we going to put it?"

"I'm not sure, but I want to see it first thing when I wake up every day."

I looked at Mike, wondering if the meaning had gone deeper with him that day. Mandy was happy to relinquish the artwork. As soon as we got home, I put it on the fireplace wall directly across from our bed. There, four foot square, would be the daily reminder that Jesus wants to pull us out of the messes we make when we try to do things our own way.

Easter dinner was delicious, lilies were in bloom, and the egg hunt was a great success. Anna always got to hide the eggs again for us, so we must have hidden the eggs about four times back and forth until we settled down at last in the living room, enjoying duck and gravy sandwiches for supper and a last handful of chocolate eggs from the baskets. We kissed and hugged our little bunny, tucked her into bed, and went down to our room. There the painting loomed in front of us and we settled next to each other in bed.

"Mikey, what does that picture mean to you?"

"Well, Fran, today I gave my heart to Jesus Christ."

Wow. This was a day that many, many people in his life had prayed would come. I could almost hear the rejoicing angels, heaven ringing with cheers, and see God smiling, whatever that actually looks like. Shimmering light? Intense radiance? Fireworks?

Jesus told a story about a shepherd who loses a sheep. He said that a good shepherd will leave the ninety-nine sheep that are on the hillside and go after the one that is lost. When he finds the lost sheep, he returns rejoicing.

My heart bubbled with joy.

"Really?"

Mike was completely serious, not shy and not hesitant.

"Yep, I asked God to forgive all my years of fighting him off and thinking that I was at the helm and could walk on water. I told him

He could have everything. My business, my life — everything. I feel tremendous peace."

And in that moment I wanted to believe in the magic. I wanted to believe that now our troubles would be made right and that things with Mike would start to get better.

Thanks, Lord. Okay, is this where we get blessed? Is Mike going to get better?

The answer was not what I wanted to hear.

God so loved me.

CHAPTER 29

Shutting Down

THE NEXT SUNDAY MORNING was sunny and breezy as Mike and I sipped coffee on the porch before church.

"Are you planning to go in today?"

Mike looked down. "I probably should. I have lots of paperwork to do"

I reached over and touched his hand. The fingers were dry and wrinkled.

"Tell you what. Why don't you let me go down and see if I can organize the paperwork for you? Stay here with Anna. She misses you. I can get it all ready for you and you can tackle it tomorrow. Would that be OK?"

Mike looked at me and smiled. "That sounds great. But you have never done anything like that before and it might make you crazy."

I gave him a stern look. "I can open mail and I can make piles just as good as you can!"

He laughed. I continued.

"I promise I'll label everything and I won't ruin anything. Let me do this, okay? After lunch."

I didn't do a plead and pout, but close. I really wanted to help.

"If I run into anything I don't understand, I'll call you."

Mike finally patted my hand nestled underneath his wide palm.

"Yes. Go ahead. It can't get any worse than it already is."

"I do have a master's degree."

Mike smiled again.

"Not in paperwork. And especially not in Yacht Outfitting paperwork."

"I bet I can help," I said with sass.

"Oh, I bet you can," said Mike. "Let's head to church."

The perfect weather made me miss my blue convertible. That car had been totaled the year before, hit by a drunk driver on the night before our vacation as it was parked outside the dealership where I had taken it for a pre-vacation check-up. Apparently the car had saved the driver's life, buffering him against smashing into a high brick wall along the sidewalk. Angels were watching over that drunk guy.

Now I was driving a zippy little KIA Sportage, black with wavy decals on either side. It looked like it should be driven by one of my sons, not a fifty-year-old grandma. We had also purchased a used Ford Explorer that was large and cumbersome for me to drive, but easier on Mike than his massive…well, large truck. Not only that, the ignition was out on the truck and the only way to start it now was by fiddling with wires under the dashboard.

Our kids labeled half the vehicles in our community "needlessly large trucks." Mike's Ford didn't fit that category, but was an old, pristine F350 with an ancient camper painted to match. Mike bought the truck from a client whose family had used the camper for forty years. It had vegetable-print curtains, wooden oak walls and ceiling, gold-flecked counters, and an avocado green stove when we acquired it. Now it was a crisp red, white, and blue with starred cushions and red checkered curtains and navy bedspreads. The next project would be painting the stove and refrigerator, and meanwhile the gold flecks and the honey oak walls had a retro look that was growing on me.

Mike had taken the camper to work on boats in other cities and I think he loved the freedom of having it. We spent much more time fixing up our "land yacht" than actually taking it to a campground. It was something I never expected to be part of my life. But as long as I had my season tickets to our local Repertory Theatre, I could still think of us as well-rounded instead of feeling like I had disappeared completely into this strange life belonging to someone else.

After ten years of marriage, I was learning to take it all in, keep an open heart, and be grateful for all of it. I had a full and active family, a gorgeous husband, a big house, a successful career, a neighborhood pool and tennis court just five doors down and a killer 180-degree view that looked like Tuscany itself.

This is what some Christians call "blessed." Then again, even rock stars call themselves "blessed" by success. Even homeless drunks call themselves "blessed" when they find half a sandwich wrapped in paper. Beauty queens and lottery winners are "blessed."

When they win.

I guess none of us really believed in Jesus' description in the book of Matthew about who are really blessed in this world: the poor in spirit, the mournful, the persecuted. Those sorry souls would find their blessing in heaven, I had always been taught. Here they just had to suffer through it.

So, in my mind, we were blessed. And now Mike was willing to let God be the leader of our lives. Icing on the cake.

That week we slept locked into each other arms. Mike made time for us to talk on the patio at the end of the day and at night I felt content and loved and safe. Thank you Jesus! So this is what Christian marriage was going to be like. Bring it on!

* * *

At the service the next Sunday morning, Mike sang loudly in his deep, unmusical voice, and his face shone without a trace of confusion or illness. He held my hand and squeezed it when the pastor talked about giving your heart and life to God. During the coffee time between services, he talked in a group of other guys, joked and laughed with them, while I caught up with my girlfriends and went to tear Anna away from the kids in the youth room.

After lunch I got the two of them settled and hopped in the KIA to make the thirty-minute minute trip down to the waterfront. The water was glorious, sparkling like diamonds. I loved the dance of boats. I loved that we could jump on one and sail around the bay if we ever made the time. Nothing was more beautiful than wind at our backs and the mysterious sea, alive underneath us.

I opened the door to the little office and slid the window wide so that the sea breeze could cleanse the smell of boat workers out of the air. Near the dock, adorable little houseboats bobbed up and down and I thought how great that would be for a retirement spot — rocking us like a waterbed into a heavenly sleep.

Then I sat down at the desk and surveyed the piles. Lord, have mercy. The watercolor paintings of sailboats and cabinets filled with yacht keys faded while I concentrated on figuring out what it all meant.

First I matched work orders to client folders. Lots of jobs had a series of work orders, or scraps of paper that needed to be converted into work orders. Like plumbing, the mantra for yachts was, "The more you fix, the more you fix." Also the time-honored, "While we are at it…" came into play. If you pulled up a teak floor to add a bow thruster, wouldn't that be the best time to install a new set of speakers? A navigation station? Engine-room storage? If none of these add-ons made it to work orders, Mike was working for free.

Next, it was time to go over the yellow slips. These were Mike's copies of parts receipts. Each needed to be labeled with the owner's job number, the date, the name of the boat and the part number to go on the invoice. Most were good. I could see Jim Stone's handiwork in the filing of the yellow slips. But there was a growing "unknown" pile that simply had a nickname for the owner, or the name of the boat and no owner, no job number, no date. This was information locked into the mind of Mike — scribbled at the counter of Marine Exchange and unidentifiable to anyone unfamiliar with the job. I looked for clues to see what parts went with what job, and found many of them from a partial name of an owner or the name of a boat.

Finally, I sorted the mail. Stacks of mail. Tucked under invoices, behind the telephone, on top of the file cabinet. Mail was everywhere. When I organized it into stacks, I used the metal letter opener that rested in a big captain's mug next to the fax machine. Most of the pieces were bills; these also had parts numbers that could provide clues to dates and jobs. Sorting through the yellow slips against the bills to see who worked on what boat on which day was probably another whole day of work. When was Teru reupholstered? What was a bill from Yacht Docktor doing here that was six months old?

Some of the mail held checks, which was like finding gold. I carefully copied them and attached the payments to the invoices in the folders, writing the job name and number on the copies. Slowly the stack of mail was getting sorted.

Finally, I looked out of the window and saw that the brightness of the day was starting to wane. The sparkle was off the water and it looked dull and the bay was heaving. The breeze was blowing off shore, toward home. I was hot and getting tired. I needed to hurry up.

I spent a little time writing notes and explaining what I thought needed to be worked on first thing in the morning, particularly having everyone going through yellow slips so we could invoice real amounts and not have this pool of expenses as overhead.

I was procrastinating.

Finally, I took the huge stack of unpaid bills and lined them up next to the old adding machine that made a *cha-ching* sound with every entry. When I had a total I put my head down. Tears started to fill my eyes. My nose started to drip and I grabbed a tissue, but the flood continued.

Through my tears I started over. I cleared my throat and raised my chin. One by one, the bills were entered again, the button pushed again, the grinding noise of the adding machine rang out over and over, like the clang of a prison lock-up. When I came to the last paper on the stack, I forced myself to push the TOTAL key. I did it all a third time.

I had to be absolutely sure that I wasn't using the machine wrong or pushing an accidental button or entering anything twice. All three totals came out the same.

$56,000.

Yacht Outfitting had $56,000 in unpaid bills.

* * *

Monday morning I called Jim and Mandy. I wanted to see if Jim could help with getting out the invoices. It was awkward. I talked to Mandy first, checking in to see how things were going with the kids, her mom, and plans for visual arts at the church. I told her the good news that Mike had made the decision to surrender his life to the Lord and that her painting was now a permanent part of our décor. Early Sermon Illustration.

When Jim got on the line I asked if there was some way that he could help with invoices. We seemed to be behind in sending them to the owners, I explained. There was a pause.

"I don't really know anything about the day to day finances," Jim finally said. "Mike keeps me away from all of that. Most of what I've done has to do with systems and analyzing clients.

"By the way," he continued, "I want to thank you again for taking us out for the bay cruise. It made a huge difference for me."

I smiled. It had been an amazing evening. Jim was hoping to join a software start-up with some former partners and they came to San Diego to talk with him. As a treat, we planned an evening on the water on Mike's client's powerboat, *Teru*, one of the largest boats in the San Diego Yacht Club cruising fleet.

As the group relaxed on the expansive forward deck, I made dinner in the galley and we looked out on the spectacular shoreline of San Diego Bay. Heading around the bay, the busy airport was on one side and the impressive aircraft carriers at the naval base on Coronado Island anchored the other side. Then the high rises of downtown came into view — hotels and quaint Seaport Village along the boardwalk across from condos and the Ferry Landing shopping area on the Coronado side. Next, the sail roofing of the Convention Center, white and gleaming against a blue sky, stretched along the waterfront.

Just as we crossed under the lovely curve of the Coronado Bridge, the shipyard and port hosted massive ships under repair or bringing containers of fruit from Chile, our South American mirror climate. Swinging the boat to the right into Glorietta Bay, our small crew was greeted by the red turret of the Hotel Del Coronado, like graceful royalty. As Mike maneuvered *Teru* among the anchored sailboats, breezes drifted across the bow. We finished the crispy crab cakes, pungent cabbage, and grilled corn on the cob. Cookies ended the meal on a sweet note. On the way back, gliding toward the sunset, the ideas flowed between Jim and his colleagues. What a way to do business. A great evening.

It had only been a few months but I now doubted if Mike could even take Teru out without assistance, even though he had done it thousands of times in twenty years.

Jim's voice ended my reminiscence.

"—So I'm not sure what kind of help I could be, but have Mike call me if there is something I can do."

"Okay, Jim, will do. In fact, I'm sure of it."

I put down the phone and stared out over the hillsides rich with colorful wildflowers, red and orange bougainvillea, oleanders in pink and white, and palm tree silhouettes against the sunshine.

What am I going to do? What is going to happen? Lord, give me peace, give us direction.

The day went by quickly. I called Mike a few times but he never had a minute to talk. He had been working all day on an invoice for a $12,000 job and was almost done. That was a relief. Maybe God was answering our prayers and his brain was going to hold it together enough to get some billing done.

It was time to make dinner. I had learned when my family went from three to nine that the secret to a meal is not to make large portions of a few things, but medium portions of several things. Anything left over then became a part of "Saturday Night Soup."

This night I made a big pot of pasta and some homemade meat sauce — small pieces of ground beef browned in olive oil and seasoned with fresh herbs and garlic simmering in crushed tomatoes. When it was done, I laid out a buffet, which is how our large family (and usually a friend or two) did dinner. A stack of plates and silverware were at one end of the counter. Then the pasta, a bowl of sauce, green beans, and chunks of eggplant sautéed with red cabbage. Garlic bread slices were lined up in a basket. A yellow bowl of ripe plums gave it the perfect look of spring. The kids were called in; they filled their plates and sat at the table. The head seat near the door was saved for Mike.

We got started. About halfway through the meal, Mike walked through the front door. I jumped up gave him a huge hug and led him to the sink to was his hands.

"It's all there, honey. Just fill up your plate and join us. Do you want something to drink?

"Just water, thanks."

Mike looked tired. He took a plate and I went back to mine at the table, bringing the bread basket with me for the rest of the family. We started up our chatting and continued with stories of the day. Mid-story Mike sat down and we were all watching Anna when suddenly she gave her dad a strange look and there was silence. We all turned out heads.

Mike sat down at the table with a flat dinner plate that had a slightly raised edge. The plate was filled with sauce, nothing else. Slowly and deliberately, Mike took his spoon and dragged it across the plate, his hands shaking. When he raised it to his lips, he bent his head forward and concentrated on the spoon. Without spilling, he sipped the sauce, then brought his spoon down again for another scoop.

Anna stared. Then all the kids stared with their mouths open. Mike concentrated on his next sip. My heart was gripped with sadness and tears came to my eyes.

I jumped up from my chair.

"Honey, I think you forgot to get the pasta."

Whipping the plate off the table, I jumped over to the counter.

"How about some green beans, does that sound good? And I'll put a little of this eggplant and cabbage on the side? Okay! I had fun cooking all of this. It turned out so good. There's a little wine in the eggplant. I think you'll love it."

I set the plate back down in front of him piled with food. He stared at the plate, then picked up his spoon.

"Try using the fork, I think it might work better."

The kids looked away with their heads down. One by one they excused themselves from the table. I sat alone with Mike, adjusting his napkin and watching him silently eat his meal bite by bite without looking up.

CHAPTER 30

The Last Time

MIKE LEFT IN THE Ford Explorer before I was awake. I opened my eyes and stretched out across the empty space in the bed, sunlight streaming into the room from the sliding door and the arched window in our bathroom. Then I remembered the night before and slipped to my knees, rested my arms on the mattress and put my head down in my hands.

Lord, what is happening to Mike? He's your child now...do something! I don't know how to respond! Should I call the doctor again? Should I get more involved with Yacht Outfitting? Should we shut it down? How do I bring up this debt? Why is he hiding it from me? Does he even know? Help us, Lord, help us!

I stood and walked toward the bathroom. There, on the table by the television, was a single penny. My daily penny. *Mike is my gift to you.* I picked it up and rubbed the copper between my fingers, then set it on the sink where I could see it when I brushed my teeth and washed my face.

While I was getting dressed I stared above the fireplace at the huge hand of God reaching into swirling waters to save a drowning Peter. *What did that incident really mean, anyway? Was it a test of Peter's faith? Was Peter being arrogant? Was it about pride or being humbled? Does Jesus expect us to walk on water?*

God so loved me.

That night I couldn't wait to meet with our counselor. I stepped into the slow elevator and listened to the slow hum. When I stepped onto the courtyard balcony, my phone rang.

"I'm going to be late," Mike said.

"Is everything all right, honey?"

"Oh sure, I just have to finish up a few things."

"Okay, I'll see you in a little bit. Be careful."

"Always, Fran. I love you."

"Love you, too."

When Peter came out to the waiting room, I let him know that Mike was going to be late, but maybe that was good thing because I had to talk about him about Yacht Outfitting. We went into his office and sat down.

Step by step, I talked about the history of Mike using our family resources to support his business. I told Peter about the night that I turned down a loan to Yacht Outfitting and that had caused him to, essentially, go crazy and about trying to smother me with a pillow. All of the details about the boat show and Mike's inability to track with reality came pouring out. Just after that, my phone rang. It was Mike.

"Honey, I don't think I'm going to be able to make it over there."

"Are you feeling okay?"

"I'm just so exhausted. I'm starting to feel dizzy."

"Are you sure you are able to drive? Would you like me to come get you?"

"No, no. I'll be fine. I'll see you at home."

"Okay, be careful, Mikey. Call me back when you get home."

When I flipped the phone shut, Peter indicated that he'd caught the gist of the conversation. He asked me to continue my story. It was almost time for the appointment to end so I moved ahead to Sunday's trip to the office.

"—And I read the total of the unpaid bills and it was $56,000."

"What did you say?"

"Fifty-six thousand dollars in unpaid bills."

Peter paused for a minute, looking away and shaking his head. Finally he turned to me.

"Well, there's really only one thing to do."

"What's that?" I asked.

Peter cleared his throat.

"You have to shut down Yacht Outfitting without Mike's knowledge."

The words hung in the air. I pictured Mike's love of the water and the wind and how his business came first in his life; how his "boys" meant everything to him. I could imagine the pain and hurt he would feel if I even brought it up and how much he would hate me for even suggesting such a thing.

"No way. There is no way that I could do that."

Peter spoke firmly. "You don't have a choice. Clearly Mike is not mentally or emotionally capable of doing it. You have to be the responsible adult. You have to shut it down." With that, Peter stood to let me out the door.

"I can't."

"You have to."

Walking down to the car, I tried to wrap my head around Peter's words. *Why did it have to be me? Was it really appropriate for me to trample on Mike's livelihood, his dream, his love?*

I know the plans I have for you, said the prophet, *plans for a future and a hope.* Deep inside, I knew that the truth was not referring to a gender-based spiritual hierarchy. God was not going to work in my life like some kind of proxy through Mike's life. I was a daughter of the Creator. He had been holding my hand as a child, teaching me his Word at seminary, loving me through my divorce, carrying me through years of estrangement, and eventually reaching out to me through the love of a good man. I had returned to my faith and now God was giving me a task — a huge one — that required me to do what was best for my family even if it cost me my marriage. And I was supposed to just trust and obey?

Wait a minute. Haven't I been through that kind of decision once already?

All these thoughts went through my mind as I drove home in the dark. My little KIA raced over the freeway and I got off at my regular exit. Suddenly I remembered that I needed something from the grocery store so I took a different turn and drove up Navajo Road. As I headed up the block, just under the freeway overpass, the KIA stopped. In the middle lane of three westbound lanes on a six-lane street. I flipped on my hazard lights and cars honked and whipped around me on the left and on the right.

Help me, Lord! Just help me get to the side of the road!

For about fifteen minutes I prayed and cried and turned the key in the ignition. Nothing. The car was just stopped. I looked down at the mileage, which had just turned over 104,000. The car had a 100,000-mile warranty. I tried again and something caught and the engine engaged. Waving my hand out the window, I edged to the right and turned in the first driveway next to a Starbucks, a nail salon, a game store and a bank. Pulling across empty parking spaces, the car stopped again. For good. I called home.

Molly answered.

"Molly, I need you to do me a favor."

"What now?"

"I need you to call Fletcher Hills Towing. My KIA just died. I'm on Navajo Road, just on the right in the parking lot next to the Starbucks. Tell them to come right away and tow me to La Mesa Auto and Tire."

"What's the number?"

"You'll have to look it up. My phone battery is about to die and I don't have a charger. Fletcher Hills Towing."

"I guess I can."

"Thanks, Molly, I really, really appreciate it."

"Okay, bye."

I fumed for a while, wishing that I had kept my AAA membership, but we always said that with six drivers around, we would always find someone to help out. And normally we were right, this kind of thing had not been a problem before.

The phone rang.

"Mom, they said they won't come."

"What?"

"They said it was too late. They won't come."

"I've never heard of that!"

"And Mike wanted me to tell him what was wrong, but I wouldn't."

"What?"

"He'll want to go get you and look at the car, but he will just break it!"

"You told him that?"

"Yes, I told him he couldn't go."

"Molly!"

"Well, Mom, you know it's true. He got really mad at me. Really mad."

"Molly, listen, tell him where I am and keep trying the tow companies. Try Two-Bit Tow."

I dreaded watching the Ford Explorer drive into the lot. Mike and Molly got out. Mike was furious. He came over to me and asked me to lift the hood. Molly came to my side of the car.

"I wouldn't let him come alone. Mom, he can't really drive at night. I don't know what he thinks he's going to do."

"Molly, he's a mechanic! He's been working on cars since he was fourteen."

"Hey, would you shine this flashlight under the hood," Mike hollered.

"I'll be right there!" I whispered to Molly, "keep a lookout for the tow truck, are they coming?"

"Yes, they are sending someone."

While I held the flashlight, Mike was tinkering with this and that under the hood, having me try the ignition now and then. I was trying to be careful not to flood the engine. At one point, Mike stopped and came over to my open door.

"Molly crossed the line with me. She tried to refuse to tell me where you were. Who does she think she is? I know I never do this, but I raised my voice at her and lost it."

"She was just trying to handle it on her own. I'm sorry that happened. I don't think she realized that she was being disrespectful."

Oh, what a mess that must have been!

Finally the tow truck came. Mike and the driver worked on getting the car loaded. I worked on getting Molly calmed down. She worked on getting me to admit that Mike had lost all capability. I tried to tell her that Mike was feeling very desperate about the losses of his abilities. When the KIA was almost locked down, Mike spoke to me again.

"Molly was completely wrong. I should be the one handling this. I've done this a thousand times. She is just making up trouble."

I stared straight ahead. Mike went with the tow truck, while Molly came home with me in the Explorer. I had no idea how Mike intended to fill out the shop's overnight drop-off form and I made a mental note to call Matt at La Mesa Auto first thing in the morning to explain everything.

As we pulled the cumbersome Explorer into the driveway I said, "Thank God I don't have to drive this thing all the time. It's huge!"

Molly said goodnight. As I waited for the tow driver to bring Mike the few blocks home, I sat on the front step to watch the stars.

Where was I before the car crisis and Molly got reamed out by Mike for telling him that he wasn't capable of handling the car trouble?

Oh, yeah. I was figuring out how to tell Mike that he wasn't capable of running his business.

CHAPTER 31

Can You Spell That?

THE WORST DAY OF our lives was the best day of spring. Warm and breezy. The birds were singing like they lived in the forest with Snow White. But inside our house at the top of Windmill View, there was tension, just a hint of what was coming. I made morning coffee and set it on the counter as Mike climbed the stairs.

"Want some breakfast?"

"No, I've gotta' get going. I'm late."

"Are you sure? Maybe we should take a minute to talk?"

"We'll talk tonight."

I walked over and put my arms around him.

"Promise?"

Mike looked down at me with his blue eyes and kind face. The face I loved so much.

"I promise. We'll talk, we'll sit on the patio and talk about everything there is to talk about. We'll talk until there are no more words."

He leaned down and kissed me and the tension between us dissolved.

"We'll talk. Tonight. I promise."

He refilled his large ship captain's mug and walked toward the front door.

"By the way, I'll hotwire the truck, so you can have the Explorer if you need it. And I'll call Matt to talk about the KIA."

I followed him out the front door. He set his cup on the blood-red vinyl front seat and fiddled around with the wiring under the dashboard until the engine rumbled to a start.

That diesel engine was such a familiar sound by now. Down at Alberto's taco shop, if they heard Mike's truck coming they automatically started a breakfast burrito. If he left the house the other way, down the hill, it meant he was going to stop at Mary's donuts.

"All good trips begin at Mary's!" was our family anthem and for the most part, it was true. Trips to the cabin at Crestline, road trips to visit family, trips to colleges and trips of kids moving away from home. Certainly Mike and Anna's weekly trips to the office began at Mary's. In fact, the walls of Mary's were covered in photos and somewhere among them was a picture of a seven year-old Anna and her giant daddy smiling and happy.

After spending about an hour at my desk, I called La Mesa Auto to see if Carlos or Matt had heard from Mike. They were a great shop and had helped us out with our six cars many times. But the best thing about the shop was that it was just a level half-mile walk back to the house. Matt said that they noticed the KIA was there and got some kind of scribbled note with our phone number, but hadn't heard a word. I explained to him that the KIA had just come to a cold stop the night before.

"That doesn't sound so good, Francine. Why did you buy a KIA anyway?"

"I thought it was cute. Why else do you buy a car? And it had a stadium back seat so I wouldn't break my back getting Anna out of her car seat."

Matt laughed. "Well, I have to say, it doesn't look good. Looks like the engine seized."

"What does that mean, anyway? It sounds like some kind of mechanic code."

"You're right, Mike would know what I mean. It's code for 'We have no idea what happened and we don't know how to fix it.'"

"Okay, take a look at it and call me back if there's any way to save it. If Mike calls, let him know that I talked to you already."

"Will do."

I wonder why Mike forgot to call Matt.

I started rummaging around the kitchen to find something for lunch when my phone rang. I ran over to the dining room table and looked at the caller ID. It was Mike.

"Hey, babe, what's up."

There was a moment of hesitation.

"Fran, I think I'm having a stroke."

I pulled out a chair to sit, instantly panicked.

"Where are you and who is with you?"

"I'm on Harbor Drive with Chris. Can you come get me?"

Chris was Mike's young intern.

"Mike, you need to have Chris call an ambulance."

"I'd rather wait and just have you come take me to our hospital."

"No, honey, I can't drive thirty minutes there and thirty minutes back here. You need an ambulance. Let me talk to Chris."

"Hello?" said Chris.

"Chris, call 911 right now and give them your location. Keep Mike's phone on you and call me right back."

"He fell down! He's on the ground!"

"Call 911!"

The call ended and I put my head down on the table, my heart racing. *Oh God! Oh God! Oh God! Please watch over Mike and protect him!*

The phone rang. I realized that I was holding my breath.

"Hello?"

"Is this Francine?"

"Yes."

"This is Lori from the bank. We thought we should call. Mike was just in here and he wasn't making any sense. Everything he said was just garbled."

"An ambulance is already on the way. Thank you for calling. Thank you so much."

"Well, we thought you should know. Hope that he is okay."

"Me, too. Oh, sorry! There's the other line."

"All right. Good luck."

I hit the flash button and heard a man's voice.

"Francine Phillips?"

"Yes."

"Are you related to Michael Canrinus?"

"He's my husband."

"He is unconscious. We are getting him into the ambulance now."

"Where are you taking him?"

"I'll call you back."

There were muffled voices, the whine of a siren and then silence.
Deafening silence.

I looked around the room. It was like being in a silent movie. I could not hear the birds, traffic noise, the ticking clock or my own breathing in and out, only this loud pounding. It took a minute before I recognized it as the pounding of my heart.

Then I went into crisis-mode calm. While I waited for the call from the ambulance driver, I contacted my nextdoor neighbors and asked them to be there when Anna got off the school bus and then take her to their house. I left messages with the other kids and let them know they would be updated. I called Jim Stone and asked if he could go to Yacht Outfitting in the morning and see if he could help out with getting everyone going on their jobs and give me a status report when I called. I typed up a list of names and phone numbers that I would need as emergency contacts.

Suddenly I realized two hours had gone by. The EMT had never called back. Now it was going to be up to me to find Mike. By some miracle it never occurred to me that Mike might be dead. I began to methodically call hospitals, starting with ones that might be nearest to Point Loma.

"UCSD Hospital, can I help you?"

"I'm looking for a patient, Mike Canrinus. He was taken in an ambulance from Harbor Drive. Is he at your hospital?"

"Where did they take him?"

"They never told me. They were supposed to call me back."

"How long has it been?"

"It's been about two hours. Can you tell me if he is your patient?"

"I don't think they would have brought him way up here."

What? I'm not asking you to guess where he is, lady – just tell me if he is there!

I took a deep breath.

"Can you please tell me if he is there?"

"What's his name?"

"Mike Canrinus."

"Can you please spell that?"

"C-a-n-r-i-n-u-s."

"No, he's not admitted. Should I check the emergency room?"

"Did I mention that he was in an ambulance?"

Did I mention that he is my husband and that he's only 57 years old and we have seven kids and he just gave his heart to Christ and he's very tall with blond hair and soft blue-green eyes and large hands with stubby fingers that can fix anything and he loves me? He loves me? And I love him?

"Oh, that's right. Let's see. No, I don't have anyone here by that name."

"Thank you. Goodbye."

"You might try Mercy."

"Goodbye."

Next call.

"Mercy Hospital. Can I help you?"

It took four calls to find him.

"Memorial Hospital. Can I help you?"

"I'm looking for a patient, Mike Canrinus. He was taken in an ambulance from Harbor Drive. Is he at your hospital?"

"What's his name?"

"Mike Canrinus."

"Can you please spell that?"

"C-a-n-r-i-n-u-s."

"And what is your name?"

"Francine Phillips. P-h-i-l-l-i-p-s."

"And you are...?"

"I'm his wife."

"Oh, here he is." I pictured the volunteer peering at a computer screen showing a list of patients. "He's in the ER. They've been wondering where you've been. They want to speak to you."

"No one told me where they were taking him. Can you tell me where you are located?"

"Well, you can take the 15 or the 805 off the 8 east, then you get off before Genessee."

"What's the address?"

"It's called Hospital Drive."

"Aren't there about four hospitals around there?"

"Right. The ER is around by the parking garage. We have Children's Hospital, Mary Birch Hospital, the Polansky Center, and a rehab all next to each other. Look for the smaller tall parking garage."

"I'll be right there."

I climbed into the Explorer and headed to Interstate 8. The hospital was in an area called Kearny Mesa that I considered to be the black hole of San Diego. I had never been in that neighborhood without getting lost or turned around. My hands were shaking and the car was large and unfamiliar and the roads all looked the same – block after block of car dealerships, cheap restaurants, light industry strip malls, and stucco apartments with cement courtyards. Neverendingly the same.

I made a turn to a small winding street and saw the hospital sign as I passed it. I found a place to turn around and go back and there was a parking garage. Tall. Smallish. I turned in and wound upward several flights until I found a parking spot on the far left row, away from the stairs.

Something hit me. *Why were they looking for me?*

Entering the ER, I waited in line at the visitor's window, then told them my name and Mike's name; spelled Mike's name and spelled my name. I was not told to take a seat in the pool of human misery suffering in the lobby and felt a little guilty that I was able to walk right in. There is a hierarchy of illness openly enforced by emergency rooms that don't take into account pain, tears, inconvenience, hunger, children, time away from work or transportation problems. It has to do with severity of illness. The fact that I was immediately ushered to a cloth cubicle was, in some sick way, the good news that my case was the worst in the room.

Mike used to tell a story about how he worked for a while in college for a mental institution. He thought he was picked for the job because he had a sensitive side and was understanding and could be fearless and kind. Later he realized it was because he was six foot four and could outrun any inmate, pick him up, and carry him back into a building. He told me they had an inside name for much of the behavior that was exhibited by patients:

"Just Crazy."

I heard him before I saw him. Moans followed by screams followed by inhuman growls. The bed was in a sitting position. On the floor were tatters of Mike's clothes that had been cut off his body. His feet hung over the edge so that the restraints that were supposed to tie at the ankles grabbed just beneath his calves, stiff and twisting against the wide Velcro bands.

His nakedness was more frightening than shameful. A tiny hospital gown covered only one shoulder and was bunched to one side at his waist. The small, white tie at the breaking point. His arms jerked wildly through the air, pulling at the restraints on his arms, just above the writsts. The tethers tied to the frame of the bed strained with each burst of anger.

He threw back his head in agony, veins bulging. The soft, kind face that I loved was sweating and grey and facing the ceiling. Screams bit the air outside of his twisted mouth, like the snarl of a wild animal, and tears flung from his eyes as his head relentlessly shot left and right like a jackhammer.

Just Crazy.

I gagged in my mouth and turned and saw a bathroom marked "Employees Only." I ran to it and did not hesitate before pushing open the door and leaning over the toilet. After a few dry heaves, I vomited and vomited and vomited until dry heaves started again. I wiped my mouth with toilet paper then cupped one hand under the faucet while I had to use the other hand to push down on the button to release the water. After about six handfuls of water, the taste was out of my mouth and I wet a paper towel and wiped my face. I looked at my bleary, blotchy face in the mirror, then bowed my head.

Father, please be with Mike, help us! Please let me know what to do! Be with the doctors and give them wisdom. Keep me in your care. Please heal Mike.

When I lifted my head I saw a penny on the floor.

I bent down to pick it up. God told me to marry Mike. He knew this would happen. I felt like a cosmic fool.

As I pushed open the door I heard a voice in my heart. "My strength is made perfect in your weakness."

CHAPTER 32

Falling into the Rabbit Hole

"**A**RE YOU THE WIFE?"

The question broke the spell that had me transfixed to the bed once I returned to the room. Instantly the smells, sounds, and movement of the ER broke through. I noticed a couple of nurses had entered the room and were trying to hold Mike down while another tried to find a vein so they could insert an IV.

"My name is Joe. I'm his nurse," one of them said, looking back at me from over his shoulder as he held Mike's arm steady. "We need to get a little background from you."

Just then, a man in a white coat with shoulder-length, bleached-gold hair — sprayed and stiff — came down the hallway. His upper body was extremely muscular and he wore a blue shirt with a white collar, a gold watch and a stylish tie.

Fabio. Why would a doctor try to look like Fabio?

"Are you The Wife?"

"Yes, my name is Francine."

"So, what is his baseline?"

"What do you mean?"

"Is this his normal state?"

What kind of idiotic question was that?

"His normal state is to get up, get dressed, kiss me goodbye, get his truck started, take his cup of coffee and drive to work."

"That was recently?"

"That was this morning."

"Hmm. Does your husband use drugs?"

"No."

"Has he been tested for AIDS?"

"Not that I know of.

"Okay. Joe is going to get some history from you and we'll see if this medication can calm him down. Then you and I will have a talk.

Nurse Joe started shooting me questions. We were squeezed between the row of curtains and the wall. My mouth was dry and foul. I said Mike had called that morning, saying he was having a stroke. Then I explained the recent memory-related lapses and my concerns about early Alzheimer's disease. I even included Mike's shingles and his mother's disabilities resulting from a head-on collision.

People were rushing around outside the cubicle; machinery whizzed by. My head ached. I then covered the diagnostic tests Mike had taken and how he looked "good on paper," according to our physician. Then, finally, about our primary doctor's feeling that anxiety was at the root of everything and, given Paxil and counseling, he would be fine.

Joe stared at the keyboard and shook his head. I was so tired. I'd been standing for at least an hour. He searched behind several curtains until he found a hard metal stool to steal from a bedside so I could sit.

I could hear that Mike was no longer agitated. I had to see him.

"It won't be too much longer," said Joe. "We want to make sure we haven't missed anything."

Finally I was released from the information-gathering and pulled the curtain back to see Mike. He was asleep. Still the sweet sleep of a child that everyone wanted to capture on film. Only this time he was covered with a light sheet, his head turned to the side, his tired muscles heavy and immobile. I pulled my stool next to the bed and rubbed his arm with light, long strokes, whispering, "I love you, I love you."

A few minutes later, Dr. Fabio entered the cubicle.

"Well, what are we going to do with this guy?"

I looked at him and wrinkled my forehead, trying to puzzle out his meaning.

What do you mean "we"?

"I don't see any reason to keep him here."

"What are you saying?"

"I'm saying that you can take him home now."

It took a beat for me to gather my thoughts, while he stared at me. Maybe another ten seconds to decide to confront the doctor who was clearing his throat and preparing to move on.

"He's tied to the bed, has an IV and a catheter. How am I supposed to get him home? Tie him down in the back seat with seat belts? He can't talk, can't eat, can't walk or sit. I wouldn't even know how to get him out of the car, let alone up the stairs and into the house. This morning he drove to work and now he's incoherent. Are you telling me that you don't intend to find out what's wrong with him?"

Just then Mike let out guttural sounds in rhythmic staccato. Suddenly his back arched and his eyes opened. Then bulged from his eyelids. His body started jerking. His legs flopped and head twisted.

"Seizure! Ativan!"

Nurses scurried to the bedside. They released the right restraints and turned him to the left while his body jerked uncontrollably. Mike started to foam at the mouth and it kept foaming and dripping down his chin. They pushed the drug into the IV and it took about sixty seconds for it to reach the brain. The seizure did not stop completely for about five more minutes.

My arms ached to reach him and hold those shaking shoulders, and throw my body on the bed to comfort him. It bothered me that no one wiped his chin. Joe held my arm and then said quietly, "This is a good thing. This is good for them to see this."

When the seizure stopped and Mike's head flopped against the pillow. Dr. Fabio turned to me. "That was a grand mal seizure. Have you ever seen that before?"

"Never," I said, shaking my head slowly.

"Are you sure?"

Was this guy crazy? Why didn't he believe me?

"Of course I'm sure! And I'll never forget seeing this one."

He looked at Joe. "We'll keep him overnight for observation." Then he turned to me. "Make sure that we have your phone number."

Walking away with a cocky gait and, flipping his coifed hair over his shoulder, he looked back at me and said, "Be here tomorrow morning at 7 a.m. We'll have you meet with the hospitalist."

Joe began typing furiously into Mike's records. Once again he looked over at me and said with conviction. "That was a good thing. You're lucky. This changes everything."

What's a hospitalist?

Mike was not admitted to a room, but was kept in the ER overnight. It only took one wrong turn before I found my way to the freeway and got on the road to home. I was going to my warm, cozy bed while Mike was not able to understand, speak, or move — legs hanging over the bed and half-naked. One of the nurses had asked me if she should bring a warm blanket and I told her to bring two, but who knows if anyone was there to pick it up if he kicked it off the bed.

I did not yet realize — and the realization would come slowly — that I had entered the broken world of The Sick, just as Alice in Wonderland had tumbled down a rabbit hole and nothing ever made sense again. In this world I was both critical and irrelevant; necessary and ignored; the decision-maker and expected to blindly go along with the decision of anyone in a white coat. I had no idea that such a world existed before Mike and I fell into it. And it wasn't Wonderland.

God so loved me.

CHAPTER 33

The "Please" Prayer

WAKING UP AT FIRST light, I called the hospital and learned that Mike had not slept peacefully. He had shown several bouts of agitation, had pulled out his catheter, and was confused. He had experienced some seizure activity and had been given Dilantin. I told them I was on my way. I fell to my knees beside the bed.

Lord, I don't know what you want. Please be with Mike and touch his body. Please keep him safe and calm his brain. Father, I know that you are in control. You are over all things. Be with Mike right now and let him know that you are near. Give me strength. In the name of our savior, Jesus Christ. Amen.

I got up and found myself pacing the room, not able to focus on brushing my hair or choosing clothes. Instead, I flitted around like an injured bird, brushing my teeth, running upstairs to the laundry room, checking my email, taking a shower, back upstairs to make coffee dressed in a towel.

Calm down, calm down. You're okay.

I threw on clothes and shoes and started out the door, forgetting to check Mapquest to check where to turn. Then I thought of Anna. I went back into the house and woke her up.

"Anna, Anna, honey, I have to go. Daddy is in the hospital. He's going to be fine, but I have to go see him. Molly is going to get you ready for the school bus."

I leaned over her a hug through the covers. She gave me a one-eyed half-smile and made the motion of a kiss.

"Love you! Call my phone when you get back from school. I put the number by the telephone, in case you don't remember it."

I made a mental note to give Anna a list of numbers and put it on the white board in the laundry room, including the folks next door, her friend's houses and the phone numbers of her sisters and brothers.

When I got to the ER, I went straight to Mike's bed His blankets were on the floor and I spread the sheet over him. After a minute or two, he opened his eyes.

"Fran—"

"Hi, baby."

I kissed his cheek, prickly with stubble, and rubbed his arm above the restraints.

"Hi," he said weakly. He tried to smile.

I reached down and held his hand, fingers intertwined. His palm was sweaty and he smelled like a rumpled pillow covered in drool. The floor of the room was covered in discarded wrappings, tubing, tissues, and towels. I was disgusted.

A man walked into the room, declaring himself the hospitalist. Mike was restless but half-asleep. I asked the hospitalist what he did and he had a rehearsed explanation.

"My job is to see if the patient needs hospitalization and, if so, to coordinate his care during the hospital stay."

"So, what have you decided about Mike?"

"Oh, we are admitting him to the ICU, the Intensive Care Unit. There are a number of tests that we would like to run on him to see if we can find out what is causing his problems.We should have a bed soon. There's a social worker we can have you talk to, if you like."

"Yes, please write down the name and the phone number for me."

"Of course. Now, do you have any further questions for me?"

"And will you coordinate with his primary physician?"

"Let's see, yes. He'll be informed of everything."

"Do you want my phone number?"

"I'm sure we have it in the records. I'll contact you if I need anything. We'll be scheduling an MRI and a lumbar puncture and we'll need your authorization on that paperwork.

"Lumbar puncture?"

"The common name is a spinal tap. We're going to be looking for a virus in his spinal fluid."

Isn't that supposed to be the most painful test you can take?

"You can wait in the lobby."

I not going anywhere.

Medical Record

PATIENT: Canrinus, Michael A
AGE: 57
CHIEF COMPLAINT: Weakness

HISTORY: Mr. Canrinus is a 57-year-old that has had altered mental status for a long time, actually since September, he has had it mild and has been only moderately disabled off and on but today he was disabled worse and his co-workers called 911. He was brought in here by ambulance. He was confused here on arrival. He knew his name and he knew his wife but did not know the day, date, or place. He knew he was at the hospital. He was altered and denied any overdose. Denied suicidal ideation.

REVIEW OF SYMPTOMS: No headache or neck pain. No sore throat or earache. No fever or sweating. No double vision or blurred vision. No stiff neck. He had blurred vision this morning but he denied blurred vision now. He denies tinnitus. He is smiling. He denies cough or productive sputum. Denies shortness of breath or chest pain. Denies nausea, vomiting or diarrhea. Denies dysuria, urgency or frequency. Denies weakness, numbness, tingling or dizziness. Denies back or abdominal pain. He denies constipation but he does have fifty-pound weight loss over the last six months.

He has depression but no insomnia. He has anorexia but no falls or stress. He has never had seizure activity but did have an EGG showing frontal lobe activity in January. He does have a neurologist. He has never been on anticonvulsants. He denies pulmonary or breast disease by admission. He does have a history of hernia. He has had shingles before, depression and a fractured left rib previously. This is the worst he has ever been according to his wife.

The patient was observed in the ER for many hours. He continued to have atypical psychosis. The patient received stable on oxygen. ICU bed was ordered. The patient was admitted to the hospital in guarded condition.

Please note: Unless specifically stated, all procedures mentioned, tests done and medications given were performed/ interpreted by the emergency physician, or were under the direct supervision of the emergency physician.

Mikey finally got a bed just after dinner and we moved into the ICU. They stuffed his shoes, wallet, glasses, and soiled, tattered clothing in a plastic bag and I carried it upstairs. I followed Mike's gurney and the IV stand and tried to keep track of the twists and turns of the hallway, but I was completely turned around.

Earlier, Mike had gone to another department on another floor for an MRI — magnetic resonance imaging — that would map his brain. I had to sign paperwork that he did not have any metal inside of him. They had me sit in a small lobby with magazines. After a few minutes a technician came to the door.

"Would you mind coming in and helping us? He's a little upset."

We quickly took off my watch, my wedding rings, and my necklace, and tucked my purse in a locker in the corner of the room. Inside, Mike was halfway into the machine, strapped to the table and fighting against the straps, shouting. I ran to him and wrapped my arms around his legs.

"Mikey, Mikey, It's okay, I'm here." I patted down his legs and rubbed his feet.

"Fran?"

"Yes, honey, I'm here. Jesus is here. You are fine. They are going to take a picture of your brain. It's going to take a while and it's going to make weird noises, but I'll be right here. Can you feel my hands? I won't let go."

"Don't leave me!"

"I won't, sweetheart. I'm right here."

I continued to talk to him and stroke his legs and feet while the machine made the sound of gunfire bursts that caused Mike's legs to jerk in fear each time. The technicians stood in the observation room watching the monitors. Periodically, they would say over a loudspeaker in the room, "Can you please keep him more quiet? It's not too much longer."

"How much longer?" I hollered back.

"Not too much."

After about forty-five minutes the procedure was over. I was exhausted. As Mike was rolled out of the machine, I kissed his forehead and hugged him, reassuring him that everything was going to be all right now.

On the way to the ICU, I ran into Dr, Fabio again.

"Looks like there is no brain tumor."

"Oh, that's good."

"No, that's not good. A brain tumor would be the good news. Then we would know what to do. Now we have no idea what is happening. What are you going to do with him?"

"Well, I'll wait until we know more."

He flipped his stiff blond hair over one shoulder and looked me in the eye.

"You're going to wish that he had died."

I was too stunned to speak for a moment. Then anger rose up.

"My husband is 57 years-old. I am 52. We have seven kids, including a 10 year-old daughter. I am never going to wish that he had died. You don't know what you are talking about."

He turned his back and, with his cocky walk and not a word, left the room.

Once Mike was settled, I saw the dry erase board that listed the name of the nurse and the place where I was supposed to write my name. There was no marker, so I went to the nurse's station. There were plenty of people milling around, the ones in front of me keeping their heads down.

"Excuse me," I finally said.

Heads still down.

"I need a marker to write on the board."

Someone slapped one on the counter in front of me.

"Thank you," I said to no one.

In Mike's room, I wrote, "The Wife: Francine Phillips"

Then I put my phone number in large letters underneath.

Taking the marker back to the counter, I ventured again.

"Excuse me."

No one responded.

"I need to have the phone number of this floor."

A woman looked up at me.

"I need a number so I can check on him since he can't answer the phone."

The woman wrote the phone number for the nurses station on a piece of paper and handed it over the counter.

"Thank you so much."

They all looked at me like I was crazy.

"See you tomorrow," I said.

Driving out of the parking lot in the dark I took a wrong turn and couldn't find my way to the freeway. After detouring north, I finally exited, crossed over, and found the ramp going south, and headed toward East County.

As the Explorer picked up speed, my eyes filled with tears. Everything felt like a blur. I took our exit and somehow made it to the last stop sign close to our house. I took me several moments to notice that the car in front of me did not go forward. Suddenly man shot out of the driver's door and came at me, shaking his fist.

"What are you doing! You've been on my tail just inches behind me for blocks! Back off, lady! What's the matter with you!?"

My mouth dropped open and before I could respond, he jumped back in his car, turned the corner and tore down the hill.

If he had waited to hear the answer to his question, he would have heard that I didn't know how to drive this car, that I hadn't eaten all day, and that I had been told my husband had literally had lost his mind and probably was going to die.

Slowly I turned the corner and drove the huge car into the driveway. Inside, I looked in on Molly, kissed sleeping Anna on the cheek and tucked up her blankets around her shoulders then went to bed, exhausted. I started sobbing and couldn't stop. I kept whispering, "My husband is dying, my husband is dying," and I couldn't stop. I must have said it a thousand times, each time penetrating a different part of my understanding and sending despair to my heart and fresh tears to my eyes.

"Help me, God. My husband is dying."

CHAPTER 34

Who to Trust?

D URING THE NIGHT I called the hospital twice. The report was mixed. Mike had had a restless night, at some points raving and incoherent, at others sleeping and snoring. I knew he needed me to be there. But there were other matters that needed my attention.

First, I needed to let the family know what was happening. Then I had to call the pastor and ask for prayer. I had to let the Yacht Outfitting employees know what was happening. And the ship yard. And the clients. Arrangements had to be made for Anna. I had to call about the KIA and figure out what to do with it. I had to figure out a way to get Mike's truck back home.

I slipped to my knees beside the bed.

Father, please go before me today. You know what's going to happen. Help me to put my trust in you and to hear your voice. Please guide me through this list and help it all go smoothly. Help me to be strong and to accomplish everything that needs to be done. In Jesus' name. Amen.

When I headed into the bathroom there was a penny on the counter. When I picked it up, God spoke again.

My strength is made perfect in your weakness.

Did that mean that God would *not* help me to be strong? Where was that passage in the Bible? I made a mental note to look it up later. I had to get to my to-do list.

First, I called all of the kids and Mike's sister about his condition with a promise for a follow-up email with more details.

Next, Matt at La Mesa Tire informed me that the KIA was not going to be resurrected. I asked for him to wait until he heard from me and then called for advice from a few other guys from the Stone's dinner group.

"I think you need to let it go," said one, agreeing with what the others. "There is no point putting money into it at this point. You have other cars."

He was right. They were all right. I had to let go of being the mom in the fun, zippy car that made me feel like a teenager. My energy was needed elsewhere. I called Matt back and told him to tow the car to the junkyard. I would drop off the pink slip.

Next, I called the church and left a message on the answering machine.

"Hi, this is Francine. Please put Mike on the prayer list," I said. "He's in the hospital after having a seizure. They think it's pretty serious, but don't really know what is wrong. He's at Memorial in ICU, so if someone could go visit him, that would be great. I have a list of things to do before I can get over there today. Thanks."

Lastly, I called Jim and set up a time to meet him at Yacht Outfitting. I got right to the point.

"It doesn't look too good. The doctor told me that a brain tumor would be the good news."

"Do they have any idea what is wrong?" Jim asked.

"No idea. Just that it's bad and he is likely dying."

I couldn't believe I was saying those words aloud, without emotion. But I knew I had to hold it together.

"What? I had no idea. I'm so sorry, Fran."

"I don't know what to think. I'll meet you at the shop and maybe we can put together a plan of some kind for the business. Sound good?"

"Sounds great," said Jim. I knew he was trying to match my detached emotions. "I might actually know someone who would buy it. I'll see you there."

Next stop was the school. I asked for a minute with the principal and outlined what was happening. We enrolled Anna in the after-school program, which she had attended when I worked the year before, so that was a smooth transition. I called her best friend's mom, our neighbors, and a few others who agreed to be emergency back-up help when I needed it.

My next door neighbors were retired and let me know they were "infinitely interruptible." They had been watching and doing homework with Anna during the evenings Mike and I were in counseling sessions and thought she was adorable.

Clearly God had gone ahead of this crisis. Mike was known and loved at the church. Anna was familiar with after-school care, and had been staying with the neighbors for several weeks already. Jim Stone was involved with Yacht Outfitting and I had made the video and spent days at the office, learning more about the business than I had known in 10 years.

There was another important detail that had already been addressed. On April 1, we had signed trust documents putting all of the assets in a family trust and naming each other as Power of Attorney in case one of us was incapacitated. All of that was in place.

I felt like I was walking through a dark and scary forest of the unknown, but could make out the footsteps of God through the brambles ahead of me. He knew about this. He knew this was going to happen. He didn't stop it from happening, but silently had been creating a path for me to follow through the fear and uncertainty. I felt on my own, but not alone.

King David apparently felt the same and wrote lots of songs about facing all kinds of threats, including jealousy, revenge, swords and arrows.

> *In you, Yahweh, I take shelter;*
> *Never let me be disgraced.*
> *In your righteousness deliver me, rescue me,*
> *Turn your ear to me, make haste!*
> *Be a sheltering rock for me,*
> *A walled fortress to save me!*
> *For you are my rock, my fortress;*
> *For the sake of your name, guide me, lead me!*
>
> — *Psalm 31*

I admit that my prayer was not so eloquent. I just wanted to get through the day.

My next stop was the Harbor Boatyard where Yacht Outfitting was located. The manager of the boatyard was a fellow named Robert Boney who had a reputation for being tough.

The boatyards along Harbor Drive were all tenants of the Port of San Diego. In turn, they leased space to various yacht vendors – repairs, reupholsters, refinishers, yacht sales and more. I didn't know much about Mike's business, but I did know that "the Yard" seemed to require fees coming and going. Many vendors, including Mike, felt that Robert was one of the most unscrupulous of all the boatyard managers.

I was on my way to see him.

First stop, though, was at the office where I met with Jim and the employees. Everyone gathered in the small space, perched on the black leather seating or on the edge of the desk. Sunlight streamed in from the high skylight.

"Mike has some kind of brain disorder that they are still trying to identify," I told them. For now, Dan will be in charge of the work and Jim will oversee the billing and the invoicing until we have more direction. I don't know if Mike will bounce back in a few weeks, or if he'll never recover. So, this is the plan for the next two weeks until I know better. In the meantime, I'm going to pay the rent, stay open and try to find a buyer for the business."

Dan spoke up. "We've had to cover for Mike for a while now. He hasn't really been with it and we're doing our best to keep things going. I think we're doing pretty well, considering."

"I do too. I definitely do. Thank you so much, guys, for your loyalty and for doing a great job in difficult circumstances. I know that Mike loves you guys and really cares about you and appreciates you so much.

"I also think you should know that they ruled out any toxicity or anything that might be contagious," I continued.

"So nothing in the yard can be blamed? I thought questionable chemicals are dumped on a regular basis around here," said Dan.

"Well, I don't doubt that, but that is not the cause of Mike's brain problem. If anything, it's the cell phone, don't you think?"

They guys all laughed. "So you can't sue the Yard?"

"Doesn't look like it. I'm on my way to talk to Robert Boney right now."

They all looked at each other. Finally Lucas piped up, "Good luck."

Outside, I walked along the wooden balcony and down the staircase to the expanse of asphalt where yachts of every size and color were perched on steel stilts and surrounded by scaffolding. The activity was like a beehive: Here masked sanders removed debris and paint from a hull. There a propeller was replaced. Under a shroud of canvas, the hiss of a paint sprayer brought newness to an unseen boat. At the other end of the expanse, I went up to a glass door with the words "Office" painted in gold. When I walked through, all eyes looked up.

A woman came up to the counter – "Oh, you are Mike's wife, Francine? I'm so sorry that he's sick. How is he doing? I'm Marilyn."

"Hello Marilyn, nice to meet you. It's a little too soon to tell about Mike. He's still in the ICU. I'm here to speak to Mr. Boney."

An older man lifted his head, his white hair wiry and short. I immediately thought of the word "wizened" from old fairy tales, with his skinny, crooked arms and leathery skin. I had heard he was in his 80s, but no one at the yard knew his age for sure. He stood up, taller than me, but bent a little at the shoulders. Before he reached the counter he started hollering.

"Your rent is overdue!"

I let that hang in the air for a minute until he reached the spot where I waited across the counter. I had no intention of engaging in a shouting match.

"I'm here to pay the rent, and have put a plan in place for the next two weeks."

Getting out the big, blue checkbook, I paid the balance and a month ahead on the rent. He snatched it from my hand.

"I want you to know that if Mike isn't running Yacht Outfitting, there is no Yacht Outfitting in my book."

Looking at those hard, grey eyes and the grimace on his face meant to intimidate me, I pulled my shoulders back and spoke quietly and firmly.

"Mr. Boney, Mike is sick. He's been in the hospital less than a week. He's not dead, so I would appreciate it if you would not get ahead of yourself. I'll keep you informed of his progress. For now, please see Dan if you need to discuss anything."

"No Mike, no business."

With that, Robert Boney turned his back, returned to his desk and started writing. There was silence in the office, Marilyn looked at me in fear, then looked down. I walked out the door composed and resolute.

As I crossed the yard, tears started to well up. The sights and smells and sounds were all the things that Mike deeply loved. Here was the realm where Mike was a prince, respected by so many – rich owners and low-wage workers. This had been more than his work. It was his family, his church and his home for many so years. I was sobbing by the time I reached the shop and grabbed a clean blue rag to wipe my eyes. Time to go see Mike.

CHAPTER 35

The World of the Sick

I SLIPPED INTO THE HOSPITAL lobby restroom, shut the door and turned on the cold water. Handfuls were splashed over my swollen eyes and wiped with a coarse, dry paper towel. Then I carefully re-applied my make-up over tired skin and put on fresh lipstick. I brushed my hair. It had only taken a few days to learn that I was now part of the world of The Sick.

In the world of The Sick, you are expected to be helpless and lost. You are The Wife, your husband is The Patient, anyone with a blue scrub is The Nurse and anyone with a white coat is The Doctor. Hospital waiting rooms are filled with The Family. These depersonalization techniques are necessary for hospital staff who see people come and go, get better or die, suffer silently or with raging screams against the pain. How could they otherwise cope? I get it.

As The Wife, your role is to be mild, sad, prayerful. You are not expected to understand the procedures, question anything, or violate the corridors and closets on your own to find blankets or water. You are not expected to take the morning food tray off the bed and plop it on the floor outside the door, no matter how many hours it has been sitting there. No one expects The Wife to use the The Patient-only toilet in the room, learn how the bed works, figure out the lighting in the room and make sure that the call button is within The Patient's reach, then track down the nurse when no one comes. No one thinks that The Wife will examine The Patient's body for bedsores, reposition the restraints so that The Patient can lie flat or turn to his side or scratch his nose or brush his teeth. The Wife is expected to wring her hands, ask to speak with the chaplain, and not use the cell phone.

When I looked inside the world of The Sick and saw desperate women in rumpled muumuus with unwashed hair being pushed aside by hospital personnel, I decided not to be *that* Wife. I decided to be The Wife who dressed smartly and attractively every single day no matter how I felt inside.

I wore make-up. I read his chart (when they would allow it) and did my homework. I learned the difference between physical therapy and occupational therapy. I found out what the medications were called and what they did. When I walked onto the hospital floor, I made a point of introducing myself to the nurse for that day and asking for a status report; finding out if the doctor had come by yet, if there were any procedures scheduled and when they would have results.

As much as hospital routine called for depersonalization of every patient, my job was to personalize Mike to everyone who took care of him. Photos of the family posted everywhere, visits every day from a variety of people, staying at his bedside for hours, bringing in his own blanket and slippers — all of these were efforts to humanize the man hallucinating and wetting the bed.

Mike once told me that his mother always responded best by talking about long-ago events. Her short-term memory was fuzzy, but she had clear recall of family vacations, dinners with grandma, road trips and hikes, so those were the topics he would bring up. I tried that tactic with some success. I brought up famous car break-downs, our skiing lesson with eleven kids, his birthday weekend sail, watching fireworks from the deck of the yacht *Teru* and Molly falling into the water on the Fourth of July. Each story brought a smile and a bit of recognition that brought focus to his flailing brain. Each reminded Mike a bit about his identity.

Back at home that night, I was exhausted. I looked up the new message from God associated with the penny and found it came from a passage in the Apostle Paul's second book written to the believers in Corinth. The church was questioning Paul's credibility and mission, which caused him to tailspin into a long list of boastful credentials to prove his worthiness.

Then Paul mentions that he has a "thorn in his flesh" — something that caused him to be mocked and disregarded; perhaps some kind of physical disability. Some experts suggest it was epilepsy; some think a disfigurement. It's a mystery that has never been solved, as far as I know.

Whatever it was, Paul wrote that he pleaded with God to take the "thorn" away. God's response to him was, "My strength is made perfect in your weakness." At the end of the paragraph in Paul's letter, he says, "When I am weak is when I am strong."

What was God trying to say to me? Two things, I think. Yes, I would need to be on my "A" game and offer the best of my mind, sensitivity, creativity, and skills to Mike, but never forget that the outcome was in God's hands. The second meaning was that when we are completely surrendered, overwhelmed, hopeless, and paralyzed with fear, we will find strength in trusting God. When we acknowledge our weakness, God provides strength.

I hated that second meaning. I hated feeling weak. God knew that about me and tried to make it as painless as possible while still making sure that I got to that point. Surrendered while overwhelmed, hopeless and paralyzed with fear.

That night began a ritual that would last for a long time. I crawled into bed after kneeling in prayer, started the Annie Lennox *Bare* album playing in the darkness, and cried myself to sleep, whispering "My husband is dying, my husband is dying." This was the weakest moment of every day when I simply wept and waited for morning and God's strength.

> *Oh God…*
> *Where are you now!*
> *And what you gonna do about the mess I've made?*
> *Now where do I come in?*
> *Gone and broken everything so I hope you'll understand*
> *If someone needed a helping hand*
> *It must be now.*
> *It must be now.*
>
> *Oh God (Prayer)* Annie Lennox

Email to Friends and Family – Day One

Dawn is breaking on the third day of my dear husband Mike being in the ICU of Memorial Hospital. We were in the emergency room most of Tuesday with Mike incoherent, but with no sign of stroke in the CAT scan. By 4 p.m., the ER doctor was not sure whether to keep him hospitalized or have me take him home. Just then Mike started to become very agitated in ER and at 6 p.m. he had a severe seizure, so was admitted to the ICU and so began an aggressive campaign to find a cause.

The next day, he spent most of the day sleeping with a very slow heartbeat. I repeated, "I love you," and he replied, "I love you too, Fran." Great! He had not been able to identify me or himself the day before. Around 8 p.m. he was sitting up and eating for the first time in two days. It was good to see some normalcy even if he didn't know how old he was.

"I'm 22," he said when asked. "And I have 22 children."

The bad news was that they had been unable to do another MRI because he would not lie still, but persisted in trying to get unhooked and out of there. We got him calmed down a little and I decided to head home. I got a call to come back, though. He had unscrewed his IV (only a mechanic could do that, they told me) and he was given anti-seizure meds and sedatives.

Today he is rescheduled for the MRI, an MRA and a spinal tap. Now that he can safely have sedatives, he should be much more comfortable, although it complicates trying to determine his cognitive state. Please pray for our doctors, for solid test results, and, of course, for Mike's peace and healing.

Thanks,
Francine

Email to Friends and Family – Day Six

Mike is moved out of ICU! He is putting two words together that make sense and is more comfortable. He's talking to visitors and recognizes them with bursts of total clarity, then bouts of confusion. Yesterday he started seeing water spurting out of the IV and thought it was all over the curtain and my sweater. When we said, "No, there is no water," he had to touch everything before he would accept it. Then he realized that he's a little nuts and let out a big sigh.

Many, many times Mike told me the story that after his mother's accident she spent three months in a coma, but the hardest times where when she was aware enough to realize her loss. This is what Mike is experiencing and it's his nightmare come true. Lots of tears coming from him. My prayer for him is total peace.

Last night he had two very agitated episodes and managed to pull out his IV each time and security had to be called. He also would not swallow a pill this morning so he is getting a mild sedative every four hours through the IV. Yesterday I bought a card and candy and I had him sign it to take to the ICU where he had hit two nurses.

The doctors say that he will stay hospitalized until they have a diagnosis – about two weeks, they are hoping.

Thanks for all the assistance, from a new cell phone battery to taking Anna for a few days and help with Yacht Outfitting. I'm asking that we forget world peace for the next few days and just concentrate our prayers on one little confused frontal lobe.

Francine

CHAPTER 36

Let's Try This

WHILE I WAS STRUGGLING with spiritual weakness, Mike had to deal with real weakness — the plain old kind that does more than make you feel helpless, it makes you actually helpless.

We had gotten some opinions from other neurologists and most suggested a consult with a brilliant doctor, Dr. Leon Thal, who was the head of the neuroscience department at University of California, San Diego. As it turned out, San Diego is the nation's hub for neurology, with the country's best brains at work on studying brains. And the best of the best was Leon Thal.

I wrote him a letter outlining Mike's condition, the mystery of the disease, and his young age and otherwise general health. At the end I wrote, "Help me, Obi-Wan, you're our only hope."

I'm not sure if that's what got his attention, but we got the consult. His colleague, Dr. Lasko, would see Mike in a few weeks.

In the meantime, the hospital team wanted to try one last approach. Most of the symptoms were consistent with some type of virus. Mike's history of shingles came into play because in some cases the shingles virus can grab onto a nerve ending and crawl its way into the brain. Although viral causes had been ruled out by the lumbar puncture, it was a last ditch effort to try something. And it would also keep Mike as their patient instead of turning him over to the UCSD system.

There was a facility in their system that was a cross between a rehab, nursing care, and long-term care. It was decided that Mike would be sent there for a two-week course of acyclovir, a heavy anti-virus treatment. It was one of those long shots where, on television, Dr. House would be saying, "It'll either kill him or he'll get better. If he gets better, we'll know it's viral. If he dies, we'll know it wasn't." Of course, no one told me that at the time.

I did have a final conversation with Dr. Fabio before Mike was moved.

"So, have we ruled out a brain tumor?" I asked.

"A brain tumor would be the good news" he repeated. "What we do know is that your husband's brain shows signs of atrophy."

"Atrophy? It's shrinking?"

"Yes, which is normal with aging, but for some reason his process has accelerated. He has the brain of a seventy-year-old. It would be best if you looked for a good nursing home for him that you can afford."

I was stunned. *Nursing home?*

"I'm only fifty-two years old and strong. Mike is going to be coming home. I will take care of him." *How hard could it be?*

The doctor looked at me for a long time without speaking. Then he abruptly turned and started to walk away. After a few steps he looked back over his shoulder and said, "You're going to wish he had died."

What a little creep! He doesn't know anything about Mike or about me or what I might be feeling. Clearly he doesn't have any hope for improvement. How can I live without Mike? He's my best friend, my husband. What an idiot! A nursing home!

Medical Records – Discharge

PATIENT: CANRINUS, MICHAEL A
ADMITTING DIAGNOSIS:
1. New onset grand mall myotonic-clonic seizure.
2. Encephalopathy of unclear origin.
3. Chronic cognitive dysfunction, progressive

DISCHARGE DIAGNOSIS:
1. Right temporal lobe abnormality of uncertain etiology

2.   Chronic neurodegeneration of unclear mechanism.
3.   Seizure disorder, nonrecurrent.

HOSPITAL COURSE:

Difficult analysis. It is difficult to separate acute from chronic in this unfortunate male.

He has had a chronic memory loss that dates over the last year, but there have been no other constitutional symptoms other than weight loss. The possibility of neoplasm was raised and, indeed, infectious disease consult ordered a CT scan of the abdomen, pelvis, and chest, which failed to reveal evidence of neoplasm. A serum protein electrophoresis is also noted to be negative and HIV was negative. An MRI scan and EEG were marginal last year. He may have had small vessel white matter disease at that time. Nevertheless, it is clearly evident now that he has a seizure. Is this an acute process superimposed on a chronic one? This seems very unlikely but, of course, a possibility.

It is doubtless that he now has an MRI finding that was not present a year ago and has an EEG abnormality that correlated with this abnormal MRI finding in the left temporal lobe. I have shared with the patient's wife and an interested and intelligent brother-in-law, who is actively researching his condition on the Internet and with friends in higher institutions.

A lumbar puncture did, indeed, show a pleocytosis as well, but in a small number of inflammatory cells. These are all lymphocytes, indicating a chronic process. An infectious disease consult indicated that herpes was entirely possible. A negative PCR in the spinal fluid markedly lowers that probability, but infectious disease does point out that it is possible to have herpes integrated in the brain, but not in the spinal fluid. Therefore, it is reasonable to cover against this possibility and infectious disease recommends a 21-day complete course of IV acyclovir.

However, all are in agreement that this is a very unusual case of herpes. The patient's sensorium, it is of note, is completely intact. He is alert, interactive, polite, cooperative, though he has very poor short and long term memory. He is a resourceful man and confabulates; he does not indicate that he does not know the answer to a questions, but reasons around things.

This is unusual to have an indolent course for herpes encephalitis. I presume varicella zoster encephalitis is also possible, again, very unusual to have such an indolent course. Nevertheless, we will complete a course of acyclovir and repeat a spinal tap.

Alternatively, one might consider other inflammatory processes. Is this abnormality on the left temporal lobe associated with his symptoms or not? There are some chronic degenerative conditions that can have abnormal temporal lobe degeneration. These, unfortunately, are difficult to diagnose with brain biopsy or by process of exclusion. I have shared with the family that the patient may well need a brain biopsy in the near future after a reasonable trial of acyclovir is completed.

An early neoplastic process is entirely possible, though it is unusual for patient have symptoms for a year of neurodegeneration without more progression. Nevertheless, a repeat MRI scan in six to eight weeks is reasonable.

Overall, the rarity of expression of this man's symptoms and finding was shared with the family and they understand that this is not a usual presentation of any classic disease. We welcome a second opinion and I personally put in a call to Dr. Thal at UCSD, who is Head of Neurology (family was also actively involved in researching this.) I am arranging for him to have an outpatient clinic visit and have arranged through his insurance for this to be approved for second opinion.

I have prepared wife for the probability that, even if he is given a diagnosis, the majority of remaining disease states are incurable and that she should be prepared that he will be *chronically disabled. We will hold out for hope for the rare possibility of a treatable condition, or, perhaps, to modify his regressions. She is prepared for the possibility of nursing home placement.*

Once Mike was transferred I was hopeful. The facility was lovely and, the aides seemed caring and understanding. For the first few days, Mike seemed to improve. All the usual signs were posted on the door: fall risk, soft food diet. But here they were neatly typed instead of scrawled in marker by a frantic nurse.

Mike's sister and brother-in-law — Kate and Don — came down from Palo Alto for a visit and he knew them. We had a nice chat on the patio and they even brought Murphy, the dog, which made Mike very, very happy.

Mike looked thin and frail. He *did* look like a seventy-year-old. But his long arms still draped me in a strong hug and his sense of humor was evident when he could get a sentence out.

He was in a wheelchair with a safety belt loose around his waist. These belts help with standing or "transferring," which means moving from one place to another — chair to toilet or chair to car or chair to bed. Physical therapists were seeing improvement in standing and taking steps, so it didn't look like the wheelchair would be permanent.

Maybe this acyclovir is working?

A few days later, my sister Joleen and I went to visit, and Mike didn't look so good. He couldn't get out of bed and wasn't too responsive. I noticed that the bedding was wet. I went to find the nurse.

"Hi, I'm Francine, the wife of Michael Canrinus. Can I speak to his nurse?"

"Room?"

"Room 342."

"You're The Wife?"

"Yes."

"What is the patient's name?"

"Mike Canrinus. In room 342."

"Can you spell that?"

"C-a-n-r-i-n-u-s."

"Let me find out who the nurse is."

She worked the keyboard and after a moment said.

"His nurse is not here."

I decided that I would be more direct.

"My husband is not looking good. I need to talk to someone about his status."

"The doctor is not here."

This was getting ridiculous.

"Who can I talk to right now? My husband is not responding and his bedding is soaked in urine. Has he been up today? Has he eaten? He is on a soft diet, right?"

Just then another aide who was standing at the counter spoke up.

"There is a lunch tray in his room!"

I stood my ground.

"We need to change his bedding right now. Please bring clean bedding into the room."

"There's bedding in the closet."

I turned abruptly and walked back to the room, noting again the soft foods/swallowing risk sign on the door. First I found the closet and pulled out sheets, a plastic bed pad and a cotton blanket and set them on the chair slamming the cabinet door in frustration. Then I noticed the tray across the room on the table. There was a Styrofoam box on the tray. I opened the lid.

Inside was a cold slab of hamburger with wilted lettuce on a thick, white bun. *This is the soft diet?*

"Joleen, can you go to the Mexican place across the parking lot?" I handed her a few dollars. "Get some refried beans and a side of rice and bring it back quickly."

Rolling him to his side made Mike became aware that I was there. He smiled and I reassured him that everything was fine and we were going to clean him up a little. I asked him to stand up so we could transfer to the chair by the bed. He followed my instructions. His blue gown was soaked with sweat and urine. I had to be careful with his catheter as we pivoted in front of the chair. After we finished the transfer, I pulled off the wet bedding and rolled it in a ball by the door and rang the nurse button.

A weak voice came through the speaker, "Hello?"

"Can you please get someone to help me with the bed."

"You are changing the bed?"

"Of course I'm changing the bed. Can I please have help?"

"Someone will be right there."

I removed Mike's drenched too-small gown and soaked a wash cloth in the sink. Slowly, I wiped down his face, neck, and shoulders. Rinsing the cloth, I applied some soap and more water, then raised his weak arms and washed underneath them on each side, then his chest and down his legs and carefully rinsed his feet. His toenails were thick and long, twisted into strange shapes. His skin hung loose on his arms and across his chest. I switched to warm water and gently washed below his waist, around the catheter, and between his legs. He responded to the warmth and I was sure that his skin felt better in the hot room.

At that moment I was overwhelmed with a sense of joy. I understood how helping a helpless human being can bring great satisfaction. God had chosen me for the task of caring for Mike and it felt like a privilege. An honor. All of my education and professional success and my creative efforts and parenting and keeping up the house and knitting beautiful scarves and being team mom and getting writing awards disappeared like a vapor and it was my hand, a wash cloth, and this sagging, weak skin that mattered. I finally got it. All those people who adopt disabled kids, parents who say their Down syndrome kids are a blessing, strangers who take the time to volunteer for those who are helpless. I was swept with a sense of peace. I said a prayer of thanks for this new understanding.

I wished the feeling had lasted longer. Joleen came with the food just as the nurse finally bustled into the room. Joleen and I fed Mike while the nurse put on the clean bedding. Then she helped me guide Mike back to the bed and started out the door, leaving a stinking pile of sheets on the floor.

"Could you take the dirty sheets away, please?"

She threw me a resentful look, then turned and stalked out. I went over to the damp pile of linen and kicked it out the door behind her and then shut it. We raised the head of the bed and turned on the television. Mike was more alert now. Joleen started talking to him. I took the tray of the cold hamburger and put that outside the door as well. I knew he was supposed to have afternoon medications and I started noting the time to see how long it would take for his medications to be brought to him.

They were promptly brought in. As the sky darkened Mike was tiring and I kissed him goodnight.

The next day I got a call from the hospital. Mike had taken a slight downturn.

"We're going to need you to provide a sitter for him."

What's a sitter?

"I don't understand."

"Your husband needs to have someone in the room with him overnight each night. You need to get some family members or friends to come at night and stay with him overnight. Or you could pay someone. They usually charge about $30 an hour."

This seemed very weird. I couldn't stay all night because of Anna. For another ten days? How was I supposed to ask people to give up a night of sleep to sit with Mike?

"Uh, I'll see what I can do."

When I got to the hospital later that day, I understood Mike's need. There was a wide smile of joy on his face as he saw me. I sat on the high bed and put my arms around him. He squeezed me so tight and didn't let go for a long time, my head tucked below his shoulder and my fingers tracing his unshaven face. Then I felt his tears wash over my hands.

When I stood up, I raised the head section of his mattress and looked around for his hospital kit. A hospital kit is a plastic tub that usually has a washcloth, booties to warm and protect the feet, lotion, and a rinse container holding a toothbrush and toothpaste. Some have items such as mouthwash, nail clippers, Q-tips, dry shampoo and tissues, depending on the hospital. The patient is charged for these items even if they are ignored. I found his in a locker-type closet behind the door, tucked on the top shelf. There was an identical one right behind it.

"Come on, Mikey, let's brush your teeth!"

He was still smiling as I put a little water in the bottom of the curved rinse container, opened up the toothbrush and spread some toothpaste. Then I ran it under the faucet and leaned over. Putting the rinse container under his chin, I inserted the toothbrush between his teeth. He clamped down on it and wouldn't let go.

"Mikey, open up a little. I'm going to brush your teeth. Go like this," I said as I spread my lips into a clownish grin. Mike made his face look like mine. "That's good!" I said starting to brush up and down both sets of teeth. In a few seconds I removed the brush.

"Now spit down, if you can."

Saliva and toothpaste spattered all over my face and down my blouse. I grabbed the washcloth and wiped it off, keeping the rinse basin at his chin. Balancing it there, I reached over and poured a little water into a cup with one hand. Then I gave him a sip.

"Let's try that again. Swish it around your mouth and spit it into this container. Can you try that?"

He swished the water and swallowed it. I put in the toothbrush back in his mouth and tried to get to the back teeth. He clamped down. "Like this!" I said with the stupid open lips. He copied me obediently like a toddler. I wanted to scream. So much for feeling like this was a privilege. We were done with the teeth brushing for now.

I found a clean gown and took off the old one that was somehow soaked. When he was cleaned up and tucked back in, I put the chair next to his bed and turned on the television, hoping that the sound would woo him into slumber. I fluffed the pillow under his head and grabbed another one out of the closet and set it on the bed next to the chair. Flipping through the channels, I found the beginning of a Harry Potter movie, laid one arm on the pillow with my head on it and, with the other, held Mike's big hand. Soon he was softly snoring and my eyelids got heavy.

Suddenly there was screaming.

My eyes opened and I saw on the television a huge snake, the basilisk, rising up and slithering around the chamber. But the scream was behind me.

Mike was sitting up and waving his arms, ducking his head and cowering. He batted his hands at the imaginary beast and started swinging his pillow through the air.

Grabbing the channel changer, I tried to turn the set off, but it went slowly through every channel until there was finally a dark screen. Then the only sound was the high-pitched cry of a six-foot-four man fighting off an invisible, magical snake that wasn't there.

CHAPTER 37

On the Receiving End

I HAVE NEVER HEARD A sermon titled, "10 Tips for Asking Your Neighbor to Do Something for You," or "Ask and You Shall Receive…From Your Friend in the Next Pew." Even our culture has preached "'Tis better to give than to receive." Of course, that was more of a Christmas slogan drilled into Americans since the Sears & Roebuck catalog was carried across the frontier. The church has never taught believers how to receive.

Well, not never. Early followers of Christ were so overjoyed to know a God who forgave them and feel the security of everlasting life that they sold their goods, held things in common, and met every day for a meal and prayer. Not everyone was a giver, but everyone was a receiver. Later the Apostle Paul explained that believers can behave and interact like a body: some are hands, some are feet, some are hearts, some are heads. All are needed in the Kingdom of God, and the giving and receiving is in balance.

Still, a hierarchy developed that decided the left brain was the body part that was supposed to be top dog. Fast-forward many male-dominated centuries to the post-WWII 1950s Southern California where I grew up. Men were to lead; women were to serve; and we made idols out of major donors. To be in need was a sign of weakness, possibly as the result of sin. Being on the receiving end became a cause for deep shame.

So the church began to separate the givers from the receivers. The receivers got farther away: Naked tribes in Africa, starving children in

China who wished they could eat our Brussels sprouts, Mexican orphans living at the Tijuana dump. In the meantime, the church of this era became comfortable with non-involvement with those in need next door.

This gulf of separation between the givers and receivers has created a distortion of the Kingdom of God. So pronounced is the belief that God loves the giver more than the receiver that it's common now to hear that a life with Christ will result in prosperity, high status, political dominance, expensive clothes and hot cars. Christians in need can ask of God, but not so much their Sunday School class.

So how was I supposed to go about finding a "sitter" for Mike? I took the route of least resistance. I let the church do the asking. I called the church office and they sent out a blast email asking if anyone was available.

By the end of the day a few folks in the church had offered. One volunteer, a tall single man, had a sailboat and knew Mike. Another, a naval officer, agreed to take the overnight "watch." A woman, Lisa, was planning to come the next night. I tried to explain to them some of the extreme behavior they might encounter.

I was so embarrassed. I called Lisa, who was much older than I was and suffered with arthritis in her hands. She had gone through several painful surgeries, but always appeared in church with a smile. Did she realize what she was getting into?

"Are you sure you want to do this, Lisa?"

"Oh, I'll be fine. I don't sleep too much at night anyway."

"Well, call me if it's too much. My cell phone is on the board in the room. Feel free to call me and leave if you get uncomfortable."

The first night was fine. Mike was fairly quiet and was able to sleep. The next night was a different story. Lisa was halfway through her "shift" – about 1 a.m. – when Mike woke and was hallucinating, screaming for help, clawing at the tubes and IV and catheter. In the eerie light of the hospital bed console Lisa found the call button. The nurses were able to find a doctor to sedate Mike.

I was awakened from a fitful sleep just before my alarm was set to go off at 5:45 a.m. I jumped in fear, just as I had with every ring of the phone since Mike collapsed.

"Hello?"

"Is this Mrs. Canrinus?"

"This is Mike's wife. Who is this?"

"This is the rehab. I'm Dr. Howard. I'm afraid we had to transport Mike back to the hospital. We called an ambulance about 1:30 this morning."

"What happened?"

"He became pretty ill. His creatinine levels shot sky high so we had to take him in, but he'll be fine. He is probably still in the ER but they will have to admit him for a few days. I'm sure if you call over there you can get more details."

What's creatinine?

"Okay. Thanks for calling."

Hanging up the phone, I fumbled through my purse and found the number for Memorial and dialed. When I got through to the ER and asked for Mike's nurse, Dr. Fabio got on the line instead. Just what I needed.

"Mrs. Canrinus?"

"Yes, this is Francine."

"Your husband is going to be fine."

"His creatinine was high. Did he go into kidney failure?"

"No, no, no. We stuck a catheter in him. He'll pee like a horse for a couple of days and then he'll be fine."

I rubbed my eyes and cleared my throat.

"So, I guess the acyclovir isn't going to help."

"Not at all. The problem must not be viral. You have that consult with Dr. Thal's colleague soon, don't you?"

"Yes, it's in a couple of days."

"That's good. This will be good information for them. I'm going to go ahead and admit him here. We'll arrange for his transportation."

I took a deep breath and managed to say, "Thanks, doctor."

* * *

I decided to check on Yacht Outfitting before I went to the hospital. I knew that the guys were still working and Jim had mentioned that we might have a buyer. When I got to the office I was saw that our attorney son-in-law, Rob, was meeting with Jim, discussing the possible buyer. It was an established company of yacht repair that even Robert Boney couldn't fault. I was paying the rent and trying to keep the payroll going but the bills were continuing to pile up.

The new company was offering $40,000 for Yacht Outfitting and was going to keep the employees, the tools and equipment and take over the lease. Our offer specified that I pay the overdue taxes and assume the bills accrued before the opening of escrow. This was a miracle! Was the Lord going to give me a little break? A little relief? Gratefulness flooded over me. I was so thankful for the help. Now I could concentrate fully on Mike.

My heart was a little lighter as I sped over to Memorial and zipped into the parking garage — now familiar and routine. In the lobby I asked the volunteer to look up Mike's room. It was a different floor; not the ICU floor, which I thought was a good sign.

At Mike's room, 357, the door was almost closed. On it were the familiar signs -- *Fall Risk, Soft Diet* — and an unexpected one: *Doesn't Speak English*. Just as I opened the door, a woman cried out and a man moaned in pain.

Mike's bed was nearest the door. He was sitting up but half on his side, a grimace fixed on his face. He was sedated and didn't acknowledge me. The blue print curtain between the beds was only halfway closed.

Behind the curtain, the patient's wife sat in the chair by the window rocking herself with her arms around her waist, head down. She cried and muttered aloud in a strange tongue, working herself up into periodic screams of despair. In the bed next to her was a man writhing in pain. His exposed legs were black, filled with gangrene and weeping pus. A modulated moan rose and fell in decibels so that there was a consistent scream about every ninety seconds, like a church death knell. His moaning and screaming and her crying and screaming were out of sync, disharmonious and dissonant.

I would learn that the man, Boris, and his wife were from Russia and he was awaiting a double amputation. We were no longer just falling down a rabbit hole. We were at the Mad Hatter's Tea Party.

I turned on my heels and went straight to the nurses' station. I did not wait for someone to lift their eyes, which could take forever.

"I need to speak to the charge nurse right now!"

Several personnel looked up at me but no one spoke.

"Right now! Who is the in charge here?"

A small Filipino woman spoke up. "Shall I go get her?"

"Absolutely get her now."

Another nurse came toward me.

"Would you like me to contact the patient advocate?"

What's a patient advocate?

"Yes. I would absolutely like to speak to a patient advocate."

The tiny nurse came back down the hall with a tall woman in a white coat with a nametag, carrying a clipboard. She came toward me with her hand extended.

"Hello, I'm Doris, the nurse in charge. Can I help you?"

"Could you come with me, please?"

We turned toward room #357. The screaming and moaning were on the ascent toward a crescendo. As I opened the door wider, I turned toward Doris.

"This is my husband, Mike. He is suffering from an unknown brain disease and is confused and disoriented. He's not sure where he is" — we were interrupted by the crescendo of Boris's screams — "where he is or what is going on. Do you really think that being in a room with a screaming man, a crying woman, both speaking Russian, is really the best environment for him to get calm and oriented? Would you like me to give you some material on optimum conditions for someone with confusion? I would be more than happy to do that. In the meantime, this room is completely unacceptable. It is not in the best interests of this patient, is it?"

Doris looked at me as the screams were gathering steam again. Mike was crying. She walked over to the curtain and swept it across the metal rod with a screech to close off the scene from the next bed.

"No, this is not in the best interests of your husband. We'll see to it that he is moved to another room this morning."

"I would appreciate that," I said to her back as she left the room. "You can cancel my request to see the patient advocate."

I sat on the bed next to Mike and took his hand. He opened his eyes and looked at me in fear. Leaning toward his face, I said his name over and over until he became aware of me and started to focus.

"We're going to get you to a quiet place," I whispered. "I'm here. I'm here. I'm here."

Tears streamed down his face and I cursed the medical system that would think it was okay to lump the crazy people together in one room and warehouse them away from the "normal" sick people. I climbed onto the bed and sat close, held his hand, breathed a prayer and continued to hold his frightened, confused body.

"I'm here. . . . I'm here. . . . I'm here. . . ."

After he fell asleep, I went down to Medical Records.

"Do you have my husband's records from rehab? He was there about a week and was brought back last night by an ambulance."

"Let's take a look. Name?"

"Mike Canrinus. C-a-n-r-i-n-u-s.

"And you are?"

"The Wife."

He worked the keyboard and then seemed to find what he needed.

"Do you want all the records or just the ones from rehab?"

"Oh, I'll take all of them, I guess."

"There's a charge per page."

"That's all right. I'll take them all."

The technician got the printer going and about fifty pages came out. I thanked him, then went upstairs to the waiting area. I sifted through the paperwork until I came to the discharge orders from rehabilitation. There, in large letters, were the words *Renal Failure.*

Kidney failure.

I was stunned by the lie Dr. Fabio had told me. I also found out that the facility is supposed to be responsible for hiring a "sitter." It is never the responsibility of the patient's family. Why did they lie?

Late in the afternoon, back at our house, I was sitting on the porch when I got a call from Lisa. I thanked her profusely for helping us and agreeing to spend the night with Mike and hoped that she was not too traumatized.

"Oh no, it was fine. I was fine."

Then she went on.

"But I'm so very sorry that this has happened to you two. It's such a tragedy. You were both such wonderful people. Mike was so nice and you were so kind to everyone. I thought you were the best-looking couple in our church."

I'm sure I projected a soft tone in my voice and thanked her again. Inside I was completely shocked by what she had said.

What the…? What does how we look have to do with anything? Mike is crazy and I'm halfway there. And why is she talking about us in the past tense?

God so loved me.

CHAPTER 38

All the King's Horses and All the King's Men

Thornton Hospital, so named because of a major donation from San Diego philanthropists Harry and Sally B. Thornton, is the crème de la crème of healthcare facilities in San Diego. The lobby is an indoor garden, filled with trees and giant urns of flowers, reaching toward intricate skylights in the towering ceilings. A gift shop is filled with comforting and thoughtful robes, smart clothing, jewelry, decorative items, gourmet candies and spectacular floral arrangements. A grand piano plays soft, calming music by an invisible pianist, reminding me of the effort to maintain the invisibility of pain, fear and death that resided in the wide, carpeted corridors of the floors above. The pretense that all nurses are kind; doctors are brilliant; wellness is inevitable.

Our visit to Dr. Lasko in the lovely office building attached to the hospital was finally happening. I met Mike's transport at the reception desk and we ascended to the neurology floor and wrote his name on the patient sign-in sheet. Mike was in a wheelchair but aware that he was going to see a doctor and that I was his wife.

The doctor *was* kind. He gave Mike a mental test: what day is it, what month, what year, who is president, what is your name, how old are you? Mike wasn't agitated or concerned, but simply said that he had no idea of the answers, although the last one gave him pause. He thought for a moment, his face showing how much he was concentrating on finding the answer.

Finally, he said, "I'm 18, but she—" he turned and pointed a stubby finger at my face "—is 52."

Then Mike's face and voice changed from that of an eager child to his normal adult self, like a switch being flipped.

"You know, doctor, I've been tied to a hospital bed for six weeks. They don't tell me what day it is and nobody discusses national politics."

He was rational, displayed sophisticated humor, and he was right. My heart soared with hope. Mike was there. He was not gone.

Dr. Lasko wrote in his notebook.

After several more tests, all of which Mike failed completely, Dr. Lasko had him walk across the room, touch his finger to his nose, stand on one foot, put his right hand on his left shoulder, and then the reverse. Finally, the doctor turned to Mike.

"I'd like to do more tests, perhaps an MRI or a lumbar puncture. I think I would like to admit him to Thornton for a few days for observation."

"He's had four MRIs and two lumbar punctures already, doctor," I said.

He looked at me patiently and kindly.

"We like to take our own images here and run our own labs. I'll arrange for his admission tomorrow and for transportation from the hospital. If you could be at the hospital in the afternoon to sign off on the tests, we can get going. I'll meet with you when we have the results. Do you have any questions?"

"What do you think happened to him?"

Dr. Lasko looked at us both thoughtfully. "I'm hoping that we can find out but right now it's a mystery."

Mystery! That's not a word that you expect from one of the world's most renowned neurologists. Maybe scientists don't know as much about the brain as everyone thinks.

Mystery is not an unfamiliar word for people who are on a quest to know God. How did God fashion the universe? A mystery. How is God three in one? A mystery. How did a virgin become pregnant, God become Jesus, and Jesus die and rise from the dead? How does the Holy Spirit dwell within believers? A mystery. If you accept that you are created and there is a creator, you kind of get used to knowing that there are things you will never know. I knew all of that in my head, but not in my heart.

For those who are on a quest to *be* God, like the fallen angel Lucifer, knowledge is the golden apple. Mystery is, however, a big, fat reminder that only God is all-knowing. Mystery is unacceptable.

So when I fell to my knees at night before crawling into my lonely bed, continued to ponder deeper into mystery by asking God.

Lord, why is this happening? Why did this happen to Mike? Why Mike? Don't you love us anymore? Is this punishment? A test? What are you trying to teach us? Do it quickly, Lord, so we can put things back the way they were! Help me understand!

Further in the night, I tried to let God know that mystery was okay with me. It was starting to dawn on me who Mike and I were and who God was; and I was seeing that having answers wasn't going to happen. I wasn't going to get to understand. Things were never going to go back to the way they were. God is God and I am not. His strength is made perfect in my weakness.

The next day I was driving back to La Jolla to meet Mike at Thornton Hospital when I got a phone call from Dan at Yacht Outfitting.

"Hey Dan, what's up?"

"Robert Boney took a check out of our mailbox."

"What?"

"Robert Boney opened the Yacht Outfitting mailbox and took our mail."

"That's illegal!"

"I know! I know!" said Dan.

"What check was it?"

"It was for that job we finished recently."

I didn't know what he was talking about.

"Okay," I said. "How much was the check?"

"Twelve thousand."

My heart sank in my chest and a fire started burning there.

"Robert Boney stole a check for $12,000 from our mailbox!"

"That's what I'm trying to say," Dan answered.

"I'm going to see him. Thanks, Dan."

I held my head high and straightened my shoulders while I stalked into the dreary office of the Harbor Drive Boatyard. Diesel and ear-splitting noises spilled inside until I could shut the door behind me. Maybe I slammed it a little. Everyone looked up.

"Mr. Boney, is it true that you opened the Yacht Outfitting mailbox and stole our mail?"

He got up slowly from his desk, his craggy face stretched hard across his jaw.

"That business owes us money—"

In the corner of the room, a small, mousy man jumped up from his desk and came to the counter. He was in a rage, his teeth yellow, his breath bad, and he strained his neck muscles to get inches from my face.

"It's our money! It's our money! I do the books and it's our money!"

I recoiled from his scream, grateful for the counter between us. Shaking, I took a breath and asked, "Whose name is on the check?"

"Yacht Outfitting," spoke up one of the secretaries in the room.

"So it's not your money, it's Yacht Outfitting's money. Yacht Outfitting will decide which bills get paid, not you. That money belongs in my account."

"Well, just try and get it back," said Boney. Then he turned and sat back down at his desk.

I slammed the door a bit louder on my way out. I kept thinking about scriptures that talk about the church protecting widows and the widow who sought a judge's help from her opponent. I thought about people I knew at the Port of San Diego and about going before the board during the public comment and presenting my case. My mind was racing, my heart pounding. I got in the car and called Jim as I drove down the boulevard, shops and businesses a blur on either side. When he answered, I pounced.

"Jim! Robert Boney stole our money."

"I know. I know all about it."

"That's against the law. He stole our money!"

"Francine, let it go," he said.

"What! No way! He is the devil himself!"

"Francine, let it go.

"How can I let that go? He had no right to do that!"

"Francine. It's already done. I just had Dan endorse the check."

"What?!"

"You are in the middle of dealing with neurologists, doctors, hospitals and taking care of Anna and trying to make sense of this. Yacht Outfitting is the least of your worries. You have to let this go. Yes, there is no justice. But you have to let it go. You can't fight this battle right now. Let it go."

I said nothing for a minute, the tires making a rhythmic pounding on the asphalt. I felt helpless and alone.

"You're right," I said as tears started to fall. "I can't do this. I have to let it go."

I slowly shut off the phone and let the pain run through me. God would take care of Robert Boney. I was weak and helpless and on my way to see a neurology specialist who called my husband's illness a "mystery." Another neurologist thought I would wish that Mike was dead and a third said that he probably *would* be dead shortly. Nothing was going back to the way it was. The business was over. My husband was dying. God was going to take everything away. I stared out the windshield, passing cars and racing to La Jolla.

"Thy will be done. . . . Thy will be done. . . . Thy will be done. . . ." I whispered to the heavens through clenched teeth.

At Thornton Hospital I entered the peaceful atmosphere a bundle of nerves. The receptionist directed me to the correct floor and then the nurse showed me Mike's room. It was large, tasteful, and had a wide bay window with a padded window seat. A chair, sink, and bathroom were like a standard room, but the writing desk, lamp, dresser drawers and shelves for flower arrangements and photographs set it apart from other hospitals.

Mike was transferred from the wheelchair to the bed when I came into the room and sank into the soft pillows. I had brought Mike's flannel blanket to warm him. Its nautical red, white and blue made a sharp contrast to the pastel green and lavender walls. An intern came by and introduced himself to us. He let us know the testing schedule; I signed the authorizations.

I spent the rest of the day there, holding Mike's hand during the lumbar puncture and rubbing his feet during the MRI. Platoons of young doctors came by to see the crazy man with the mystery disease and his exhausted wife. I left as Mike's dinner tray arrived and let the nurse feed him, while I sought refuge in the dining room. Keeping some knitting and a book in my car at all times was my saving grace. After a couple more hours of sitting by Mike's side, I let the night nurse know that I was heading out to go home.

"Call me if you have any questions," I told her. "I'll probably call around midnight."

I went down the silent elevator and walked under a starry sky to my car in the open air parking lot. The ocean breeze was chilly but brought a freshness my mood. I just needed sleep.

The drive home from La Jolla was about forty minutes. I was just cresting the hill of State Route 52, just above a flickering valley of city lights twinkling a welcome when phone rang.

"Hello, is this Mrs. Canrinus?

"Yes, my name is Francine Phillips. I'm Mike's wife."

"We were wondering if you could come back."

"Is something wrong?"

"Your husband has become quite agitated. I think you'd better be with him. The window seat can be made up into a bed. We would really appreciate it."

"No problem. I'll be right there. I'm about a half hour away."

I got to the end of the freeway, spun the Explorer into the opposite westbound lane, passed Mary's donuts and headed back to my frightened husband and the prospect of a sleepless night, knitting and reading between soothing pats and reassuring hugs. I checked in with Molly to ask her, once again, to take over getting Anna ready in the morning.

Back in his room, staring out the wide bay window, I looked over at Mike. He had calmed down after about an hour and was asleep for now, so I tried to quiet my mind. Jesus promises to carry our burdens, so I tried to give them over, naming them one by one. Mike's health, my fears, Yacht Outfitting, the kids, the finances. There were parts I wanted to hang onto. I wanted God to solve these things *my* way, of course. The perfect buyers of the business, the children united in prayer, a publisher for my book project. God could do those things, couldn't He? Didn't He want to preserve my husband, my family, my home, my career? Make them all better? Did I really have to let it all go?

Over the next couple of days, Mike was poked and prodded and examined and observed. He grew more calm each day, his brain rebooting itself like a computer that has crashed. He began to be more oriented to his surroundings, which always brought a flood of hope to my heart. Maybe this was all a huge test from God and if we passed the test, we could get our lives back again, like the ancient story of Job.

Actually, though, God did not test Job, but allowed him to be tested. There is kind of a big difference and I was trying to figure it out. Once you start digging into it, you see that Jesus talked a lot about times of testing, of rejection, of suffering and endurance. But does God create or just allow pain in our lives?

Like every other high school kid, I had studied "The Grand Inquisitor" chapter put forward by Dostoyevsky in *The Brothers Karamozov*. In it Jesus is put on trial and condemned because of human suffering, no matter the how it originated.

I read, "The Lord chastens those whom He loves," in the books of Proverbs, Hebrews, and Revelation and wondered if Mike and I were being punished to bring about a greater good.

One morning that week, a group of church friends had invited me to join them at a great breakfast place in Hillcrest where the pancakes were the size of a twenty-inch plate, hash browns were piled high, and slices of ham were an inch thick. We were all having a great time with lots of laughter, but inevitably conversation turned to me and Mike and the overwhelming pain we were experiencing. Without warning, tears came flooding.

"Yes, I feel that God does punish us," I blurted out. "But my great fear is that Mike is being punished for *my* faults. That he is paying the price for the rotten things that I have done in *my* life."

I hung my head and let the tears fall. Now there's a conversation stopper. Then everyone talked at once claiming that would never be the case, they were sorry, God isn't like that. Everyone was stumbling over each other to be reassuring. But in reality, it was the last time I was invited anywhere by anybody except our best friends, Betsy and Steve. My thread-hanging friendships snapped to a close.

Days later, the specialists at Thornton Hospital and Dr. Lasko's team of residents had come to a conclusion and we set up a time to meet at Mike's bedside. By now I was used to the lush lobby and the piano music had become repetitive. Stepping into the pretty room with sun streaming in from the window, I saw a team of eager young men and women surrounding Mike and asking him questions. Mike was smiling at all of them, gracious and polite, but not really making sense with his answers. After a few minutes, one of them spoke to me.

"We have come to the conclusion that we've done all that we can do without a brain biopsy. We see that there is a temporal lobe lesion, but it is too close to the brain stem to do a biopsy. The risk of death is too great. So we are putting him on massive doses of steroids, which should stabilize the inflammation in his brain somewhat and extend his life.

"So, the good news is that we are sending him home. He'll be discharged around 3 o'clock today."

I was struck with terror as questions filled my mind. *That's good news!? What was I supposed to do? How would we manage? He couldn't talk, walk, eat, use the toilet, or use the phone or the remote. He couldn't make a decision, cook a meal, manage money or cross the street, let alone drive a car, mow the lawn or take out the trash.*

Panic continued to rise and my hands started to sweat.

Wasn't there anything more that anyone could do for him?

On the outside I struggled to remain calm and in charge.

"I'd like to speak to you alone," I said to the doctor. "Please."

Out in the pleasant hallway, I fell apart.

"I can't take him home today! I'm not prepared. Aren't you supposed to have a social worker do a home inspection? Do I need a hospital bed? Grab bars? A commode?"

I looked him hard in the eyes. He had no response.

"What am I supposed to feed him? Is he supposed to have a wheelchair? Can he stay alone? Is he supposed to have home health care? Who pays for that? Is he dying?"

The doctor looked at his feet and then lifted his head to return my stare.

"I am a neurologist," the young man said. "I don't know the answers to any of that."

I looked at him, trained in an ivory tower of medical expertise with no clue about the impact of his words on an everyday family. I decided this could be a teachable moment for him, far beyond rounds and differentials and speculative diagnoses.

"Well, it's your job to know," I countered in a softer voice. "You're not treating just a brain, but a whole person, a whole family, in fact. Six weeks ago my husband drove to work in his truck. Our lives are now devastated and you can't tell me why or even what to do about it?"

He was silent.

I turned and walked down the soft hall carpet to cool off. He went back into the room with his team. After a minute or two, I turned around and gingerly opened the door to Mike's room. The team was there and the same young doctor spoke up.

"We've determined that your husband could probably benefit from rehabilitation," he announced.

That was an interesting determination, moments after my meltdown. He went on to recommend two weeks of rehab.

"Longmont Hospital has one of the best rehabs in the state," he said. "Isn't that near your home? We will transfer him there and they will work on his walking, eating and talking. If he shows improvement, he may stay longer."

I began to breath. He plowed on. "Before his discharge they will send a social worker to your home for recommendations and tell you the resources available for home therapy."

I glanced at Mike. Maybe we were going to make progress after all. Then the young doctor finished his comments.

"It's also possible that he will not improve, but get worse. It's possible that he will not live very long."

Well. At least we have some direction. I shook the neurologist's hand and thanked him, then breathed a prayer.

Thank you, God! At least I have some direction.

"It's been a pleasure to meet you both," he said and he led the group filing out the door, others murmuring pleasantries as they passed me. Then they were gone. I looked over at Mike.

"Well, honey, you're going to another hospital, but this time they are actually going to let you get up."

Mike smiled and tried to say something. I leaned over him and gave him a big hug, trying to feel some of the warmth of the old Mike. But his arms were weak, his shoulders boney, his skin hung loose. There was nothing familiar in that hug. His body is becoming a stranger. It broke my heart to think of him becoming a stranger.

I got out my knitting and sat down, but before I started a single stitch I made calls to my friends and the prayer chain with the news. The good news.

Poem

Without warning, my eyes fly open.
When they connect with the clock, I cringe.
2 a.m.
Again.

I try to force myself to stay away from email.
No, close your eyes,
deep breathe,
go back to sleep.

I tell myself that if I won't put on my slippers,
I won't go outside to the garage office, where the email lures.
I'll be cold. My feet will freeze.
Breathe deep.
Go back to sleep.

So, yes, my feet are starting to get icy because here I am at the keyboard.
Not sure how I got here, but it's 3:30 a.m. now and there is no more email to open.

Hit the Send and Receive and watch the bold-faced lines dance down the page.
Viagra for cheap.
Millions available from a Nigerian prince.
Travel and hotels.

People going places and having vacations and living lives *and*
needing Viagra.
Gagging down the page like a throat spasm.
Interspersed with comfort and criticism.

What am I looking for?
If I can only open the right message.
If only I can click on something that says:

This horrible thing will soon be over.
You can get back to your real life.
There will be a large funeral, flowers, appropriate music,
readings, perhaps.
It will all be lovely and touching and nice.
Everyone will remember Mike as he was.

Hurry.
I can't see your old face anymore,
or hear your old laugh,
or feel your skin the way it used to be.

Death, come quickly if you must,
before the other Mike,
the real Mike,
is extinguished completely.

So I keep opening email, clicking and clicking, with cold feet
in the middle of the night.
I definitely am getting cold feet.

CHAPTER 39

Battle!

For the first time since that day in April, I felt that there was something I could actually do for Mike. And I had learned to ask for help without humiliation. It was a great lesson to learn that most people want to help and felt good when they could; they just don't know what to do. When you ask for help for something specific, it's a relief to most people. It was easier, of course, because I was asking for Mike, not for myself.

I asked Mandy Stone if she could create a smaller version of Mike's favorite image, Jesus pulling Peter out of the water. I readied his favorite blanket and pillow. I picked up shirts, underwear, pajamas and socks, then packed them with his comfy sweats. I got a portable CD player for music and a DVD player so he could pop in his favorite movie (*Holes*). I had read that brains can be soothed by the sound of water so I bought a little table fountain and was actually able to put it together by myself. Being productive felt so good!

Thinking through Mike's disabilities, I became inspired. Using a small three-ring binder, I created "The Book," which became a mainstay that Mike carried everywhere with him in his backpack and showed to everyone. On the cover was a great photo of Mike laughing at the helm of a yacht with his employee Lucas. The first page showed a picture of Mike and me, and in large letters were his name, my name, and our relationship. Then, beginning with the oldest, there was a page for each child with photos, their names, status (such as married or in college). More pages included his sister's family, my sisters and their husbands, his family friends the Earley sisters, and key phone numbers. The Book sat on the bedside table in rehab and his speech therapists said she would recommend it to all of her clients. The Book kept him grounded and connected to our family, and humanized him as a patient to all of the hospital staff.

When Mike came rolling into the rehab in his wheelchair he was able to touch, see, and feel a bit of home. Always a gadget lover, he quickly figured out the electronic devices and was able to listen to music on his down time.

Not that there was much down time. Mike was put on an aggressive schedule of walking, talking, re-learning basics like brushing teeth and taking a shower. The physical therapy area was extensive with equipment including steps and ramps. There was a full kitchen, speech therapy labs, a pool, and a lounge area where families were allowed to come watch movies with the patients on Friday nights. He was in a ward of six, with just two other roommates, so he immediately made friends. At meals, they were rolled out to long tables and were assisted in eating and then given time to have conversations.

"There's a black guy that I noticed no one sat with, so I made a point to be next to him," Mike told me. "He's had a really interesting life. He served in World War II and is a hero. He's a great guy," Mike continued with a smile. "We're friends."

I hugged his neck. "You always make a friend, honey, wherever you go and wherever you are."

He turned to me and I leaned in to his shoulder to hear his whisper. "Some of these old guys are real jerks."

I smiled a little, thinking, *There! That's Mike! That's the same Mike. He's still there. We just have to be patient until his brain reorganizes and more of the real Mike will come forward.*

Clearly the Mike that is tender, observant and loving, was not gone. Mike was not gone.

Once he moved to rehab, he was back in our neighborhood and more accessible so more of our friends were able to visit and help. One man arranged for his brother, a hairdresser, to come and give Mike a great haircut. Others brought audio books, flowers, and clothes. Many families took turns watching and entertaining Anna, bringing meals to the house, and being available for whatever needs arose. All of these gestures helped him regain his identity.

Because Mike was making progress, the therapists agreed that it would be helpful to continue rehab. Because he was still Dr. Lasko's patient, he ordered a transport up to Thornton Hospital for the evaluation.

Medical Record

PATIENT: CANRINUS, MICHAEL

DATE OF SERVICE: JUNE 17

> *This 57-year-old man was evaluated recently during an inpatient admission at Thornton Hospital for progressive decline in cognitive function and one seizure. He now returns for follow-up. The history is difficult to date precisely but apparently he had some cognitive and affective symptoms in November. In April he had more marked cognitive decline, with some word-finding difficulty. He had an extensive evaluation at the end of April which included the notable finding of 20 WBC in his CSF.*
>
> *Remainder of the work-up was negative except for an MRI of the brain that showed an area of increased signal to the left temporal lobe and a small area on the right. An MRI/NRA showed temporal lobe atrophy, left more than right. He was discharged at the end of May and spent two weeks in rehabilitation. He is now able to walk better with the use of a cane. He's had smaller gains in his ability to speak and communicate. He is still unable to read and has difficulty maintaining orientation and planning this. He also has trouble writing. He has not had further seizures.*
>
> *He has mild expressive aphasia. This was slightly better than when he was in the hospital a few weeks ago. He named seven out of eight objects or their parts correctly. He produced seven names of animals in one minute, with one paraphasic*

error, but only produced the names of two vegetables in one minute. He had difficulty with initiating naming for either of those categories. He was oriented for the year, but not month or day. He correctly subtracted 3 serially from 50, He spelled "world" backwards as "drod." He could follow two-step commands.

The CSF pattern is suggestive of an inflammatory or infectious process and the MR studies suggest that this is selectively involved in the temporal lobes. It would be highly unlikely to have these CSF results if he had Alzheimer's disease or a similar degenerative process. Tests for a paraneoplastic limbic encephalitis were negative and it would unusual for the CSF picture to improve and for this order to stabilize spontaneously. I think it is most likely that he had encephalitis and is left with fairly severe damage to the temporal lobes. Although PCR and studies for herpes virus were negative, some other virus may well have been the culprit.

He will continue to have rehabilitation. There is no specific treatment to recommend. It is not clear that further diagnostic testing will be helpful, although several tests have not yet come back which were ordered during his hospital stay.

It was time to prepare for Mike coming home, but first I organized a way to attend Jesse's graduation from U.C. Berkeley. We were in the middle of retiling our front entry, so my sister came down from Orange County to supervise that task. Friends took Anna camping that week, and two of the Earley sisters came down to visit Mike. Mike's sister's family joined us at the graduation in Palo Alto and it was a lot of coordinated effort that let me enjoy that happy occasion.

Our neighbor and church friend, Dan Bernard, kindly helped me remove the glass shower doors and put up grab bars in the shower. I also got a commode, a rubber-clad mattress, a shower seat and hand-held shower heads. Sliding doors led to a patio and garden and we buried the above-ground stepping stones to have a level surface for Mike to have access to the lounges outside.

My brother-in-law came and reinforced the bannister to the lower part of the house that contained the master bedroom, bath, and Anna's former nursery which had become a craft room that Mike nicknamed "the Martha Stewart room." In fact, Mike told me after I finished the room that he was going to form a support group named, SPAM: Spouses Against Martha. Maybe he would remember that he was funny and clever and loved to tease.

This flurry of activity was fueled by hope. Hope that Mike would be so much better if he could just come home. Hope that being surrounded by familiar things would help him become oriented and that his old life would seep back to the forefront. Hope that holding his own mug, petting the dog, hearing the sound of birds, and seeing the sunset from the patio would trigger memories and cut through the inflammation that ruled his brain.

There were flashes of the old Mike that were getting stronger with every visit. One afternoon I decided to videotape him and create a thank-you video for the church. So many people in our little church had stepped forward to help.

He was sitting in a wheelchair on the patio of rehab – a completely amateur set-up with noise from the air conditioner and overhead airplanes drowning out the audio. He was very thin and his skin had a grey pallor. His eyes were rimmed in red. But he had great presence of mind, and found the words to say that he appreciated everyone and that the love that the church people had shown him was astounding. Then he began to weep. As he wiped his eyes with his stubby fingers he stopped, looked at the camera and said, "Do you know what *faklempt* means?" After more words of thanks, Mike ended his comments with a completely straight face:

"I want you to be aware that if I see you, I *will* hug you."

A couple of weeks later, Mike was ready to visit home. We were all excited about proving wrong the medical "experts" who had given up on him. It was going to be fine, I just knew it. Everything was going to get back to normal. Thank God. "My strength is made perfect in your weakness," was the voice of God that I heard every day when I found the penny. Didn't that mean that everything was going to be perfect?

God so loved me.

Email to family and friends *June 9*

A quick update because this morning I have the big pow wow with doctors and the home evaluation this afternoon. Mike is coming home!

No more tied to a wheelchair, or setting off alarms when he turns over in bed! We will be setting new limits at home, but I know that he will be more comfortable and hopefully brain cells will relax in more familiar setting. We are determined to get him reading again.

The plan is for him to come home on Saturday, the 12ᵗʰ. He is walking, dressing, eating, doing tasks, etc. He will be going back for rehab regularly and still many tests ahead from the experts at UCSD. Still don't know what is wrong inside the brain—don't much care at this point. Mike is coming home! And they told me he would never come home again! We will find out what's wrong and of course I do care with a vengeance.

What happened to Mike?

Thanks to so many for prayers and sacrificial efforts. God has truly been here for us through you.

The next 10 days:

Sale of Yacht Outfitting

Complete San Diego Foundation work

Jesse's Cal graduation party

Take care of all the home evaluation recommendations by Saturday

Mike's appointment with Dr. Lasko, neurodegeneration specialist at UCSD

Anna's end of school parties and promotion on the 18ᵗʰ – dinner celebration

Doctor's appointments for me and Anna (she's been having headaches again – too scary)

Drum up more freelance work

Yikes!

Francine

Poem
Waiting in Line at Starbucks

If it's a normal day, there's a long wait.
And you hold your personal cup, deciding your personal order
Ordered by name.
Give your name and your order.

Everyone watches everyone in line, normally.
And, if it's a normal day, there's a good ten minutes to pretend
That everything is normal.
That you are hip and you have a life to go to,
Thumbing through the latest CDs or
examining the espresso machine as if you might buy it
or be comparing it to the one you have at home.
And the biggest decision you have to make
is between soy milk or hazelnut.

When the real decision is between brain specialists,
Which hospital will find the answers,
And who the person that used to be your husband
will be today.
A 70-year-old with a stroke?
A 3-year-old trying to read?
A middle-aged, macho guy who drove to work one day and
forgot how to sign his name and now waits longingly, tied
to the bed, for your face to come round the hospital curtain.
A normal face.
Even though he can't remember your name.

But for ten minutes every morning, that goes away.
You are not poor or unfortunate or pitiable or an example,
or exhausted or strong or amazing.
You can pretend that you are normal.
Things are normal.
You have a name.

You have an order.

At the hospital they have a cart.
Same colors.
Same choices.
Same coffee, even.
But it's not the same as waiting in line at Starbucks.
Nothing, personally, will ever be the same.

CHAPTER 40

Home

T HE DAY OF MIKE'S homecoming was a bright summer day, kissed by
our constant breeze off the ocean thirteen miles to the west. Since the
home visit everything had been made ready. He could make the downstairs
his "day room" with the TV, music, audio books, outdoor space, easy
commode access. Sleep was going to be important and was scheduled
for every afternoon, even though he had therapy three times a week and
a schedule of walking once a day with his cane. In the evening he would
join the family for dinner and sit upstairs with us until his bedtime at
around 8 p.m.

There were about twenty-two pills a day that we kept track of in a
seven-day pill organizer. Heavy steroids were recommended by Dr. Lasko
that could extend his life by five years, so they had to be carefully regulated
and dispensed along with anti-seizure, anti-depressant, vitamins and other
medications to make him stronger.

Later Anna told me that she remembered Dr. Lasko saying that her dad
could live for five more years, and she thought, *I'll be fifteen when he dies.*

Along with the pills, we organized Mike's closet and drawers for simple
decision-making and easy wear-ability. Stacks of Depends were in easy
reach and socks, pants, shoes with Velcro ties and over-the-head shirts with
no buttons were available when he was ready to dress himself.

Mike stepped out of the car, and I ran around to guide him up the
three front steps through the wide double doors into the entryway. He

sat upstairs while I unpacked and then led him to our room downstairs. My hope for an epiphany of familiarity with our home of ten years was slightly premature.

As I closed the draperies and got Mike tucked into bed after practicing the stand, swivel, and sit routine for the commode several times. I tucked in his covers and leaned down to kiss him.

"I'm not crying," he said. "It's good to be home and in our bed. I love this bed." He stretched out and smiled. "I only cry in the morning when I wake up and remember what happened. Isn't it funny? I cry in the morning and you cry at night!"

Mike threw his head back and laughed. Then I kissed him again, adjusted the monitor so I could hear him upstairs, and dimmed the lights. As I walked up the stairs, tears filled my eyes. *Yes, I cry at night, but what Mike doesn't know is that I cry in the morning too.*

* * *

The next step in dealing with Yacht Outfitting was the mountain of debt that we owed. As I met with Rob and Jim, they came up with a suggestion that led to one of the hardest things I have ever done.

"One thing that you should do is make a list of all the venders that you owe money to and ask them to forgive the debt. Businesses can write off $3,000 in bad debt per year on their taxes. Some may do it and some may refuse, but it can't hurt to ask."

"You want me to ask them to forgive our debt?"

"It can't hurt."

Armed with a list of names, business names, phone numbers, and amounts that we owed, I started out the morning with a strong cup of coffee and several prayers. Sitting in the kitchen and looking out over the valley, I felt the opposite of the scene outdoors. Cool breezes blew across the sunny landscape dotted with swaying palms and fragrant eucalyptus. Inside I was hot, sticky with fear, and overcome with sorrow.

How do you ask for someone to assume your debt?

Lord, you died for me and Mike. Nobody had to ask you to do it. You freely offered your life and paid the price of my mismanagement, my brokenness. Lord please take my pride and make it that same humility. Help me to ask for help. Help me to receive it graciously. Help me! Help!

Slowly I dialed the first number and for the next five hours, one by one, I explained about Mike's illness and asked perfect strangers if they would be willing to write off what we owed as bad debt and set Yacht Outfitting free from this enormous burden. Some people said yes – more than I expected. Some refused, feeling abused and angry. As I ticked off each call, the forgiveness began to outnumber the refusals.

The largest debt, Marine Exchange, was almost half the total. The owner, Mike's long-time friend, had died a few months before.

"I can't make you pay that debt, Francine," said his widow. "I'll just let it go." We cried together. It felt as if there were angels on the line with us. Her offer of debt forgiveness was unbelievable.

I ended the day with a new perspective on the power of forgiveness and the gift that God so simply offers to everyone who wants to be set free. Offers to me. Offers to you.

Email to Friends and Family

June 22

Time to give a final thank you and update to those who have faithfully been supporting us through prayers, thoughts and deeds, the major upheaval that has taken our lives in a completely new direction.

Mike has been at home for just over a week. He uses a cane to get around and is pretty steady up and down stairs, around the house, out in the yard, getting in and out of the car. Still some spills and accidents, mostly due to vision/ cognitive errors. For instance, last night he saw the table between two living room chairs, perceived it as a chair and tried to sit – of course landed on the floor! That's been the worst mishap, but that's an example. I opened the silverware drawer and found coffee grounds poured into it. Little stuff and nothing compared to the joy and peace of knowing that he is alive and here. So grateful to have him back at home when some doctors said it would never happen.

He attends rehab at Longmont Hospital three mornings a week for three hours, physical, occupational, and speech/ cognitive therapies. This should continue for about two more months and perhaps longer if he continues to show improvement, which he does. Even in the last week, there is improvement. His mechanical abilities and curiosity are pushing him to learn more – work the coffee machine, get his laptop and printer hooked up – all those things that need to be put together are what he loves to fix.

Cognitively, Mike has much of his complex thinking. We are able to talk about what has happened and the implications for our lives and for Anna and the rest of the family and our future. He has retained his wicked sense of humor, for the most part. And there's a lot to laugh about as we adjust to being side by side 24-hours a day. He wants the challenge of being independent and friends are coming alongside to take him places without me or visit on the back porch while I run errands. So grateful for this. He has many more gaps in his simple, immediate brain tasks – what does the clock say? How do you get ice from the refrigerator? How do you use the remote? (My God, the perfect husband!)

How is it working? We got the disabled placard, which makes some things easier. Mike comes with me to the bank, the grocery store – other errands are more difficult and tire him. Where I used to get six things done in the morning, I can get 1 or 2. Huge adjustment for me and probably will save my life. We are cleaning closets and getting rid of unused stuff. Simplify. Unclutter. Yes, the plastic bins of this and that that I've saved for "just in case" must go. Let it all go. Agonizing reappraisal. Mostly this is good for the long run, if exhausting for the moment.

We are going to stay in our home at this time, and have refinanced back to a 30-year loan from a 15–year to lower the payment. The sale of Yacht Outfitting is close to completion and, although it leaves us several thousands of dollars in debt, at least it will be one less thing to worry about. For the time being, I will continue to freelance, carving out writing time in the evening and during rehab and visits. Mike's disability will cover the house payment so I need to earn enough to cover living expenses. If the right job comes along at the right time when Mike can be alone or with the right caregiver, we'll see what happens. Meanwhile, want to write that book you've been meaning to write? I'm available!

This experience has shown us how important love is, and how important it is to give and receive it. There are amazing tales associated with this journey since April and they will make their way into print, I'm sure. Example: After sharing the poem, Waiting in Line at Starbucks*, my friend Tricia sent me, what else, a Starbucks card in the mail. These types of kindnesses make us feel very rich indeed.*

We had our big meeting with Dr. Lasko, the dementia specialist from the UCSD Neurodegeneration unit. Wonderful man. They had no additional findings from the Spectro (contrast) MRI. Turns out they were looking for additional lesions that they may have been able to biopsy, but none were there. Good News/Bad News. Bottom line from him: Mike had a devastating event – virus? Inflammation? Who knows? He no longer has it. It has left him with brain damage, brain shrinkage and impairments. There are no more tests, no more treatments, only waiting to see if he improves or gets progressively more out of it. See you again in two months.

For now, Mike is improving. We have no dramatic cause to blame, or treatment upon which to pin our hopes. Our hope is in things unseen, untested, unknown. We are living day to day, grateful for those who show us so much love and concern. Unbelievable love and concern. Some days we cry and mourn the life we had wanted – more possessions, more travel, more success, more things to see and do. Underneath is a growing understanding that there are other measures to the good life.

We have been thrust into a life with different values, different pace, different challenges than most our age, but not most 20 years from now. By then I will be an old hat at many of the life changes that will be thrust on most of my friends. How I hope I will be in the position to give them the consideration that I have been given.

So, thanks a million times over for so much help, humor and prayer. Our door is open, our hearts are open and hopefully we are a little wiser and have a little more to offer you when your time comes to need a listening ear. We're here.

God bless,
Francine Phillips

CHAPTER 41

Surrender, Surrender, Surrender

TRUTH BE TOLD, MIKE'S first week at home was horrible. When I crawled into bed with him that first night, I was terrified. There was no comfort in having him next to me and there was no comfort for him.

He tossed and turned constantly, hitting me with every roll in my direction. He talked out loud every few minutes, a tortured gibberish that was a sickening mixture of words and angry sounds. My few snatches of sleep were interrupted by him getting up and peeing around the room. I would cry "No!" each time and scramble to put a towel under the stream, then guide him to the commode.

Then at 3 o'clock in the morning I woke up and he was gone. I got up and looked around the room, in the bathroom and in the craft room.

Could he have gone upstairs alone?

Finally, I heard movement outside. I slipped, barefoot, out the sliding doors into the cold, damp early morning. Mike was naked, walking in a panic around the yard and peeing into the garden. His pale body shone in the moonlight.

I took his hand and guided him back to bed. Under the covers I held him close until he was warm, turned on some music and prayed that he would fall asleep, but his eyes were wide open in confusion and he continued to move about in the bed. No wonder he was exhausted and confused. He needed sleep.

After four or five nights of this, I needed sleep, too. I was a weeping basket case, absolutely broken down and unable to cope with any decisions.

God so loved me.

The Bible character Gideon again came to mind. He was called by God to conquer the Mideonites. The book of Judges tells the weird strategy that led to victory. Gideon had managed to muster up 22,000 soldiers from the surrounding tribes. The morning of the battle, God spoke to Gideon who had worked hard, sent out recruiters, and sounded the trumpet of battle.

"You have too many men."

God went on to explain that if they had a victory under those circumstances, the nation would disregard God. Each man would think, "My strength has saved me." So God made Gideon undo the hard work of recruitment. First, Gideon announced that anyone who was trembling in fear could go home. Immediately 12,000 turned on their heels and ran.

Then God said there were still too many. He had Gideon take them all down to the river to drink. Some of the warriors knelt and lapped up the water, while some cupped it into their mouths. God had Gideon send the men who lapped the water home.

Three hundred were left. Gideon got the point. He worshipped God and let God lead the battle. And the strategy was all God. In fact, it made fun of conventional battle. Three hundred men surrounded the Mideonite camp, blew trumpets, and broke glass jars. It created such confusion that the Mideonites fought and killed each other.

I was getting the point, too. I was like John Travolta playing an angel in the movie *Michael* whose blood pumped, wings raised, and eyes glowed at the prospect of battle. I saw Mike's illness as call to arms. I gathered my warriors, armor, and weapons to save Mike. God had kept telling me day after day, "My strength is made perfect in your weakness," but I didn't want to hear it. What I heard was more like, "My strength will show up when you've done everything you can do," or "If you do a good job, I'll come alongside and boost you up."

I prayed for strength and God answered that prayer by giving me utter weakness. It turned out that what I thought was my strength was helplessness like Gideon's army — blowing a horn and shattering an empty jar.

* * *

It was almost Independence Day – July 4. Mike was becoming more and more oriented to home, figuring out details like pouring milk, finding his way from room to room, turning on the television, putting on socks and buttoning a shirt (although not necessarily putting the right buttons in the right buttonholes). He was getting used to using a cane, although neighbors told me they often saw him take a walk and hold the cane up high off the ground as he walked. They all watched out for him as he would stride to the corner and back, passing the four houses and returning home with only a couple of slip-ups.

I found a cool way to celebrate Mike's independence. The local municipal airport for general aviation was a big part of our lives. When we were dating, we would park by the runway and have serious talks. Later, we would sit on the patio and identify the planes that circled for landings.

Mike's dream had always been to build a plane and become a pilot. We had been collecting monthly copies of *Plane & Pilot* for ten years, and he and Nick had been refining their design since they had first glued balsawood wings and a tail on a pencil and flown it across their yard. We had measured the driveway for an Ultralight trailer hitch and joked for years about whether I would ever want to fly in a plane that Nick and Mike had built. After all, they designed and built a sprinkler system that required getting soaked to turn on and off.

In the local paper was an advertisement for airplane rides on July 3 to benefit the airport's junior aviation club. There was a cook-out, plane rides, and early fireworks for only $15 per person. I knew Mike would love it. We packed our beach chairs in the car and drove down the hill, ate undercooked hot dogs on paper plates, and sat on the tarmac until it was our turn to fly. Mike sat in front and Anna and I in the back.

It was glorious. One of those crystal clear days where visibility was infinite. The little plane rose into the air and circled over our house as the vista widened to include the nearby college, Mission Trails Park and Cowles Mountain, then further east over several lakes and swaths of pines. Mike was as enthralled and excited as a boy.

"Look! Look!" he said with every tip of the wing, sending us into a new direction and providing a completely different perspective. After a perfect landing, we disembarked, thanked our pilot, and wobbled back to our chairs. Heads lifted back to feel the evening breeze on our cheeks and necks, the sky was finally dark. We wrapped ourselves in knitted afghans and looked for stars.

Suddenly, the first flare rose with a whistle, then burst into a canopy of flickering lights directly overhead, diving and fading near the ground. Then another. Then another. Red, white, and blue in spirals, in the shapes of arrows, or like a broad umbrella of fiery light. Close enough to touch, it seemed.

The next day, the real July 4th, we relaxed and went to the neighborhood pool. Mike was able to paddle around the shallow end on his own. In the afternoon I fired up the grill and we had *perfectly* cooked hot dogs, burgers, and corn on the cob.

So many other years we had spent the holiday on San Diego Bay, right underneath the fireworks displays. Tonight would be a little more subdued, but still beautiful. We could see about five distant fireworks displays from our vantage point on top of the hill and even more when we climbed a ladder and sat on the roof of the porch. That wasn't in the cards this year, but there would be plenty to enjoy, far enough away to be dazzled, but not bombarded by the explosion of sounds.

Just as we were getting settled on the porch, Vanessa and Rob called.

"Can we bring the kids and our friends and their kids over to watch the fireworks from your house? We don't want them to be scared by the noise."

"Of course, we'd love it."

So we got out blankets to set on the grass as the grandkids and their friends sat down and turned their faces toward the sky. Mike and I scanned the kid's faces as they settled on their parents' laps with shining bursts of color reflected off their cheeks and mirrored in their widened eyes. We sang softly at the finale and could hear voices from the streets below join the song as bursts of color and the echoes of pounding booms filled our hearts. What could be a more breathtaking sight than fireworks filling the sky and reflecting off the joyful faces of those you love?

After sleepy hugs and tired kisses, the kids were bundled into the car, and Mike and I went down the staircase. I went first to break any possible fall. Mike grabbed the banister and made it down thirteen stairs, one foot at a time. Content, warm, and grateful, we felt so fortunate for the heroes we knew and the magic vision of light and color sparkling in the night sky. Through the night, an occasional BOOM! broke through our sleep like a wrecking ball, but we just rolled over and slipped back to sleep, never imagining that it was a battle cry.

At first I imagined that the sound I was hearing was the snap of more fireworks. Then, more awake, I noticed the methodic pounding coming from the room just above my head.

What now?

I grabbed my robe and started up the stairs. Mike was already up, probably eating a bowl of cereal, usually with milk but sometimes with water if he was confused. He had a special spot for eating at the large kitchen counter. Keeping routines made a huge difference in organizing his brain.

But this sound was coming from the living room. *Pound, pound, pound.*

Halfway up the stairs I hollered.

"Mike, are you all right?"

"No!" came his answer. The pounding stopped.

"I'm not all right. I'm blind."

CHAPTER 42

A Totally New Level

I was able to get Mike into a chair and held him while we both cried. It felt like a kick in the stomach. I did all those things you see on television, snap my fingers, wave my hands over his face and clap loudly. Yep. Mike could not see. Everything was completely black.

Blind!? Are you kidding, Lord!?

Because Mike had just endured months in hospitals, I stayed calm and suggested a strategy. We would get him a good shower, then pack clothes, The Book, and the electronics – cell phone, clock, music player, and fountain. I planned to print out a medication list, and then we'd drive over to Thornton Hospital to the brain specialists.

I got him downstairs and the water at the perfect temperature before I undressed him and guided him into the shower.

"Is this your way to get us to take a shower together?" I teased.

I asked Jesse to stay with Anna. Then I alerted Thornton ER we were on our way. Mike put on his own tennis shoes and we started up the stairs. First the cane on the right, then the left foot, then the right foot. Hold the rail. Try to keep your hips straight forward. Other hand on my shoulder. Here we go. Okay, second step.

We almost made it. About two steps from the top, Mike suddenly pitched forward. He did not hit his head, so Jesse and I were able to turn him to his side. He threw his head back. His eyes fluttered and he shook like a leaf in a hurricane. His mouth oozed foam.

A grand mal seizure.

"Call 911!"

Jesse ran to the phone. The seizure didn't stop until the emergency team was coming through the door with a gurney. Then as the four men got their bearings, Mike started seizing again. Jerking and shaking and groaning with a heavy pant. He had not had a seizure since that first time in the ER about four months ago.

"I was taking him Thornton Hospital. Can you take him there?"

"Sorry ma'am," said one of the EMTs. "State law requires that we take him to the nearest hospital. We're going to Longmont."

My heart sank.

As they rolled out of the house, I grabbed the bag, my knitting, and some granola bars and jumped into the cumbersome Explorer. Mike had two more seizures on the short ride to the hospital. I learned later that at one point, his heart stopped. Of course, no one told me, and they hadn't asked if he had a Do Not Resuscitate (DNR) order.

I arrived in time to wait in the lobby for a half hour before they would let me in. They were giving Mike a CT scan when I walked through the curtain. He lay on the ER bed, ashen, sedated, and unable to speak. His left side was paralyzed. He was blind. He was in restraints. I sat on the awkward stool and bowed toward the bed, throwing my arms over his body.

Lord!

I know that you are in control and that you have gone before us. You knew this was going to happen and nothing that happens on this earth is unknown to you. I trust you to take control of Mike and to heal his body. I ask you to remove all of the inflammation and restore his sight. Please God, if it be your will, give Mike back his health. Touch his eyes, the lesions in his brain, the paralysis at his side. Give his brain back the connections and the pathways that can restore him. Make our weakness your strength.

I know that you are God and I am not. You provide our daily bread as you promised, you have not left us helpless. Guide the physicians, help them find the answers.

Thy will be done. Thy will be done. Thy will be done.

I ask these things in the name of your son, Jesus Christ. Amen.

The results of the CT Scan showed numerous — almost constant — seizures happening inside Mike's brain. I stayed by his side until about 1 a.m., then I drove home, exhausted, cried out and terrified.

As I climbed into the empty bed my mind began racing with all of the things that I would need to change and rearrange to accommodate blindness on top of dementia. At 2 a.m. I was on the computer looking up the Center for the Blind and the Braille Institute and other resources for the blind. I would notify Dr. Lasko in the morning to see if Mike could be transferred to Thornton Hospital. Would it be better to move Mike upstairs, or keep him more contained in the downstairs during the night? At 3 a.m. I called the hospital. They said they had a bed available and would be admitting him to a room before morning. During the night Mike had pulled out his catheter twice and the seizures had continued, but the paralysis had resolved itself. At 4 a.m. I turned on the Annie Lennox album and entered a fitful sleep.

> *…So, light me up like the sun*
> *To cool down with your rain.*
> *I never want to close my eyes again*
> *Never close my eyes*
> *Never close my eyes.*
> —A Thousand Beautiful Things, Annie Lennox

At 5:30 a.m. I got up and wrote an e-mail to family members and the guys at the office. Then I showered, dressed, put on make-up, and held my head high as I walked into the hospital just before the shift change. I met with the night nurse and got more details about his behavior during the night. Another CT scan was scheduled for later in the morning, as well as another MRI.

As I sat next to Mike, praying, I heard the voice of God clear as day. I bolted upright.

It's happening to Mike; it's not happening to you.

I repeated this out loud. "It's happening to him, it's not happening to me."

Of course! I could still drive, I could still answer the phone and write a check and open an envelope and cook a meal. This was not about me, it was about him. Mike was the one who was suffering, I was just the support.

Instantly the layer of self-pity was lifted. It was happening to Mike — not me. Yes, I felt loss and pain and it was going to be hard to be a caregiver of a blind person, but I could *see*!

The saying became a mantra that I repeated every day. It kept me from falling into a wallowing pit of self-centered resentment and despair. I didn't get to do that. It wasn't happening to me. It was happening to Mike. All of my energy needed to be concentrated on him, his despair.

Only Mike was not in despair. After about two weeks, he had improved to the point that the neurologists felt that more rehab would be helpful. This meant that they thought he would live, that recovery was happening. It also meant that *he* thought he would recover.

But the rehab experience this time was marked by a more difficult road. Mike experienced a common behavior of brain injured patients or Alzheimer's patients called sundowning. As Mike and I talked about it, he said that after a full day, his brain says, "Enough; I'm done now," and starts to shut down for the day. So, during the day his is aware and participating and improving in rehab, but at night he is Just Crazy.

In case you don't know, there are restraints used in hospitals to keep patients from falling or getting up or pulling out catheters or blowing their noses or wiping their tears. And, in the case of a careless nurse, to keep patients from using their call buttons. Okay, I'll be generous and call it careless. You can call it *care less*.

Restraints consist of wide, closely-woven cotton bands secured onto thick Velcro straps — about four inches long — made of leather and lined in sheep's wool. The bands are tied to various spots on the railings to determine range of motion. If the bands on the feet are loose enough, the patient can turn on his side to avoid lying in soiled or wet sheets. If not, the patient is simply stuck.

The hand restraints are positioned on the wrists; they don't have to be tight, just secure enough to hold. The hand bands are also tied to the railings, although hospital beds have a hook where they are supposed to be secured that allows for no range of motion whatsoever. So placement of the hand band is at the discretion of the aide or nurse. Most protocols require that the patient be able to reach the call button and have hand movement as long as one hand can't reach the other hand and undo the Velcro wristband. If the band is tied closer to the face, the patient can scratch a nose or wipe an eye. If the band is tied further down on the bed, the patient is helpless. Only the truly compassionate pay attention to this. I think every nurse or aide should spend an hour in restraints as part of their training.

I was on a healthcare online chat room where a woman once posted that she didn't think hospitals used restraints any more. Here was my reply:

Just so you know. My husband Mike was in four hospitals this past year and he was tied to the bed in every one of them. Some were more humane than others. It was torture and when he got home it took him four weeks to be able to relax at night. He was stiff and straight with his hands at his sides. It was pitiful.

In addition to restraints, many facilities use alarm pads on the bed under the plastic bed pads. When a patient lifts off the pad, whether it is for sitting, turning a bit too far or even just bending his knees, a loud alarm goes off alerting the nurse to movement. Only the nurse can turn it off.

It's annoying to a visitor. To Mike it was torture. Imagine being blind, in restraints, naked under a thin, open-backed robe, bedsheets wet and feeling a bowel movement coming. Not being able to reach a call button. Humiliated. Helpless. To a mentally fragile person, I'd say this is not in the best interests of the patient and leave it at that.

One Friday night I thought it would be fun for Mike and me to have a movie night at rehab, even though he could only listen. We pulled a wheelchair for him and a comfy chair for me in front of the large television and popped in the video about the guys who stay young because of alien pods in the swimming pool they sneak into. Mike kept asking what time it was, getting increasingly agitated.

At 8 p.m. he said, "We have to turn it off. I have to go to bed now."

"Are you tired, honey?"

"No. It's time to go to bed. I'll get in trouble if I don't get into bed."

"It's okay, Mikey, it's our Friday night movie."

"No, turn it off! I have to go to bed."

What is making him so afraid?

I wheeled him back to his room and let the nurse know he wanted to be prepared for bed. I was sorry he didn't know that he was safe with me and that there were no bedtime curfews if I was there. It concerned me that he was so docile and fearful.

CHAPTER 43

False Hope

AFTER ANOTHER WEEK HE could speak, walk with a walker, use the bathroom, and eat on his own. He could get dressed, pull on underwear, sweat pants and get a polo shirt over his head. Use of the call button, operating the television and the CD player all came back. He could differentiate light and dark and see shadows, although trying to get him to describe what he could see or not see was difficult.

Whatever the gains, the thought of him sinking into fear each night and being restrained was more and more uncomfortable for me. It was time for him to come home. Again.

They had scheduled him for another week of rehab, so I made an appointment with the rehab director, Dr. Murphy. I asked if we could switch to home therapy and he agreed that Mike was at the point where he would be better off getting assistance at home than staying as an inpatient. We agreed on a Friday discharge. Yikes!

Because Mike had spent so much time on yachts, I had an inspiration. The small room adjoining the master suite became "the Stateroom." It contained a bed with drawers underneath, the commode, and an armoire for his electronics. That was it. Everything was pretty much within reach and in its own place. His cane hung on a hook near the bed. The closet door was removed to accommodate a dresser. Everything was sleek and ship-shape. In this room, he was captain. He could keep the lights on all night, listen to music, play an audio book, and dance if he felt like it.

He didn't dance, though. The tragedy of being in restraints is the trauma that continues long after the ties are broken and you are set free. Even though Mike was back home, he had constant nightmares that were so realistic he cried for hours.

"I'm in the hold of a ship and it's very dark," he whispered when I asked him to describe the dream. "There are no windows, but there are people around me that won't answer when I call. I'm given bread once a day and some water. It's cold. I'm so afraid and I'm alone."

When he slept, he tried to stay on his back and not move. This lasted for weeks. I wondered if, in fact, he had been a prisoner of war in Vietnam or had experienced some form of imprisonment.

Holding him and comforting him for yet another time while my heart felt like a fist inside my chest, I asked, "Mikey, are you sure that you have never been captured? Are you sure this is a dream and not a memory?"

In the daylight, with sun streaming into the room from a huge window, he could stretch his arms over his head and smile. "I've never been a POW. It's just a dream."

In the book of Judges, Samson was a child that God had planned to use to deliver the Israelites from their enemies, the Philistines. In those days chosen children were set aside and called Nazirites. They were dedicated to God and had to refrain from alcohol and from cutting their hair. You could tell by looking at them that they had been chosen to serve God, the way we can look at collar and robe and recognize a priest. Aong with the exterior identification marks, there were certain expectations that Samson was supposed to fulfill.

But instead of being extra spiritual, Samson was just supernaturally strong, and he used his strength to satisfy himself. He killed animals with his bare hands; he massacred a thousand Philistines in an afternoon. He lusted after their women above the humble and circumspect good Jewish girls.

Delilah came on the scene with confidence in her wiles and nagged Samson to tell her the secret of his strength. He lied to her a couple of times about how she could overcome him by binding him in restraints, but each time he busted out of them with ease — which made her become more petulant and whiney . . . . and seductive. Finally he told her that the secret to his strength was his long hair, his last outward symbol of his vow of obedience to God. While he slept she cut his hair, and God left him. This time the restraints held. Samson became a POW. He was in chains.

As in most prison settings, a helpless victim brings out pure evil when humans have complete power over other humans. The guards plucked out Samson's eyes. He was mocked and teased as a blind person.

In his humiliation, Samson was brought to a Philistine temple years later for a public celebration of his capture. But by then his hair had grown long. Humbled and surrendered, he prayed.

"Remember me, I pray thee, and strengthen me (just this one time). . . . Let me die with the Philistines." Then, we are told, he toppled the supporting pillars of the temple and he "killed many more as he died than while he lived."

I always thought this was a weird Bible story. But when I saw my blind husband helpless in restraints, there was a part of me that was hoping for a miracle that would give him super strength and the ability to take revenge, like Samson. Instead, we learned more about weakness and humility and that God steps in when we are surrendered, not when we think we can do everything in our own strength.

The truth is, God will take care of everything if we trust and obey. Let go.

One other thing about restraints. Sometimes we put them on ourselves. Sometimes we are so caught up in pretense and trying to be "just fine" that each time we forego authenticity and sidestep humility it's like another wide Velcro band keeping us from the call button. But a little miracle happens here on the spiritual level. Whatever we do to ourselves, we can never lose the call button to God. It comes and finds us. The call button is always within our reach. And that's a promise.

I had informed Dr. Lasko's office at Thornton Hospital of Mike's blindness even though I never succeeded in getting Longmont to transfer Mike there. (It's about the money.) He was out of the country on vacation, but I made arrangements for Mike's medical records to be sent there. When he got back into the U.S. he called me.

First he said that he felt sure that Mike's condition was something known as *central nervous system vasculitis*. There was a clinic at Johns Hopkins where he had a colleague and they had been discussing Mike's case.

"I'll bet my career on it," he emphasized. "One of the main symptoms is blindness, so I didn't consider it until I heard about Mike losing his eyesight. It's like a constant, chronic stroke in his brain, but we can treat it with steroids."

Getting the sure diagnosis was a good thing. The diagnosis itself, not so good. Google it sometime. Life expectancy is about forty-five days.

"I've also arranged for my good friend Leah Levi to examine Mike," he said. "She is at the Shiley Eye Center and is interested." Leah Levi was a world-renown neurological ophthalmologist, and Shiley Center was the best eye facility on the West Coast.

Then he asked a question that made everything possible.

"Does Mike have any military service in his background? I have a clinic at the Veteran's Administration Hospital where I can see him for free. If we can make that connection I can keep him as my patient."

It seemed like an impossible task. Mike and I had met when I was 40 years-old and he was 45. I knew that he served in Vietnam for four years after high school, but I didn't really know that much about it or how to find out.

"The VA is excellent here in La Jolla. It's attached to the University of California here in San Diego and is a teaching hospital like Thornton. I know Veteran Hospitals don't always have a great reputation, but any VA attached to a medical school is going to be one of the better hospitals you can have. The best neurologists in the world support the clinic in La Jolla."

"Thanks, Dr. Laski. I'll get going on that."

"Oh, and by the way. They'll turn you down automatically, but you just have to do an appeal. I'll write a letter."

Great. Just write an appeal.

But suddenly miracles poured in. I had remembered Mike had mentioned a Navy friend, Vecchio, and dug around his desk until I found out his contact information. After we spoke Vecchio sent out an email that went nationwide. Responses flooded my inbox from his shipmates all over the country. Someone had his discharge date; another had his ID number written in the ship yearbook. I found out all of the remarkable details that I needed for the lengthy VA application. Amazing. I completed the paperwork and turned it in.

We were turned down, just as expected, but still so frustrating.

Written appeal to the Department of Veteran Affairs

Enrollment Coordinator
Department of Veterans Affairs
San Diego Healthcare System
3350 La Jolla Village Drive
San Diego, CA 92161

RE: Notice of Disagreement
Dear Sir/Madam,

My husband, Mike Canrinus, applied for benefits with the VA for 664/04C4, C-4993. He served for four years in Vietnam with the U.S. Navy on the U.S.S. Falgout. He is 57 years old.

On April 20 he was hospitalized with what appeared to be a stroke, had a grand mal seizure and was incoherent and in need of restraints. This began a healthcare odyssey that led to four hospitals, seven MRIs, six spinal taps and every test you can think of. There is no tumor, no stroke. He was released June 12 with significant brain damage and memory loss, unable to read and write, walking with a cane or using a wheelchair in public. His discharge called for 24-hour supervision. At that time, we had to sell his business, Yacht Outfitting, on Harbor Drive, at a significant loss. I have been unable to work outside the home, although I have a small writing business. He is receiving $2200 a month in state disability for 15 months and his Social Security Disability is pending.

With the loss of his business (leaving $60,000 in debt) we have had to COBRA our health plan, PacifiCare. For Mike, myself and our 11 year-old, it is more than $1100/month.

On July 5, Mike became blind and had three more seizures. He is unable to safely walk around the house without assistance, certainly cannot leave the home, can't even find the bathroom. He has fallen twice at home, even with help.

His current neurologist is Dr. Lasko of UCSD and the VA.
He has also been seen by neurologists Dr. Doug Perkins and
Dr. Chris Bradley. All will attest that Mike has a devastating
disability. His brain is atrophying and they say it is the brain
of a 70-year-old and the damage is progressive.

The neurologist at Longmont Hospital believes that his
decline may continue rapidly and result in death within six
months, whereas Dr. Lasko thinks he may survive for many
years. My concern is not just for now, but for the future when
he may need to be placed in a long-term care facility. Dr.
Lasko thinks he has a rare disease called Central Nervous
System Vasculitis and he is taking anti-seizure and steroids
medications.

We've lost our Dad.

We have raised seven children. Our son is a reservist in
the Marine Corps and served in Iraq last year. I believe that
Mike qualifies for the Priority 4 status. Enclosed is some of
the medical paperwork and I would be happy to provide
more – MRI films, discharge summaries, etc.

Thank you for your consideration,

Francine Phillips

Mike's blindness turned out to be a kind of magic "open sesame" password for some services. He was granted "devastating illness" status and admitted as a VA patient. All of his care would be charged with a sliding scale co-pay. This was *huge*! After his initial visit with the Shiley Eye Center, he would be treated at the VA Hospital for exams and free glasses. They even had a "blindness school" that he hoped to attend.

Blindness turned out to be another step down the rabbit hole that society runs from in extreme horror. It's one thing to say, "He has a rare brain disease that causes intermittent dementia and memory loss." But when you toss over your shoulder the phrase, "He's blind," no further explanation is required. Mike was completely brave in accepting what had happened and at trying to make the best of it.

* * *

Just about the time we got settled into a new routine, I got a call from one of the employees of Yacht Outfitting.

"The new buyers of Yacht Outfitting fired all of us and changed the locks on the doors."

"What?! Those are the terms of the escrow! They haven't paid us any money."

"Well, you better get down here."

When I finally reached the buyers, they explained that the business was not going the way they expected that it would.

"We thought that it would kind of run itself," one of them said.

"What small business have you ever heard of that runs itself?" I replied. "Small businesses take hard work, dedication, and customer cultivation. Everyone knows that."

"We just thought the customers would sort of come to us."

"But you owe me $40,000 dollars!" They hung up without another word.

Robert Boney had his own take on it all as head of the boatyard.

"If I don't like the business, they cannot assume the Yacht Outfitting lease," he practically spit the words at me as I entered the yard office. "I want you out of that office and out of that shop within thirty days."

I sat in the driver's seat of the Explorer and sobbed, head in my hands. It was all really gone – the business, the clients, the office overlooking the sparkling bay, the camaraderie of the boat workers, "the boys" from the shop. Over and done.

At home I called a moving company and made arrangements to empty the office and bring some items home. The employees suggested that I see if the business next door would buy the tools. I went down the next day to meet with the owner.

"Hey," I said. "I have an inventory of the tools and equipment. Since the business was assessed at $40,000 I will sell you the tools for $10,000. Mike has some very specialized and customized tools that he designed for certain jobs that are worth a great deal."

"I'll give you $3,000."

I thought for a moment and tried to find an alternative. I had already approached a good friend of Mike's who almost paid me $10,000 but changed his mind at the last minute. I felt like the helpless widow. Finally, I nodded.

"For $3,000, I'm going to go over what I think we will need at home and you can have the rest, agreed?"

"Agreed. I'll write out a check."

A few minutes later he handed me a check for less than one-tenth of what I had hoped to get for Yacht Outfitting. About an hour later I got a call from Mike's friend who had changed his mind about buying the tools.

"Francine, are you still willing to sell the tools for $10,000?"

"Well, an hour ago I accepted a check from the business next door."

"Oh! I wish you had called me."

"I wish you had called *me*."

"Sorry, well, good luck. Say hello to Mike!"

"Oh, I'll be sure to do that. You can come visit any time."

I found out a few days later that Boney had already decided to let the business next door take over our shop. He already had signed a lease and had it arranged so that I would not be able to sell Yacht Outfitting to anyone. He had planned to steal our tools for money owed, in his mind, so he thought the neighbor was gracious to give me anything. Lucky me.

When the movers came a few days later, I spent a hard, boiling-hot day in the dusty office and the chaos of the shop. Lots got tossed into the dumpsters under the balcony. Lots. The movers packed the leather chairs, the mini-fridge, the file cabinets, the computer, the office equipment and the Snap-On rolling cabinet with common household tools. The rest – I let go.

We were sweeping up the office when I thought about the beautiful, six-foot, carved wood Yacht Outfitting sign that hung on the balcony of the boat yard.

"Can you remove that sign and take it with us?"

The movers took a look. "Sure. We just need to remove the bolts."

"Do it!"

After all, Boney would just be throwing the sign away. It really was doing him a favor, right?

The sign was mine. Left at the boat yard was a gap, an empty space that looked like a mistake, like something was missing. It reflected the empty place in our lives. To me it's a monument to the hard work and successful career that brought Mike pleasure, thrills and unspeakable joy. To the career that was gone forever.

God so loved me.

CHAPTER 44

Creating Vision

Email to Friends and Family:

September 27

Hello faithful followers on the pioneer road of, "What Now?"

The good news is that Mike has been approved for disability status with Social Security, so we will be getting some long-term help from that. I believe the blindness and having an 11-year-old qualifies us for additional dollars. They said it would take six months and it did! Actually it may be another month before we get a check, but what a blessing to have it. Thanks, all of you, for that deduction from your paychecks! A tiny bit of it is going to us.

Also good news is that he has been re-classified as a devastating disability by the Veterans Administration, after a written appeal following their initial denial. The bad news is—I'm not sure at all what this means? Do I go there for treatment, do they fund our current provider – what happens now? So, more time on the phone, figuring this out. Also, the Social Security designation means he is "eligible" for Medi-Cal? Which would be better? Can he have both? Lots of new territory for me to cover and the websites don't really explain those kinds of things. I'm the worst at this stuff.

Had some fantastic visits – a great dinner with Lannie, Chris and Jake as he comes down for another year at USD; a great "chick night" organized by Gwen Houston on my back patio; then an all time great day with Tricia who came and did everything for a day – dust, vacuum, go with me to the dog groomer, held my hand while I did paperwork, made dinner and motivated me to get out my fall pumpkins. Thank you, thank you, thank you!

Nick and Jocelyn's wedding was wonderful. We had lots of family time with Melissa and Nate, Teresa, Vanessa and the grandkids, Mike's sister's family and my nieces and nephews – whew! Mike did really well at the rehearsal dinner (David and Jeri Brown made a timely visit so she could help me with 12 centerpieces.) Mandy Stone came with me to the Automotive Museum, setting aside real deadlines to help me make it beautiful. The next day the wedding went off and was spectacular. So happy for them, so in love. Mike did okay as best man with Jesse as his "attendant" standing near him and I danced with my sisters. Very wonderful memory.

Healthwise, I should look up what I last wrote, but this month has been up and down. He spent three days at Longmont Hospital for chest pain – all clear with that. A day in ER with dangerously low blood pressure (dehydrated?) and last Friday we spent another eight hours of "quality time" in the NEW Longmont ER because Mike fell coming into our front door. He cut his head on the planter and had to have about 12 stitches on his forehead. I told him it was just in time for Halloween. For about three weeks he has had virulent you-know-what and that's been challenging. We decided today to just pull out the rug in his room and put in linoleum. Doctor didn't have much to say about it. It's getting a little better.

On Nov. 4 we go again to Dr. Lasko at UCSD. He has ordered another EEG this week so see if there is continued brain atrophy or evidence of more lesions. Mike is doing well in therapy – has word problem homework that he reads and gets right (knee is to leg what elbow is to _____) but he surprised the therapist by not knowing who got married, thought the Earley sisters were OUR children, etc. Stuff I thought we were over. I had him call Bill and Linda Cooper because he told me he thought they were trying to have a baby (they're grandparents like us – but YOUNG grandparents, right Linda?)

Also on Nov. 4 we go to a very famous neurological ophthalmologist, Leah Levi, at the Shiley Eye Center to get an evaluation. So, we just have to get through October.

God bless all of you,
Francine

WHAT IS NEUROLOGICAL BLINDNESS? You can almost be on track by saying that it's when the vision damage originates in the brain and not the eye. In other words, the brain doesn't know what it is seeing and just sees . . . well . . . nothing. Mike's first visit at the Shiley Eye Center started with the standard eye chart. He did not see the big E at the top of the chart and went down the rows articulating naïve guesses at the letters listed. The next test involved flashing lights that Mike was supposed to identify. He didn't see any of them. All this time the technicians were making encouraging sounds, "uh-huh," "hmmm," "go on," while I was beside myself freaking out at the utter horror.

He can't see the big E!

But then this blindness gets very tricky. He seemed to be able to see *some* things. If you talked to him, he could look at you, even look you in the eye. If he knew that his cane was hanging on a hook next to his bed, he could not only go right to it, he could *see* it. So my explanation ended up being, he can only see what he can already see. If he saw his computer and I asked him to show me the computer, he could point to it. If I asked him to hand me the broom that was on the wall about six inches in front of him, he would say, "What broom?" He couldn't see it, it just wasn't there. If his brain didn't already know what it was seeing, there was no way that it could make sense of the image — it would stay blank. Very weird.

It was like the passage in the Bible where Jesus tries to explain something and says, He who has ears to hear and eyes to see will get it. I never understood that – ever — and it always seemed like nonsense to me. Once we entered the realm of neurological blindness, I got an inkling of what that meant. If Mike had eyes to see, he could see. But in that case it didn't make him less blind.

So, Mike had no trouble qualifying to go to the Center for the Blind to learn to cope with blindness even though he didn't *look* blind. And he didn't really think he was blind because he could see some things if he was familiar with them. The things he couldn't see – a street curb, the pole he was about to run into, the car door opening onto the sidewalk in front of him — he didn't know they were even there, so he thought he was seeing everything.

This weird kind of blindness made me realize that it was more important than ever to build safety zones into his routine — places that he got to know really well so that his ability to see them and to navigate them would improve. While most of the time he would be guided by putting his hand on my shoulder as we were trained, we needed to build places of freedom into his field of vision. Seeing the bed, the commode, the computer screen, the rooms of the house, the dirty pots and pans in the sink, the door to the patio – these navigation signposts could become visible with constant repetition.

Washing the pots and pans became his daily contribution to our household (who wouldn't want a husband to do that!). He would break glasses or dishes every day, but pots and pans he could do.

Our local Starbucks, in fact, became one of the zones. I would bring him in, set him at a table and go get our order. Eventually, his vision improved at that Starbucks. Later, when he attended the Braille Institute, that Starbucks was the meeting point in our neighborhood to catch the bus every Thursday for Braille.

Another "safety zone" that I tried to create for Mike was the church. I wanted him to know how to get around, how to find the bathroom, how to navigate from the lobby to the sanctuary, how to "see" the parking lot, the pulpit, the stained glass windows that Mandy Stone made, how to "see" the hostess table on the trellis patio where donuts were served in-between services. How could I make that happen?

Could he stuff the bulletins with the elderly ladies on Thursday mornings? Mike didn't have the capacity to do that correctly.

Then a gentleman in the church started a group called "Boat-building and Bible Study." What could be more perfect for Mike? He went several times to gather in the garage to cut and plane wood, sand and then epoxy. Mike was able to share his expertise on building boats and tell stories about building Hobie's catamaran, *Katie Sue*. When I say it was a God-send, I mean that literally. He was so proud when the boat was completed and we had a huge celebration picnic with all the families.

One Sunday there was a little notice in the church bulletin that they were looking for someone who could volunteer to water the flower pots on the patio entrance to the church. Sprinklers took care of the expanses of lawn, but the flower pots needed watering with a hose. I talked to Mike about it and then to the pastor.

"Do you think that this is something that Mike could learn to do?"

"Well, I'm not so sure. . . ."

"Can we give it a try? I'll do some training with him the first few times and let's see if it will work. If it doesn't work out, we'll bow out."

So part of Mike's week became a 6:30 a.m. Metropolitan Transit Service (MTS) ride to the church, walking to the hose, then watering each pot, counting them to make sure he didn't miss any and then getting back on the bus three hours later. Slowly he could make his way around the church without much assistance. On the bus, people asked Mike where he was headed and he talked freely about the church being wonderful and inviting them to come to the services. He was a great listener and invariably he would tell me, "I met someone on the bus today and he (or she) was really interesting." His ability to be interested in others never wavered.

There was a 6:30 a.m. men's prayer group that meet every Monday at the church and they noticed Mike was always there at that time. One time they said to each other, "Why not invite Mike to join us?" Eventually, someone from the group picked Mike up every Monday and brought him home. They made sure to include Mike in every meeting; when Monday was a holiday, they went out to breakfast. Mike was up and dressed and standing with his backpack and his cane at the door without fail. That little group of men changed his life and he changed theirs.

The first time he went to the group Mike came home and I asked him to tell me all about it. He sat at the kitchen counter and I filled his tall plastic cup with cool water.

"Well," Mike started, turning to face me. "They are reading some kind of book about men and what they should be like by a John somebody."

"You mean *Wild at Heart*?"

"Yeah, something like that."

"Do you want me to find you the audio book?"

"Maybe," he said, trying to think through the words of what he wanted to tell me. "The thing is, I guess the book says all these things about men. Men like to hunt. Men need to be in charge. Men have to take risks. Men like to be wild.

"The thing is," he continued as I reached over to hold his hand. "I can't do any of those things." Hi face had a look of guileless questioning and he rubbed his forehead.

"I can't do anything like that. But I'm a man."

My heart skipped a beat.

"Yes, you certainly are. You are a man of God and you are the bravest man I've ever known. You go out into a world of darkness with a cane and a prayer. You take more risks than any man I know. It's the faith that you have inside that makes you manly, Mike, not any of that other stuff."

I took his cup and refilled it from the water cooler.

"And you be sure and tell them that next week."

He did. Mike, his stumbling helplessness, his absolute faith that God was with him and loved him, the care and concern he showed to others and his simple prayers made him a treasured member of that group over time. And they were a treasure to Mike as well.

CHAPTER 45

Just When You Think...

O UR LIVES ENTERED A semblance of normalcy, as much as a blended family of nine with a blind, ill Dad with no memory and random seizures could get. Everything was hard, but we tried to take everything one day at a time.

Prayer was daily, not as punishment, not as requirement but simply as the acknowledgement that God was in charge and could be trusted. Too many miracles of being provided help, money, work, healthcare, and other solutions — plus the continued daily penny — could not be explained away by anything less than a spiritual power that was personal, loving and giving. Did we feel that God didn't care or had abandoned us? Only once.

It was am otherwise routine morning before I picked up a phone call at 11 a.m. and heard our 25-year-old daughter, Molly, barely audible, on the line calling from her apartment.

"Mom, I'm really sick. I've been throwing up for two days."

I knew how hard it was for an independent young woman like Molly to make that call to "old Mom." For some reason, I didn't put her off. I didn't say I had to try to finish one more paragraph or wrap up my research or whatever. "I'll be right there," I said.

I got up from my desk immediately. "Anna and Mike, you have to stay here alone because I have to get Molly and bring her home, is that OK?"

"Sure, Mom," Anna answered. "We'll be okay."

Wisely, Mike and Anna walked next door to get our neighbors' number in case they had a problem. Wonderful Tom and Mary offered to be "infinitely interruptible," at the drop of a hat. I hoped they meant it.

When I got to Molly's place, she *was* very sick and looked extremely gaunt.

"We are going to Urgent Care right now," I told her. When I got to the parking lot, I left her in the car while I went inside and got a wheelchair to bring her inside. The nurse at the desk told they had fifteen patients in the back and it would be an hour wait. I wrapped a big beach blanket over her lap in case she got sick. After about ten minutes she was hyperventilating and I went up to the desk.

"My daughter is really sick. She needs to see someone."

"We'll get her in right away," said the receptionist.

"Molly!" called the nurse at the door just as I was sitting down from my second request to be seen soon. We were brought inside, they asked Molly for a urine sample and we went into the partitioned room. More waiting.

I ventured a question that I hesitated to ask. "Do you have insurance, Molly?"

She lowered her head. "Not for 12 more days. You have to work six months to get covered."

Suddenly she bent forward, "Mom, my stomach is killing me, it hurts!"

Feeling like Shirley McLaine in *Terms of Endearment*, I went to the counter toward the nurses and doctors standing around, casually laughing.

"My daughter is in a great deal of pain, when can someone see her?"

"There's a patient in room A?"

The doctor came in and checked the urine sample. Suddenly there was a huge flurry of activity – protein in the urine, blood draw – five vials, EKG. I was getting concerned.

The doctor faced me and said, "I'm going to call an ambulance and take her to ER."

"But it's twenty feet away!" I said.

"She'll have priority if she goes in an ambulance."

Okay, I admit, I was thinking about the added $600 ambulance fee… so shoot me. It was twenty feet away.

I walked up to ER, then remembered I had left my cell phone at Urgent Care. I walked back and the ambulance was still sitting there. The attendant came out and said to me, "We did a blood sugar test and it was 170, so it's not that…" Walked back to ER and got there before they finally left one driveway for another.

Ten minutes later I went to the window at ER.

"My daughter, Molly, was just brought in and I'd like to be with her," I said through thick glass and a scratchy intercom.

Click, click, click of a keyboard. "Oh, she was *just* brought in. She's not settled yet. Give us about 10 minutes."

I called Anna and Mike. Mary, our neighbor, had decided to join them at our house and they were all watching a movie in Anna's room. Good enough. Again I went up to the window where a lovely white-haired volunteer in a blue jacket said, "May I help you?"

"My daughter is inside and I need to be with her," I explained.

Click, click, click.

"Oh, she's not settled in a room, it will take at least a half hour."

Having been in more than my share of ER situations, I've seen patients lying on gurneys for hours waiting for rooms.

"Listen, my daughter is in there and I don't care if she's in the hallway, I need to be with her," I said very firmly.

She wilted. I got my hot pink Visitor badge and was escorted deep into the ER – to a room, of course. Molly was in huge distress, blood pressure off the chart, no potassium and hyperventilating – heart rate 130, blood sugar 396. They had thrown away the vials and drawn their own blood. Did their own EKG.

The nurse was blunt.

"Your daughter is in diabetic ketoacidosis – DKA. She's fighting for her life. If you had not gotten to her, she would be dead right now. We're taking her to Intensive Care. All of her internal organs – kidney, pancreas, liver – are filled with infection."

Diabetic? Molly was never diabetic!

There was much to thank God for. She called, I answered, I went, I demanded a doctor….Thank you, God! Five nurses basically told me the same thing. She would have died if we had gotten there later.

All afternoon Molly lay, pale and still, on that ICU bed. She had deep circles under her eyes and her lips were chapped and blue. I held her hand, praying and pleading. My baby girl. My firstborn.

God, please don't take her life!

Worried about my own blood sugar, at 8:30 p.m. I went to the cafeteria which was, of course, closed. I drove to Rubio's at the mall across the street for a HealthMex bowl. As I pulled back out of the parking lot, the car sputtered. It was just above "Empty." I turned toward a gas station instead of the hospital, but at the red traffic signal, the car stalled. Out of gas. My heart was pounding.

How could this be happening? This can't be happening!

I tried to stay calm and called my house.

"Mary," I asked, "What is Tom doing?"

"He's at home watching television."

"Well, would you mind asking him to get a gas can out of the shed next to our garage and bring me a gallon of gas?"

"Sure, where are you?"

I calmly described my location, thanked her, and hung up. And waited. And waited. More than 45 minutes.

That's when I broke down. My heart gave out; my bones ached. The fear. The burden. The financial worries. The thought of losing my daughter after the stress of "losing" Mike was unbearable. People looking in the window of the strangely-angled car blocking the road with hazard lights blinking saw a tired middle-aged woman beating the steering wheel, crying out to God.

"It's too much, too much, too much! Stop it! Stop it! Why are you persecuting me?"

Finally regaining control, I called Mary back.

"Where's Tom?"

"Oh, Mike said that all of those gas cans have water in them and can't be used?"

"Mike said? And he listened to Mike?" My voice was a screech. "Mary, Molly is dying and I'm sitting here out of gas!"

She paused less than a second.

"He'll be right there! Leave the car."

In the next five minutes I lost my faith.

There is no God! God is a cruel joke! I refuse to believe that I am loved, that He cares, that He is there. God is not there! My daughter is dying, my husband is dying, and my car runs out of gas a block from the hospital! God is being cruel and I am just a plaything for him to destroy. A mouse being flung by the claws of an indifferent cat…

After the car situation was resolved, I stayed until 10 p.m. and went home. That night I lie in bed and, for the first time in my life felt no connection to God. The universe seemed immense, cold, unending and impersonal. My heart beat faster and I tossed and turned. I was afraid. How could there be no God? How could I start to unravel my faith? What alternatives are there?

First there is the conviction that there is such a thing as meaning and purpose, so that rules out nihilism. Then there is the idea of a primary force that created everything, so that rules out atheism. And if you accept that a force created everything, you have to accept that the force is smarter and more powerful than you, so you can't define it on your own terms, and that rules out we-are-all-one-with-god or we-are-god nonsense.

Once you admit that you can't define God you are pretty much left with exploring what God has to say about himself, and that gives you the scriptures, which puts agnosticism to rest. Once you study scripture, which is, basically, the history of God's dealings with humans, you have to accept a linear universe, and that rules out all the "isms," re-incarnation, and karma.

And once you accept a linear universe with a beginning and an end, you figure out that you are on the timeline for a reason and maybe you should find out what it is. So, to find out the reason, you might as well ask. Once you ask, God starts telling you to look at Jesus, because he became the incarnation of God and overcame death to teach us who we are, which puts pretty much everything else to rest. And once you see Jesus, you see your failings and how much you fall short, which makes you want to be saved from your ridiculous striving to be "good." And once you ask Jesus to be saved, you are.

I was. I was saved and had a personal relationship with the living God. He was passionate about me, not gleeful about the pain or the evil or the suffering. God was not only there, God was good. I knew that was true and could not *not* believe that.

Molly continued to have to fight for stability all Saturday. I brought Mike to the hospital and we found irony in the fact that this time he was in the waiting room and someone else was in ICU. I led him, thin, wrinkled and blind to a seating area near a television.

"I'll be right back. The rest room is against the wall."

Just then the ICU door opened and I slipped past the doctors coming out and walked straight to Molly's room. I bent over and kissed her gaunt cheek and her beautiful deep blue eyes opened.

"Mommy."

She'd turned a corner. The rest of the day I raced back and forth between Molly's bedside and Mike's spot in the waiting room, checking to make sure both were doing all right.

On Sunday Mike and I headed for church. I had told our pastor what had happened to Molly and he prayed for me on the phone. In a very lovely gesture, our pastor had Mike and I come forward in the service.

"I don't know why some people are given such hard assignments," he said. "But Francine and Mike have had more added to them."

Many, many people stepped to the front of the church and prayed for us.

Later that evening I spent some time alone finalizing my thoughts about the whole God thing. The problem with denying Him is that there is no other. There just isn't. Who am I to think I know better than my creator? There is just God and He is God and I am not. I am on the receiving end. Period.

As the sunset screamed red across the sky and the stars shone light from millions of miles away, I felt like the tiniest of specks on a spinning planet in a single universe in a single galaxy in an unfathomable world. Does God really have a plan? Does He love me; know what I am going through? Again and again I had always found the answer to be "Yes." Does my faith depend on the absence of pain? Can it be reasonable to doubt a good God because shit happens? No, if faith is faith, it has to be real in any circumstance, not just when life is good. Rain shines on the righteous and the sinner.

Lord, I am your child and this world is not all there is – I am yours for eternity. You promise to overcome evil someday and injustice. You will throw the author of evil into a lake of fire. You will take revenge against suffering. There's no reincarnation, no earning your favor, no punishment I have to endure. Jesus took it all. You promise to comfort me on Your lap. You promise that all this will come to an end. And I believe it.

Monday, Molly took a turn for the better and it was reported that she was going to survive! Molly was going to live! Mike and I loaded up in the car and drove down to her apartment to pick up her mail. As I thumbed through the huge stack of a Vogue magazine, mail and bills, and solicitation postcards, there was a stiff envelope.

"Welcome to PacifiCare," it said. "Here is your membership card."

She was covered! We confirmed it as we went straight to the hospital. That day PacifiCare called her and said they would have her diabetic pack waiting for her when she got released at the end of the week.

Good news! She was out of the woods and no new overwhelming financial burden. I had reached the end of my strength and the end of my faith and yet God was still there.

God so loved me.

CHAPTER 45

A Sick Little Twist

In the world of The Sick, life is an endless round of challenges — actually, that's too kind of a word. Obstacles? Battles? Oppression? A common sentiment that I still feel is "Everything is a fight."

Everything. A Fight.

My role as wife was transformed into nurse and caregiver, but also into strong advocate, paperwork wizard, financial expert, medication genius. One minute I was changing wet sheets, the next I was protesting a change in medication by a neurologist. An hour after that I was dealing with a leak in the sprinkler system. Wife as warrior. If you are in a similar situation, you are being called to take charge. Forget about being "submissive." God wants you to step up.

This was hard on Mike, even though I tried to protect him from the frustration and pain that was overtaking our daily life. Did Mike and I fight? Of course. We were, after all, still a married couple. Two people thrust into an unfamiliar world trying to figure out a balance and how to build trust in each other. Over time, there were highs and lows but it seemed that everything we went through had some weird, sick twist to make it worse.

For instance:

Coming home from the hospital when I was told he was dying to find that I had left the slider open in our bedroom. Not one, but TWO skunks were in the room and had sprayed everything before scurrying out – bed, loveseats, rug, throw pillows, clothing. Really?

Another time I was driving to the hospital to make an important decision about Mike's care. His sister and brother-in-law were visiting and staying at the house. I got a call from Don.

"Murphy got out." Our ancient dog.

"Did you find her?"

"She was picked up by animal control."

"What? That hasn't happened in fifteen years and she is out all the time!"

"I can go get her," he said, "but…do you think she will come to me?"

One Christmas Eve I came home to find that water had been pouring into my closet for hours, directly under the upstairs bathroom. Not pure water, if you get my meaning. Anna and I cut out the carpeting in front of the closet, which was destroyed, and dragged it outside. My clothes were all contaminated. Shoes ruined. Purses trashed.

The insurance adjuster was unsympathetic. I told him that my collection of Christmas sweaters on the top shelf of the closet were affected.

"Oh, don't worry, we'll throw them away."

"Throw them away! What part of Christmas Collection did you not hear? These are in my will, which one goes to which daughter. You need to have them professionally cleaned."

After that, he was convinced I was trying to defraud his company. Right. The Great Christmas Sweater Get Rich Quick Scheme.

He insisted that I have the bathroom inspected by a company of his choosing. They found asbestos not in the flooring, but in the linoleum beneath the flooring. The floor (also the closet ceiling) had to be removed. Remediation was $3,000, which they paid. Rebuilding the closet and putting in a floor were not covered. Another $4,000 that I did not have. Thankfully, men and women in the church came to help. Some told me I should fight it. I had too many other battlefronts that were firing.

During the weeks of blowers and no closet and chaos, I got pneumonia.

(Later, when I learned the real meaning of letting go of everything, I laughed at myself over the sweaters. But at the time, I was still clinging to everything that represented the life I had built for myself that was being destroyed.)

* * *

One morning when Mike was in a hospital I walked in about 11 a.m. He was still in restraints and soaked with urine, his sheets spread with excrement. At 11 a.m.! I went straight to the desk and firmly insisted on seeing the nurse in charge. Of course she apologized and got an aide and they hurried to get Mike cleaned up. He was crying. I was furious. The aide was defiant.

"I'm not wiping that white man's boney butt!" she said to the nurse.

After a little while they said I could come in. Mike was washed and clean, in a fresh robe with crisp, white sheets and a soft blanket over him. He was incoherent, but at least not crying. I asked him to turn to his side. Everything looked clean. But when I spread his buttocks, the area was thick with excrement from top to bottom. I took a wet towel and wiped up handfuls, then soaped another towel and rinsed him clean and put cream on his raw, sore behind.

* * *

I was at the local Christian Writer's Guild conference and Mike was in the hospital when I got a call from an intern about giving Mike an MRI. I thought about it and decided that it was not necessary. None of Mike's previous 26 MRIs showed anything new or different and they each cost a $500 co-pay. You do the math.

"No, I don't think I will approve an MRI."

"But ma'am, you have to!"

"I do not. Mike has had 26 MRIs and 11 lumbar punctures. They have all shown the same results. Is there any reason to think that this will be different?"

"No, but it's our protocol."

"So, you are not expecting anything different?"

"No."

"And you don't expect that the MRI will have any benefit to the patient?"

"No, none."

"So there isn't really any reason to put him through it?"

"It's our protocol."

"You mean, it protects the hospital?"

"Well, I guess."

"Let's skip this one. I refuse."

Later, when I bought the medical records for this particular visit, it stated "The Wife refused the MRI at great risk to the patient including possible death."

* * *

Mike had a friend at the blind service center named Sonya. I'd been there many times and knew that he was popular among the blue-haired set with macular degeneration that enjoyed the classes, the library and the camaraderie. For older folks, the center was more about coping and developing living skills and renegotiating social skills.

Sonya was going through an emotional crisis and turned to Mike. They talked on the phone for hours. I thought it was good for Mike to be needed and I knew he was a great listener and could give good advice.

It was time for the annual party thrown by one of the teachers.

"Hey Fran, can we give Sonya a ride to the party? She lives near us."

"Sure, Mike, but she'll have to come home when you get tired."

"That's okay."

The day of the party I packed the car with Mike's backpack and a change of clothes, a cooler of hors d'oeuvres, and a container of homemade brownies. We set off to find Sonya's place. Mike said it was in a complex of single housing units off the street at the end of a long driveway. Apparently he had gone there on the MTS bus once. While he sat in the car I went to her door expecting to find a pleasant elderly lady in a muumuu.

What I got was Blind Barbie. Blonde hair high in a French twist with giant cleavage wearing a tight halter sundress, red with white polka dots and high, red wedge sandals with ribbon ties that snaked up her tan legs. She sat nervously behind me in the car and talked nonstop.

"You and Mike must have such a wonderful marriage, so perfect. He talks about you all the time."

I glanced at her in the rear view mirror. "Oh, we have our challenges like anyone else."

Later Mike innocently told me that she had asked him to go to bed with her one time, but he stammered and told her, "I'm married."

Oh, and Sonya wasn't really blind. She had regained her eyesight — temporary loss from diabetes — but didn't want to tell anyone because she was on disability and was afraid she would be kicked out.

Eventually Mike regained some eyesight too: tunnel vision. For a year it was black and white, then he started to regain color. He was still legally blind. He still couldn't cross a street or find anything, but it made life easier for him. He resumed his love affair with computer Solitaire and when Jesse taught him Google Earth, he felt more free than ever, visiting his old home, his high school, and ports where he had sailed, all from his huge, overstuffed desk chair.

* * *

One result of this improvement in his activity was that people thought he was more capable that he was. It was whispered that I was getting some kind of emotional contentment out of being his caretaker. I enjoyed leading him around everywhere. I was holding him back for some kind of sick attention or appearance of sainthood. I didn't give him enough independence. Then, of course, there were those who thought I didn't protect him enough.

One day I was praying on my back porch when God spoke to me. I was given a picture of some point in the future when I was going to be blamed for doing the wrong thing, no matter what happened. I thanked God for this insight and decided to place a call. This was one fight I could nip in the bud.

After a few pleasantries, I told the person on the line that I needed to say something important. I took a deep breath and tried to keep my voice steady.

"I was just praying and heard the Lord tell me something that I want to share with you. Here's the thing. I know that you will blame me when Mike dies. I know that you will think it is my fault, no matter when he dies or how it happens. When he came home from the hospital at the beginning of this, your first words to me were, 'Well, don't kill him.' So I'm telling you now, I know how you will react and I'm ready for it and I know that it's not true. Don't worry about me being upset with you because I understand how you could feel that way, but I know it's not true. God told me that I am not to blame."

CHAPTER 46

Mike's Thoughts and Prayers

MIKE'S SIMPLE FAITH WAS growing. His participation in the Men's Prayer Group helped him wrest his hands from the helm of his life. He was no longer *Follow Me or Die*. Instead his life credo was *Follow Christ. He who would save his life must lose it*. This wasn't just a random Bible teaching. This was Mike's truth and it is true for me and true for you.

About two years into his illness, Mike wanted to be baptized. Jim offered to clean and repair his backyard spa that was a rock waterfall and pond surrounded by lovely trees. The dinner group marshaled homemade desserts. A few of us practiced our favorite choir song that fleshed out Mike's favorite painting of Jesus pulling Peter out of the water.

> *Hold to God's unchanging hand,*
> *Hold to God's unchanging hand;*
> *Build your hopes on things eternal,*
> *Hold to God's unchanging hand.*

Mike wore a white robe, about a foot too short, and our pastor Craig and Mandy guided him into the tranquil spa. Family and friends surrounding him while we offered our little anthem and a prayer. Then Mike, all six foot four inches of him, was dipped backward, sustained by strong hands, then lifted up, clean, forgiven, renewed.

It's one thing to understand in your head that you are a follower. It's another to feel it in your soul. But God created the time/space continuum so that real things would happen in real time. Physical things. Wet things. Public things. Baptism is one of these. That thing that happened. That moment in time that you can't rationalize away when you surrender everything and let go of your life. Mike rose up from that water with joy that none of us will ever forget and can never deny.

Mike had borrowed a philosophy from his first sailing boss, Bill Bailey, an inspirational speaker and writer. One day Bill had come to him and said, "Michael, we are going on a voyage," and hired Mike to crew his yacht. Kind of the way Jesus called His disciples. It changed Mike's life from that moment. Mike dropped out of his last semester at college and gave himself to the sea. He never looked back or regretted his choice. Bailey was known for championing a positive attitude and each morning Mike would call out, "Fran, today is the best day of my life!"

That year our pastor passed out lined, spiral-bound journals to each member of the church. I didn't think much about it at the time. It wasn't until many years later, when I was cleaning out the bookcase, I pulled one off of the shelf assuming that it was simply blank. Instead, I happened to open the cover and found that Mike had filled every page with letters to God. Mike, in his faltering handwriting, wrote journal entries addressed to God, misspelled and barely legible. I touched the page gently and was shocked to read what he had been thinking. His words revealed insight into the mental and emotional ups and downs and his active acts of surrender at this time period. I was astounded as I sat down and read his profound thoughts. Every page was a prayer and almost every prayer was for me.

Below are several journal entries, unedited, that let you walk a little in Mike's shoes.

Journal Entry

March 19

The thief of yesterday is gone but I love the memories. Living in it is what I do not want to do. The same about the future. Now I had a bad day, but it was the best day of my life. Now most people will think thi is stupid. It is not once you understand liveing in the present time then you

will be happier. Thank you God and Fran for helping me through this time. Right now I have deeps feeling for the.
Good might.

Journal Entry

March 20

Today was a wonderful day it started out with the Prayer group and a talk about India and how Christians have influenced them. It is surprising, then having a talk with God and breaking out in tearse for no apparent reasone. It is not because I am sad it is because I am sad for others. Now I feel them coming with a joy behind them.

Good Night Sleep tight
Mikie

Journal Entry

Friday

Started out at four in the morning with me waking to a wet bed. Bot up and changed but still wake up with a wet bed. Decided to get up and go to the office after. Spent the rest of the night playing Solitaire wining four times. Now let's get to the good part of the day. Right now I feel very good and am wearing a diaper just like a baby __ Thank you God for giving me what I have in life. Love you, Fran. It is time

Journal Entry

Sunday

Today was a day that I will rember for a Long time Church was especely something that got into my heart. The music was about Jesus getting crucified and what that ment Now I have a differernt feeling for Jesus I thought that God was all I needed to pray for. That is wrong. God is number one and Jesus is the Teacher of all.

Journal Entry

Monday

Today was a very interesting day. I went for hapy to sad to hapy. Now as I look back I see God with me all the time. I have to talk to my bible study about the diference between God and Jesus. I know the normal diference but my emushans have a hard time. I had thought about staying home so Fran did not have to spend time caring for me and she and Anna coulde have a great girl time together. She does not think I can care for myself. On this note, I will say goodbye.

Journal Entry

Saturday

Today was a wonderful day just as I wanted. The only problem was that I had 4 episodes with my brain all short and I drank a lot of water and it seemed to stop them. Now on to happy times work was fun and good, insight was excepshionaly sharp. Fran was tyierd and took a map that also good for her. Tonight will cooked dinner. Now I must get good sleep for I am going to work tomorrow without her noticing.

Bye Fran you are a spechial woman beyond all.

Journal Entry

Saturday the real one

Today was the best and worst day of my life. The past is OK and in future is unlived. The saying I am trying to live by because it make my life easier. God, Jesus, I know realy now that you are with me every step. Now I am talking to you in a slower voice. Voice tone means a lot about what someone thinks.

Love all,
Mike

Journal Entry

Monday

Spent the day with Fran She went to the hospital for an examine of her lungs. They were fine but she had other things that required a lot of meds. The church is sending us food three days a week. A Little thing that I got going. She does not know.

Good night and God Bless
Mike

Journal Entry

Saturday

Tonight I just had a experience that hit me in the heart. Laying next to Fran and hearing her cough. I cannot do anything about it. If I was able to drive I could get her meds. My feelings are dep tonight.

God is with us.
God is here
God is in charge
God help Fran
God help Fran
Not only in life but in everything.

Love
Mike

Journal Entry

Tuesday

I had a day where I just relaxed, played Sollitaire and got a lot done such as cleaning Fran's mirrors to almost perfetshion. But most important I tooke care of Fran. It made me feel loved. That may not seem normal but it is with me. God is with us and now when I stop writing I will pray and talk to God. Tears are coming down in joy.

Good night and God Bless

Journal Entry

Wednesday, April 2

Now I am sick also coughing and runny nose. God is on my side I feel him right now and know that all is going to be fine.

Good night and God bless.

Journal Entry

Saturday

Today has Just come to a great end. All the time I was having a time both questional and good. I had to stop my work because I was breathing but the plus side was beater only in a few ways but they were important to me. Fran is now telling me what she wants in a positive way. I had a hard time with that. Don't know why.

God I want to learn more about the Bible but a while ago my ego did not want to listen to the Bible CD. Tonight God look down on Fran and lead her to a happy life.

Regarde
Migelito

Journal Entry

Wednesday

Today was a great day. I swore that I would never play Sollataire again but I did and had a blast succeeding with new moves.

Thank you God for what you have given me and now it is my turn to give back. I's Bible time and not Solataire time. Love you God my creator. Jesus you gave up your life for me. Now it's time for me to give up mine to you. For REAL. I feel God with me right now because my emoshions are coming to the surface and my eyes are blinking for no reason. I sign off now with happiness in my soul.

Good night and God bless
Mike

Journal Entry

Friday

Today was a day that was bost great and bad. Some days are like that and they take all the enegy out of me. I deep looking att the picture of Jesus pulling John out of the water and I keep thinking it is me. I can not walk on water but some times I think I can. Now I am going to put down my pen and open my mind and heart to God I kow that he is here.

Journal Entry

Sunday

Today was the best day of my life Fran gave me a big hug.

Journal Entry

Wednesday

Just got to say one thing tonight is that right now I am as happy as can be. It is because I learned that I am not alone in this world. How could I feel that? I did not open my mind to all that is good and I am suronded by it. God, wife, family, friends and all that is good. Writing this brings out dep feelings in me. All is good even though it is hard.

Mike

CHAPTER 47

About the Brain

Over time, human beings adapt. Mike and I tried to establish certain routines. Trips to the hospital became commonplace. I had a hospital kit packed and ready like a pregnant woman — water bottles, a couple of granola bars, cell phone charger, cash, knitting.

Simple knitting. Once when Mike was in a coma, I decided to knit a scarf until he regained consciousness. That thing sprawls wide, narrow, tight and dense, then loose. Lacy. Long. After that, the kit was adapted to simple knitting. Over the years it was modified and expanded, but it represented the only concrete way I could prepare for a completely unknowable future.

"It's just that you have nothing to *stand on!*" said my friend Mandy. "Everything shifts constantly, just when you think that things have settled down."

I instantly thought of that old hymn we used to sing in Grandpa's church — Mom on the piano and Dad's voice rising over the congregation like a force field.

On Christ the solid rock I stand,
All other ground is sinking sand,
All other ground is sinking sand.

It was true. Of course, it's true for everyone and has been for 2,000 years of human history, but for us, it was *really* true. Everything began to sink.

Of all the difficulties that Mike and I were experiencing, two things emerged as enduring conflicts. First was the constant game of tug-of-war played by the neurologists and the two hospital systems. Because Mike had seizures he had to be taken to the nearest hospital, a decent community hospital with good doctors and okay neurologists who treated him as an epileptic and gave him Dilantin. At the Veterans Administration hospital there were the best neurologists in the world who treated him as a patient with brain disease.

Once Mike had been taken to Longmont Hospital by ambulance during a particularly bad seizure. He ended up in the stroke unit, which was good because those nurses knew how to handle someone who couldn't speak. Not so good because he hadn't had a stroke. Afterward, I took him to the VA to be checked out. They informed me that he had toxic levels of Dilantin in his system and he had to be hospitalized for a week to undo the damage done to him at Longmont.

So whenever possible, if we felt that a seizure might be coming on, we piled into the car and took off for the twenty-mile drive to La Jolla. Sometimes the seizure would come in the car and I would drive up to the ER entrance, run inside shouting for help, grab a wheelchair and he would be rolled immediately into the back room, given Lorazepam and usually admitted about five hours later. Other times he would not seize and we would wait for hours in the cold lobby, television on, trying to be polite to other patients while they stared at Mike, praying for the seizure build-up to subside.

Waiting in the ER examination room for hours was the worst. But it did serve to demystify all things medical. I searched the cupboards for cups and tissues. I figured out how the equipment worked. Mike would take his own blood pressure. I wandered down the hall until I found personnel who would bring us warm blankets. One time, after about four hours, I tried to get on the Internet from the doctor's computer. Well, why not?

Often, when the doctor finally came in, the tall blind man was sitting on the chair and the haggard woman with him was asleep on the examination table wrapped in a blanket.

The other enduring conflict was the fact that Mike thought he could take care of himself. He would go along with the boundaries and the accommodations that I wanted him to make for his illness, thinking they were unnecessary, that he was doing it just to please me, not to save his life. In a way this was fine if it preserved his dignity. In another way, it put constant, heartbreaking pressure on me. I was the one who watched him, one morning, drop a glass into the sink then pick it up, fill it from the faucet and try to drink again from pointed shards before I yelled, "Stop!"

It wasn't that he couldn't *do* things for himself, it was that he had huge lapses in judgment. How do you convince someone of that who doesn't believe it?

For instance, here's another journal entry:

Journal Entry

Wednesday

All is well and today I had a great day because primarily every thing went well. Now let's write about how God is in my life. First he guids and teaches me through many ways for example I fell and cut my knee also ran my head into a sharp overhang when leaving the back lawn. This happened two days ago but now I look back on it as a lesson for me to slow down.

Love you all
Mike and dad

Mike hid his injuries because he didn't want to bother me or his part-time caretaker. It was about five days before I discovered the cuts. Both legs were completely infected with MRSA bacteria. The sores were the size of oranges, oozing pus.

"Why didn't you tell us? Should I start doing an inspection? Please, Mike, I have to know when something goes wrong."

We went to Urgent Care immediately. He was on a five-hour IV drip as an outpatient for two days, but finally had to go to the hospital for a week. Even then the infections didn't actually clear up completely, but I somehow got the impression that it was good enough for a guy who was going to die anyway.

"He's got a lot worse problems than MRSA," one doctor said. "Doesn't he only have a few weeks to live?"

"Sixty days," I said back in his face. "He was given sixty days to live. Another specialist gave him five years."

"How long ago was that?"

"That was eight years ago."

Eight years.

The hospitalizations and seizures were becoming more frequent. The first few years of the illness there were only one or two hospitalizations per year, then more and more each following year. It had reached a point where the VA gave me liquid Lorazepam in little glass bottle droppers to see if it could stop a seizure. It did and it worked, until it ran out. When I tried to renew the prescription the pharmacy would only give me pills. What good are pills when someone is having a seizure?

Trips to the emergency were happening about every four or five weeks. The next trip to the VA emergency room had started out with twitching, which progressed to panting and paralysis of his right side (a temporary syndrome with some seizures). By the time we got into patient area, Mike was having a full-blown grand mal. His whole body was rising and jerking, the neck veins were hard as cast iron pipes, his eyes bulged, his mouth foamed. Two nurses were trying to get a vein for an IV.

Getting a vein in Mike was difficult in the best of times. I watched these two fretting and trying to poke a needle into Mike. I watched, with growing agitation and horror for over an hour.

"Give him a shot! Just give him a shot! You're not getting a vein!"

The screaming voice was me. I got up and ran down the corridor until I found a doctor and told him to come quickly. The doctor immediately administered a shot and questioned me about what had happened. The nurses disappeared. When Mike was finally stopped seizing, still unconscious, the doctor walked purposefully to a cabinet at the end of the room. Then he came over to me, bent down and looked into my eyes. His hand reached out and took my arm. He turned my hand upward and placed something in it. A bottle of liquid Lorazepam.

In the weeks to come, Mike's world was becoming smaller. He had long ago graduated from the Center for the Blind. I got a call once at work to tell me that I needed to come to the graduation that afternoon because

Mike was being awarded Best Attitude. I hung up the phone and sobbed. Hearing that your husband is being awarded Best Attitude at the Center for the Blind falls into that category of words that you never imagined you would hear someone say.

He also had been asked to leave the Braille Institute after five years. He apparently had peed in the back of the bus. Not accidentally. We had a meeting with their social worker, who tried to get him to understand that it was unacceptable, but he didn't have the capacity to see the problem. In our conversation beforehand I had suggested that she say it was a suspension and could be revisited. Two years later I finally had to tell him that he was never going back. It was excruciating for both of us.

By that time, seizures started to come with regularity. About every three weeks, Mike's brain would shut down completely, seize and he would be unable to speak, stand, read or write. His world became very limited for about a week, and then he would bounce back and be just a little below his baseline from the month before. Each time there were the phone calls to friends, an email to the prayer team at church. Tired condolences and murmured sympathy.

"It could be worse," I said to Mandy, trying to sound hopeful. I'd said that from the very first seizure.

"Yes, but the things that it could be worse than are getting more and more terrible."

Mandy had admitted that she prayed for us every day when she walked the local high school track until she finally started crying out at 5:30 a.m. on a cloudy, damp morning, "Stop it! Stop what you are doing to Fran! It's enough! It has to stop! No more!"

It was becoming clear that Mike needed more constant care, even though we had an alert system around his neck. We spent one Sunday afternoon driving around to visit residential facilities. Mike was crying and so was I. He felt that he didn't need it, but was willing to do it for my sake. There was no convincing him otherwise.

It was during one of those weeks that Mike had been hospitalized at Longmont that my nephew was getting married. Mike had been close to Jason in his troubled youth and Jason had made Mike an "honorary groomsman" in the wedding program. I felt fortunate, in fact, that I could go to Orange County for the wedding and know that Mike would be in good hands at the hospital. He would be pleased by the program. As a result of a mix-up I was the photographer for the wedding and was staying with my cousin the night before. About 9 p.m. my cell phone rang.

"This is the neurologist at Longmont Hospital. Are you Mrs. Canrinus?"

"I'm Mike's wife."

"Well, he is showing signs of a brain bleed. We need to do an MRI and then I will call you. We will probably have to do surgery on Monday."

"What kind of surgery?"

"We have to drain the blood. It's collecting between his brain and his skull and putting pressure on the brain."

"Are you sure you would do that with a DNR patient?"

"Yes, you have to do it. You have to! I'll meet you at the hospital at 8:30 Monday morning!"

"Okay," I said. "Do the MRI and call me back tomorrow. Look at his medical records and see if you can consult with Dr. Lasko at UCSD and let him know."

"See you Monday."

I immediately put a call into Dr. Lasko. I wanted to learn more about this problem. He called me back Sunday morning.

"It sounds like a subdural hematoma. Did he have a fall?"

"Well, he falls often, but nothing unusual that I know of. But he doesn't always tell me. He's been in the hospital a few days. They don't always tell me, either. What I really want to know is if you have heard of this neurologist and is he capable of performing the surgery or should I have it done at the VA?"

"I have heard of him and he is capable of this. It's not a very complicated surgery and I'm sure he's done lots of them."

"Is Mike dying?"

"No, Francine, not necessarily. But, of course, every surgery has risks."

"Okay, well thanks, Dr.Lasko."

"Oh, you are very welcome."

Sunday morning was a whirlwind of last minute activity. I went to my sister's house and we put the finishing touches on the pew bows: gorgeous bouquets of peacock feathers. We headed to the church with bins of decorations so we could start transforming the fellowship hall into a reception space as soon as the services were over.

There were fun photos to take of the bride getting ready, the groomsmen huddled in prayer. My sister's signature gift card box that she re-crafted for every family wedding. The bridesmaids, the flower girls and the beautiful ring bearers. I stood by the back entrance and thought about Mike and me having our little wedding almost eighteen years before. Afterward, we ate, we danced, we cut cake, and finally I hugged the bride and groom, slipped over to my sister and told her I had to leave.

"I've taken about 350 photos," I said. "I think there are some pretty great ones."

"Well, thanks for all your hard work. I really appreciate you stepping in to take photos. Are you sure you have to go?"

"Yes, I'm sure." I rubbed my cheeks with both hands and wiped my eyes.

"Mike is having brain surgery in the morning."

CHAPTER 48

Not Yet

IT WAS VALENTINE'S DAY. Surgery day. Anna stayed home from high school, where she was now a senior. We pulled into the familiar hospital parking lot at about 8 a.m. and walked along the sidewalk, past the rehab center and up the elevator with the broken direction lights to the surgical floor. Outside of his room, a nurse had two brain negatives called up on the computer screen.

"Here you can see what is happening," he told us. "That large white space is the pool of blood. See how it is pushing the brain aside? And there's the small pool on the other side. We will drain them both."

I sent Anna inside to see her dad.

"And what would happen if we didn't do the surgery?" I asked him.

"Oh, he'll die in a couple of weeks."

I turned and went into the room. Mike was sitting up in bed, smiling. His head was shaved and he had two Xes written in black Sharpie on either side of his head.

I sat on the bed next to him and held his hand.

"Mike, you are going to have a little surgery. It's all going to be fine and they've done it many times before. There is blood seeping out of your brain, for some reason, so they have to drain it out. They are going to drill some holes, but they will heal up. You'll be in rehab for a couple of weeks to recover, this time a different one.

"Mike," I squeezed his hand. "We have to do this or you will die."

At that moment the neurologist bustled in.

"I need to speak to The Wife!"

We went outside to the hallway and the forceful man looked at me, searching my face, then spoke.

"Don't do this."

"What do you mean?"

"Don't do the surgery. This man has no quality of life. He doesn't want to live like this."

Boy, you don't know Mike!

I was furious. Clearly this doctor had not even glanced at the chart last Friday night before he was insisting that I *had* to do this.

"Well, doctor. I just came from telling him that we had to do this or he would die. Do you really think I can just turn around, go back into the room and tell him we changed our minds? Oops, never mind?"

"Okay, okay," he said. "We'll give him one more chance. But if this comes up again, I won't do it."

"Fine. Please proceed."

"I will. It will be a few hours. I'll call your cell phone when I have results. Go to the mall with your daughter. Have lunch. It will be fine."

And that's what we did. Anna and I walked across the street to the mall and I bought her a bottle of her favorite perfume for Valentine's Day. After a while we slipped into the cool, vinyl booths of one of her favorite restaurants and looked over shiny pages of bright-colored pizzas, burgers, pastas, and lavish desserts. Once we ordered, I sat back with a sigh.

Anna had lost so much. A year or so after Mike had been sick, she looked up to me in tears.

"Mommy, it's like I don't have a dad anymore. It's like he's a grandpa, not a dad."

"I know, honey, I know. But he still loves you like a dad and would do anything in the world if he could be your dad again. Anything."

"It's so sad," she said, her smooth, pre-teen face and brown eyes looking into mine. "Why did this happen?"

It was question that I had cried into my pillow so often.

"Sad things happen, honey. I'm not sure why. But we know that there is a heaven where he will be whole again. He will be healthy and strong for the rest of eternity."

She looked down. "I know . . . ."

Now, she was seventeen. I looked into those same questioning eyes.

"Anna, are you ready for him to go? If this is his last day on earth, are you ready for that?"

She took a minute, then looked up at me, straight in the eye. "Oh yeah, Mom. I'm absolutely ready. Seeing him suffer is too much. He tries hard, but I know he doesn't like the way he is. Are you ready?"

No! No! Not yet!

From the first day of his collapse a part of me had been cringing and repeating those words in my head, "Not yet!"

"I'd like to get you through your senior year and graduation in June, so I'm hoping that Mike has a little more time."

Not yet! Not yet!

Just as we finished our leisurely lunch, the cell phone rang. It was the neurosurgeon, calling me. There was no message.

Anna and I left the restaurant and started up the steep hill leading to the hospital. We waited in the lobby and let the receptionist know that we were there, waiting for the doctor. Neither of us spoke, wondering if the next words we heard would change our lives forever. Shortly after he rushed in, green scrubs stained, surgical mask hanging around his neck, head covered with a pale green cap.

"He's fine. He pulled through. He'll go to rehab and be home in a couple of weeks."

He turned and walked away, then turned back. "It will probably come back in about six months. Don't do this again," he said pointing his surgeon fingers at me. "No next time."

So, no change in our lives forever today. Not yet.

CHAPTER 49

Enough

Mike's birthday was a two weeks after his surgery. He was sixty-four years-old. I went to the neighborhood bakery and got him a supersized cupcake that could have served two. On the patio of the nursing rehab, his scars and stitches stood out from the prickly hair that was starting to grow in. His smile was wide, although he was wrinkled and tired.

"Do you know what today is?" We had sat on the patio under an umbrella in the pretty garden.

"Yes, I do!" He eyes twinkled. "It's my birthday!"

I was surprised. For years we had a playful routine where I would take him to breakfast or spend the day with him and surprise him by telling him it was his birthday. I was so glad he was better. The surgery might have really helped.

Every day I visited, brought clean clothes, took away old ones. He was confined to a wheelchair at this facility and I knew that was hard on him. His last time in rehab he had been giddy all the time and loved his roommate. I think he had been on mood elevation drugs. This time, not so much.

I brought him home early. He was so happy to be in his room, our former bedroom.

Over the previous year I slowly realized I needed to sell the house and downsize. It broke my heart but it was a financial necessity. I painted and updated every room, including our old master bedroom. Now Mike got settled into the huge room, which had been transformed.

The bed was in an alcove. There was room for a long couch and a large desk for his computer. Next to the fireplace a bookcase held his television and audio CD set-up. The walk-in closet was neatly organized with towels, bedding, and clothes. On one side was a large table that held his coffeemaker, a basket of coffee, cereal and a small fridge with milk and snacks. The bathroom was set up with grab bars; it had a shower seat and hand-held shower head. A wide sliding glass door next to the bathroom led to the private garden that we had re-surfaced for easy access for him to enjoy sitting on the patio outside.

It was the perfect set-up for Mike. All except the 13 stairs leading to the upstairs main floor, but he never had trouble going upstairs.

Our part-time helper, Rita, who was a trained nurse choosing to work as a caretaker, was a gift from God. When we discussed various options for Mike she was a great sounding board.

"When I went to visit Mike in the rehab," said Rita, "he took me aside and pulled on my arm. 'Don't ever let me have to stay in a place like this,' he told me. 'I don't want to live like this.' I told him, 'Write that down! Make sure everyone knows this.'"

A few weeks later the effects of the surgery seemed to be wearing off. Mike was having seizures almost every day and spent much of his time sleeping. It was a Thursday night when we sat down in his room for a talk about the future.

"Mike, you just went through this surgery and I want to go over the DNR order to make sure it's exactly what you want."

"Okay. I thought we went over that."

"I'd like to do it again. You know, every time you are hospitalized it is supposed to be reiterated. They do that at the VA, but not at Longmont, so I want to talk about it. Do you have any questions about your affairs in general?

"Are we giving anything to the kids?"

"Yes. You have a life insurance policy and each child is going to get some benefit. We'll have enough to pay off the medical bills. We have our funeral arrangements made. Rob will help with the financial side."

"So, what else, Fran?"

"We have a long form and it gives you all kinds of options that you have to tell me 'yes' or 'no.' I'll just start. Do you want to be resuscitated if it is indicated that you will be brain dead?

"No."

"Do you want to be resuscitated if it means that you will be on a respirator for the rest of your life?"

"No. No way."

"Do you want to be resuscitated if it means that you will be on dialysis the rest of your life?"

"No, I don't want to be hooked up to anything to be alive."

"Do you want—"

"Fran, all I want is to not be in pain. All I want is pain medication."

I let those words hang in the air, barely breathing. This was so hard.

"Just the same, if you don't mind, I want to go over these one by one and make sure that I perfectly understand what your wishes are. I don't want to do anything that we haven't talked about."

"That's fine. But if I can't walk, can't eat on my own, use the bathroom, or can't speak, I don't want to continue on."

That was what I expected. But what he didn't know was that he had been in that condition several times. I couldn't count anymore the number of times that he had been dying. Now, though, things felt different. In the last twenty months, Mike had been hospitalized sixteen times. Clearly something was changing.

We finished the form and I tucked him in bed with a kiss and soft music playing.

About 2 a.m. I heard a loud crash downstairs. I jumped up and ran downstairs. I turned on the light. Mike was barefoot and standing in the middle of the room.

"I'm sorry. I wanted coffee. I thought it was morning. My bed was wet."

"Mike, it's okay, don't move!"

Strewn across the floor was hot coffee and a shattered coffee pot. I got him back to his chair, wiped his feet and put on his slippers. I asked him to sit back and relax. Then I went up and got into my own slippers and came down with a broom and several towels. Carefully sweeping the glass away from the hot liquid, I gathered it into the dustpan and emptied it into the trash can. Towels mopped up the coffee and then I wiped it all dry with more towels. Next, I took off the bedding and piled it in a heap with the towels and pushed it all out the slider to the back patio. I would deal with that in the morning.

Once the bed was clean, I guided Mike into a warm shower for a quick rinse, wiped him down and put on fresh pajamas. Tucking him in again, I said, "Here's the commode in case you need it. If you get up again, put on your slippers. I'm not sure I got all of the glass."

"Thanks, Fran," he said. "I'm so sorry."

"Don't worry about it, Mike. It is what it is."

"Good night, Fran."

I walked out the door.

"Good night!" I said as I mounted the stairs. It was 3:30 a.m.

I was just nodding off again when, Boom! I heard another crash.

Pulling on my slippers and running downstairs, I found Mike on the floor near his desk.

"I fell!" he said in tears.

"It's okay, it's okay. Let's get you settled."

"I wanted to get up."

"It's okay. Shhh! It's fine. I'm going to sleep down here on the couch. Let's try to get a little sleep before I have to go to work."

After a few minutes in the darkness I asked him a question.

"Mike, it would be so much easier if you would just acknowledge that I am taking care of you and you would try to do what I ask you to do? Why don't you do that? Why do you think you can take care of yourself?"

"Because I have to think that, Fran. I have to."

Once Mike was sleeping soundly, I crept up to my bed. Tears would not stop. I was so tired, in so much pain.

Help me! Help me God! We are so weary! Mike is miserable. Help me!

We all think we have contingency plans. Well, I'll just sell the house. I'll just rent out rooms, I'll just find a live-in. I'll get a second job. When those things turn out to be undoable, we realize that we aren't so self-sufficient. Not in control.

Years ago, when my mother was dying, my sisters and I did everything possible to ease the passing. We stayed by her bedside. We sang. We got the guy she wanted to sing at her funeral to sing. But she continued on for several days breathing seven times a minute. Try that out on your own.

Time it. Crazy, right? Give her permission to go, our friends told us. And through this tortuous wait and her suffering we gave her all the permission we could and you know what I learned? Permission didn't matter because it wasn't in her hands. Or ours.

Friday I went to work. Mike was awake when I said goodbye and he told me he was going to stay in bed a while. I called Rita and asked her to come in early and stay a few hours later. I told her about the night before and she kept a watchful eye until I came home.

"If you need me, call me," she said as she pulled out of the driveway.

But it was just a very normal night. I talked to my friend, Betsy, and told her about the horrible night before and let her know that I had better cancel our plans for a movie on Saturday.

"I'm sorry to call you with bad news all the time, Betsy."

"No, I want you to call me. I'm here when you need help, and if I'm not, call Steve. He'll come."

"Thanks," I said, "You guys are such faithful friends. You know you are the only people in the entire church who have ever invited us over after Mike got sick. The only ones."

"Well, we love you guys!"

"Anyway, thanks."

That night, Mike tolerated me watching my favorite Friday night show, *Say Yes to the Dress*. I was addicted. Frilly bridal gown decisions and family drama had nothing to do with wet beds or hospitals. Another favorite was the hospital drama, *House,* because we knew all the differential diagnoses and heard the word "vasculitis" a lot and Mike would whoop and laugh, "I have that!"

So, after the show Mike got up and said he looked forward to a good night's sleep. I followed him to the top of the stairs.

"I love you, Mikey" I said and gave him a hard squeeze, breathing in his skin, feeling his arms around me.

"I love you too, Fran!" Mike said in his rich, deep voice that was so soothing. He went down to his cool room without a trace of misstep.

Saturday morning was silent.

Is Mike alive?

I had awakened with that same thought for nearly eight years. Almost three thousand days.

Draging on some jeans and a top, thinking that Mike was asleep, I was happy to let him rest. I made some coffee, then filled a cup and took it downstairs.

My stomach clenched. It was a scene from a nightmare.

Mike was naked, wedged between the bed and the wall. A long, fresh streak of blood smeared down the wall. He was panting loudly and his eyes were open but there was no response in them. Staring wide. I had never seen him like that. Was he conscious?

I wrapped the sheet around him and tried to pull him up onto the bed. It took a long time, but finally I was able to inch his long torso up to the mattress. His head flung backward until I pulled it up and onto the pillow. I prayed by his side, then called Rita.

She came quickly and we both sat and just looked at him. His skin was pulled tight across his face and looked yellow. We determined that the blood on the wall came from his mouth, because there were no cuts or wounds anywhere. Probably the result of a seizure.

"Have you ever seen someone like this, Rita?"

She looked at me and paused. "He looks like this is the end."

I tried not to show my feeling of desperation.

"If I call an ambulance, they will take him to Longmont. I want him to go to the VA. Do you think we can get him upstairs?

"I think that's a good idea. I'll call around to medical transports."

"I'll call Betsy's husband, Steve."

After a few minutes of trying to reposition Mike and put him in underwear, Rita came in with the report.

"Medical transport will take him if we can get him up to the driveway."

"Okay, let's try."

Steve pulled up just then and we called him down to Mike's room.

'Let's get him dressed," I said. We had some elastic-waist shorts and a button down Hawaiian shirt to put on. *How hard could that be?*

It took three of us to get him dressed. Mike had no physical responses. All the while, he was semi-conscious, panting and staring. I thought if we could get him in a wheelchair we might be able to wheel him backwards up the stairs. But after the ordeal of dressing him, we all sat down, drank some water and caught our breath.

Finally Steve spoke. "Ladies, I'm sorry, but we are not going to get Mike upstairs. We can barely get a shirt on him."

"You're right," I finally said. "Let's call an ambulance."

"Fran," Steve said evenly. "Why take him anywhere?"

I stopped to think. I knew what he was asking.

"I promised him that he would not be in pain so I want to make sure that he's not in pain."

The ambulance driver came and the EMTs all plodded downstairs. Another crew came behind and suddenly there were six men hovering over Mike.

"Can't you please take him to the VA?"

"They aren't an authorized emergency room."

"Well then, can you just help me get him upstairs?"

The head of the team thought a moment.

"There is a number at the VA that I can call that might give me permission. . . . I'll call it," he said."

After a few minutes on the phone while the EMTs were moving the couch and estimating the wisdom of carry him or using a gurney, the captain hung up.

"We can take him."

I must have looked puzzled.

"He's not in a seizure situation. We're not required to take him to Longmont."

"Oh, thank you so much!"

I gathered the hospital kit, wrote a note to Anna, fed the cat and got changed. By the time I got to the hospital, Mike was in a single room in the ER. A resident came forward and introduced himself. He was young, very tall, and reminded me of Dr. Kildare from my youth.

"We're not sure exactly what has caused it, but he seems to be in some kind of altered state. Semi-conscious. His brain appears to be shutting down. We can start with an MRI—"

"No," I answered simply. "No MRI."

"Maybe a CT scan can tell us—"

"No. No CT scan. No more. All he wants is pain relief. Can you please make him comfortable and give him something for pain relief?" I looked at the young doctor intently.

"And do you understand what this means?"

I took a deep breath as other patients looked on and nurses scurried around the room. "Yes, I do. Can you make him comfortable?

"Yes," said the doctor. Then he turned to me again. "I happen to think you are right. You are very brave."

I had to be brave. All the months and years and tears were coming down to a moment. This moment.

"*He* is brave, doctor. He is amazingly brave. This was his choice, not to cling to life but to face what comes next."

I stayed until almost midnight when he was moved to a room. When I got home I took a call from the resident.

"We'll likely move him to the palliative care unit tomorrow."

"Thank you, doctor."

When I woke the next morning, I had the familiar thought.

Is Mike alive?

I immediately called and was told that there had been no change, no responses, nothing at all different.

That day I notified the family that Mike was in the hospital in some kind of semi-conscious state, using the words of the doctor, and we were near the end. They were invited to come and ease his passing.

Family gathered around, friends came, people visited and pitched in over the next few days, and Mike was never alone. We suctioned him and repositioned his body and made sure he looked comfortable. It was disturbing to see his body fail.

Most difficult, about every thirty to forty minutes, he would shoot upright in bed and have a seizure. Unlike any previous seizure, his eyes would bulge and he would point to an unknown place of unrest like he was looking into a world beyond. Then after a minute or two he would collapse back to his pillows. There was no tiptoeing into the dark beyond. No floating towards the light. This was death and it was hard.

Many of the nurses had mentioned the recently published book, *Heaven is for Real.*

"Have you read it?" they asked.

"Yes. My friend Lynn was the collaborative author. It's wonderful."

Is heaven real? I've believed it all my life, but is it really real?

I stayed overnight on Sunday and by the end of Monday I was drained. My brother-in-law stayed on Monday night as planned, and Anna and I spent a lot of the night talking. She wanted to go to school on Tuesday, so I informed the vice principal and the school counselor what was happening and who would be picking her up if the time came. My friend had volunteered to do that.

In the morning I took a long shower and dressed comfortably for the long vigil. Right before leaving I went into my jewelry box. There was Mike's wedding ring, gold with blue lapis and a diamond embedded on one side, like the North Star over the ocean. I slipped it on my middle finger and decided to wear it to the hospital.

The physicians asked my permission to give him an antihistamine which would stop the foaming and suctioning.

"What's causing that," I asked.

"He can't swallow, so those are his fluids being expelled."

Can't swallow.

Mike was not coming back to us with a smile, saying, "Today is the best day of my life!"

As people came and went I decided to take a break and go get some food. When I got back to the hospital, I parked the car and went in the side entrance. Walking down the middle of that wide corridor leading to the elevators I looked down at my hands. The ring was gone.

My husband was dying and I lost his wedding ring. I sat on a bench and wept for the loss. All the loss.

Poem

Set sail, my love.
Skim the glistening waters
So deep; so mysterious.
Leave the waves and swells behind.
Lift Anchor.
Set sail.

Play in the wind, instead of the sea.
Sail the jet stream.

Up, up, tilting toward heaven's gates;
Then come about at the throne of Christ.
Receive your crown.
Well done, Mike, Well done!

That evening I decided that it was my turn to say goodbye to Mike. I had borne him a child, wiped his sick limbs, prepared his meals, ordered his medication, and paid his medical bills. In four days we would be married for eighteen years. It was time for my goodbye. Instead of sitting behind everyone on the couch, I took the seat next to his pillow. Slowly, everyone kissed him goodbye and left.

Alone with Mike, I lay next to him and talked, remembering the good times of falling in love, going over the lives of the children one by one and praying for each of them, one by one. I talked with him of his bravery and how inspiring his life was to so many people. It was a time of sweetness and his seizures started to dwindle. I lay next to him and closed my eyes.

At 3 a.m. the nurse came in the room.

"It's almost time," she said. "It should be within thirty minutes."

To me he looked identical to the morning last Saturday. These nurses who see death on a daily basis see the other side more clearly than the rest of us. Again I rocked his worn, withering body. Then, quietly, I began to sing *Amazing Grace* and it was as if a gateway to heaven was opening and other voices, I swear, were joining in by the time I got to the last verse:

When we've been there ten thousand years;
Bright shining as the sun,
We've no less days to sing God's praise
Than when we've first begun.

As soon as the song finished, the panting stopped. I looked at his face and knew that Mike's soul was making its journey away from earth. I raised my head to the heavens, tears and sobs coming freely, looked at his face and grasped his shoulders,

"Well done, Mike! Well done!"

Then I rested my cheek against his cheek and whispered.

"Today is the best day of your life!"

EPILOGUE

O F COURSE, THERE WAS an unusual twist. As I sat in my bedroom later that afternoon, family bustling in the kitchen and preparing a meal while I hid in my room in pain, I had a phone call. It was from the hospital morgue. I had arranged for an autopsy so that some of his neurologists could add to the body of knowledge about this little-known disease.

"I'm sorry to disturb you, but the medical examiner's office has taken the body. They want to do their own autopsy."

"What!? Why?"

"I'm not sure. They'll be calling you."

A few minutes later, still curled up in my rocking chair, the phone rang again.

"Mrs. Canrinus."

"Yes."

"This is the medical examiner's office and we have evidence that your husband has died of a subdural hematoma. Is that correct?"

I thought back to the early morning when the attending doctor and I were trying to decide on cause of death. We figured that the brain had probably started bleeding again as expected, so we put that as cause of death. I stared at the phone for a moment. Steadying my voice and trying to sound confident.

"Well, the doctors and I agreed to put that as the cause of death. If you look at the records you'll see that he had a subdural hematoma evacuation last February and the neurologist said that it was likely to return. You will also see that he had a rare brain disease for the past eight years and was hospitalized sixteen times over the last twenty months."

"Well, ma'am, we'll get back to you."

I didn't tell a soul. For two days in the back of mind I wondered if I was going to be arrested. Finally I got another call.

"Ma'am, we have decided to drop the case. And we never did the autopsy. Do you want us to send the body back to the VA?

"No, we are done. No more procedures. Please just send it to the mortuary."

"Yes, ma'am. Goodbye, ma'am.

* * *

When Jesus was crucified by the Romans at the demand of the Jews under their rule, it was a real death — fearful, bloody, sweaty and cruel. Like Mike enacting the DNR order, Jesus allowed it to happen, although He could have stepped down from the cross as others taunted Him to do. Jesus surrendered to death and His Father turned His back on Him and allowed death to swallow Him because He loves you. He loves me. And nothing else — the things we hoard on earth, the success, the status, our health, the secrets we keep and the sum of our anxieties — is more real than that. It's real. God, Jesus, the Holy Spirit, the community of believers, and evil — it's real. If you don't believe it, ask God. He'll let you know.

But Jesus had a weird twist to His death as well.

Jesus didn't stay dead.

He came back to laugh and talk to people, eat, drink, cook and teach. He invited everyone to be humble and be on the receiving end of His love until He left this earth on His own terms. And He is alive today and is waiting for you to believe it, to start a conversation, go deep, be honest and surrender everything because it will all — all of it — pass away.

Everyone dies.

You will die. I will die.

But because I know that Jesus Christ died for me, I don't have to stay dead.

God so loved me.

> *For God So Loved the World that He Gave His Only Begotten Son, that whosoever believeth in Him should not perish, but have everlasting life. John 3:16.*

"Follow Me or Die"

He sailed through life.
Careful preparation was his secret.
Checklists.
Survival was given every opportunity to prevail over
being a helpless speck on a wide, wild ocean.
He was careful.

But once underway, he sailed into the headwind,
preferring the sail to the rudder.
He didn't like to tack.
Straight ahead.
Confident.
Capturing the wisps of air and current
and channeling them into power.
Powerful.

Until . . .
a rogue wave, strange and rare,
sucked the bottom out from under him,
pounded relentlessly,
overwhelming,
coming out of nowhere.
Slammed and tossed.
Powerless . . .
but still afloat.

And he navigated the strategy of letting go of the rigging.
Forsaking the sail after all.
No option to come about.
Allowing himself to float.
His buoyancy maintained
by being positive, cheerful, accepting and loving.
And loving.

It turned out he had an Anchor.
Jesus.
Yes, that Jesus.
"Even the wind and the sea obey him."

He survived tumultuous seas on faith,
forsaking sail and rudder altogether,
and clung to his Anchor.

Now he sails again on glassy seas, the wind at his back.

A Dozen Things a Wife Must Know to Save Her Sick Husband's Life

1. Know your financial situation, the cost of your healthcare, pension or social security income, your life insurance policy costs, mortgage and husband's social security number. Have medical power of attorney and discuss any Do Not Resuscitate (DNR) orders in advance of a crisis. If you have a trust, the power of attorney documents are usually found in the trust documents. Power of attorney and medical power of attorney are different things. Many pension plans also require documentation that you have power of attorney in order to continue making payments to the bank account. Get this all in order. For both of you, for that matter.

2. You are The Wife — their job is to depersonalize, your job is to get the best care — extraordinary care — by personalizing The Patient. Bring in pictures, encourage visitors. Check in person or by phone every day.

3. Dress up. Wear make-up. Hold your head up high when you enter the hospital, to be recognized and respected and the authority in the situation.

4. Do your homework. What are the medications? What is the differential prognosis? What is the diagnosis? When questions come up — write them down. Ask them.

5. Obtain all medical records after a hospital stay. Some hospitals will charge you a copying fee, some will charge to give you a DVD of an MRI. Buy them. Read them. You will not only catch mistakes, but you can see what they really think is happening. See what they are keeping from you.

6. Keep your own medical records. Write down dates, procedures, impressions, everything. Mistakes are made all the time. You will need a timeline. In a crisis, you won't remember anything. Things that you think you'll never forget can be overshadowed by the next crisis.

7. Ask for help. There is no shame in asking, in fact, most people *want* to do something and are waiting to be asked. Ask friends and family; post something on Facebook; set up a care page. Ask for specific tasks and pray. Ask for groups to do a project together. And remember: Church people you barely know will often respond more compassionately than family members who have their own agenda with you. Go figure. Plus family members may be suffering also and not want to believe that things are all that bad.

8. Meet the hospital's patient advocate, if there is one. Do this before there is a dispute. Just introduce yourself and let the advocate know who you are and make them aware of your husband's status — in a friendly, just-in-case way. Then, if something goes awry, be a tiger.

9. Meet with the hospitalist. These are hospital-paid doctors who manage a patient's care in a hospital in lieu of the primary care physician. They are not your advocates — they are the hospital's advocates. If they can make money on your husband, they will keep him. If they will lose money on him, they will transfer him out. On a Friday.

10. What is the Friday Dump? Hospitals try to empty their beds on Fridays so they don't have to pay for a full staff of personnel on the weekends. Ask on Thursday whether they plan to discharge your

patient the next day. Usually they give you no advance warning, just "Come get him. He's going home today!" If you haven't bought Depends or a rubber mattress cover, or cleared the room or put up grab bars, this can bring on a crisis. If you have a job, have a plan for discharge that can be implemented on quick notice. Or ask the doctors to recommend a week of rehab or convalescence.

11. Meet with a social worker to find out your post-hospital options. Medicare will pay for twenty-one days in a skilled nursing facility after hospitalization if the patient is taken directly there by medical transport. (Which will be charged to you.) They will not pay anything if the patient goes home before rehab intake. Skilled nursing facilities often bid on your loved one. A patient profile is posted, and facilities with beds and the ability to care for his needs let the social worker know that they want him. They will also have contact numbers of home health care workers or therapists. Persist in meeting with the social worker. In my husband's hospital, they had a different social worker for every floor, so I had to retell the story four times.

12. Discuss end of life preferences in advance of a crisis when you are not in crisis mode. Burial or cremation? Who needs to get ashes? Do you have plots? Did you know you can buy resold plots at a discount? Do you want a funeral or memorial service or celebration of life? Slide show or framed photos or both? Flowers or donations? Printed program? Pall bearers? Obits can cost more than $1,000 in the local newspapers — photos extra. Decide as much as you can ahead of time, especially about funeral arrangements, because it's easy to make emotional or irrational decisions when the time comes. Plan ahead or you may end up paying $1,000 for an urn that's shaped like a '57 Chevy or a golf bag.

STUDY GUIDE

At the beginning of the book, Francine Phillips writes about being away from God and building her life on girlfriends, plays, writer salons, dating, and intimate relationships. What qualities attracted her to Mike when they first met?

Once Francine invites the Lord to take charge of her relationship with Mike, what changes start to happen in her life?

When God responds with the penny and the statement word, how did you react?
Is that hard to believe?
Do you wish she had saved the pennies?
What difference would that make?

What do you think of Mike's *Follow Me or Die* philosophy?
Is that the way Christian men behave?

Does your church teach protection from suffering? Is it subtle or overt?

Francine's life changed significantly when she became married and mother to seven children. How do you think God used this in her life?

As you learn more and more about Mike's brain deficiencies, what would you have done differently? What would you do if it were your husband?

Have you ever had an experience with healthcare professionals that left you feeling helpless?

Should Robert Boney at Harbor Drive Boatyard have acted differently?

Who are the heroes in this story?

What was the turning point in Francine's relationship to God at this time?

What have been the turning points in your relationship with God?